NEW FOUND LANDS

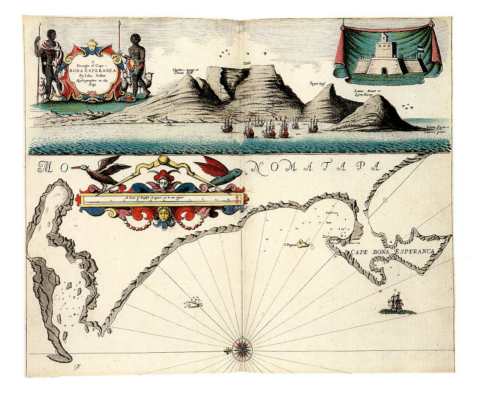

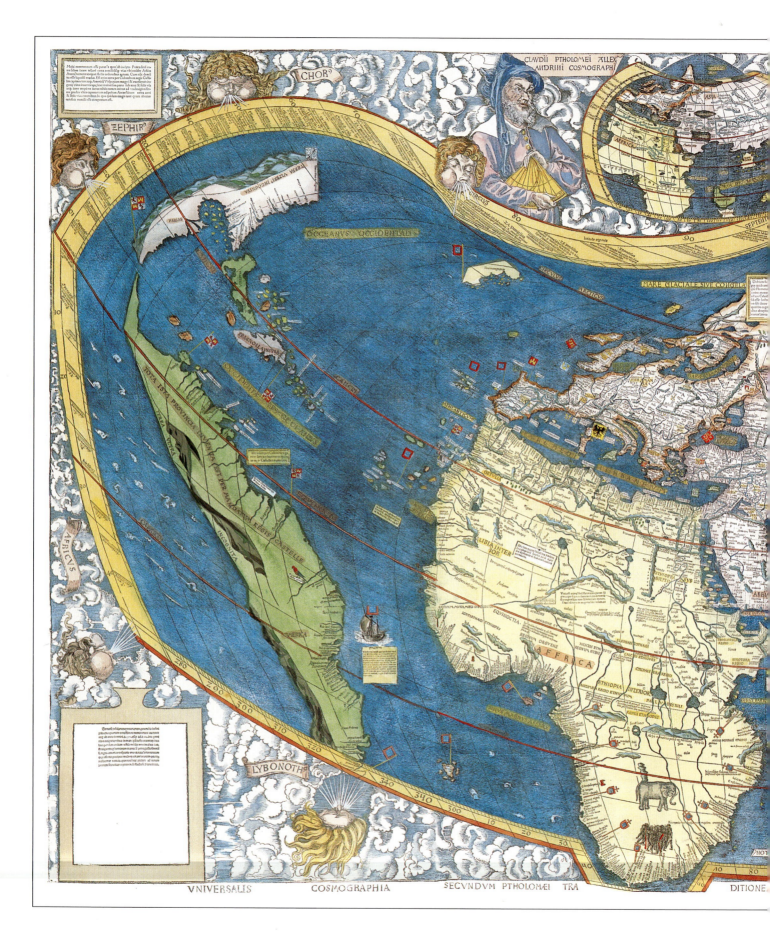

UNIVERSALIS COSMOGRAPHIA SECUNDUM PTHOLOMAEI TRADITIONE

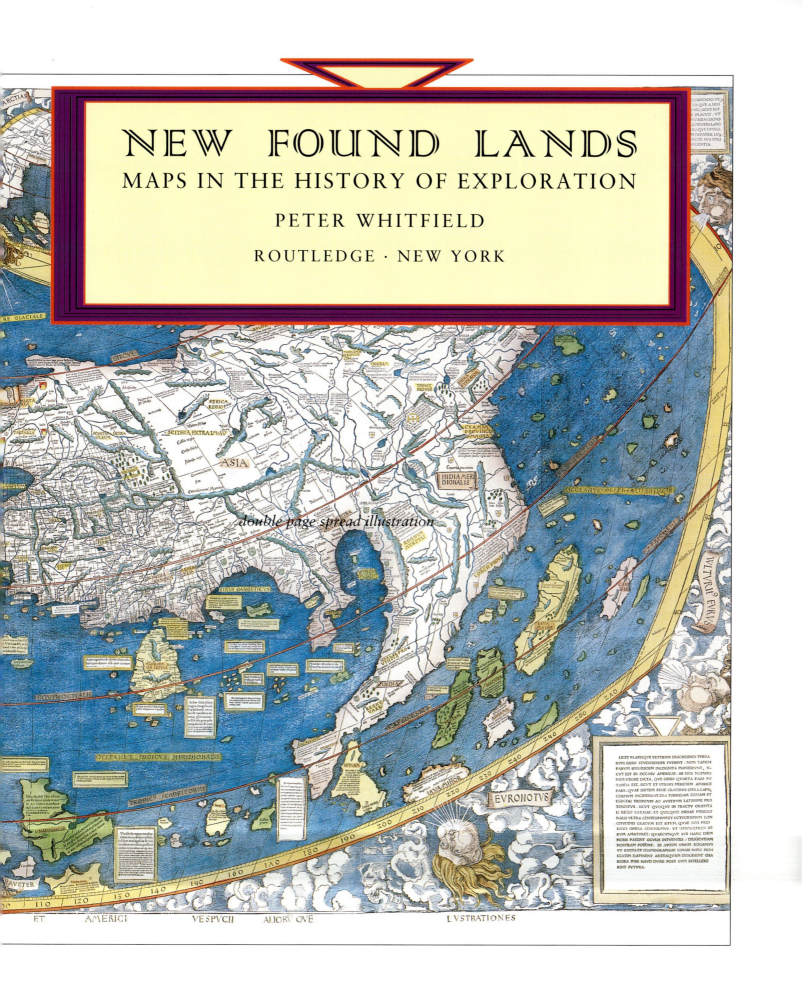

NEW FOUND LANDS

MAPS IN THE HISTORY OF EXPLORATION

PETER WHITFIELD

ROUTLEDGE · NEW YORK

double page spread illustration

Half-title: The Cape of Good Hope, by Seller, 1675. The most famous maritime landmark in the world, later the base for British expansion into Southern Africa.

The British Library Maps C.8.b.13, f.25.

Title page: Waldseemüller's World Map, 1507.

Schloss Wolfegg

Published in the United States of America and Canada in 1998 by
Routledge
29 West 35th Street
New York, NY 10001-2299

First published in 1998 by
The British Library
96 Euston Road, London NW1 2DB

Library of Congress Cataloging-in-Publication Data

Whitfield, Peter, Dr.
    New found lands : maps in the history of exploration / Peter
Whitfield.
        p.   cm.
    Includes bibliographical references and index.
    ISBN 0-415-92026-4 (alk. paper)
    1. Discoveries in geography.   2. Cartography—History.   I. Title.
081.W47 1998   97-47767
910'.9—dc21   CIP

Typeset by Bexhill Phototypesetters
Printed in Hong Kong

CONTENTS

PREFACE

LEGENDS ARE REQUIRED TO BE beautiful rather than true. The history of exploration is full of legends which, while they are not untrue, contain only a part of the truth. They are legends of men challenging the unknown, displaying heroism and endurance, or meeting death in arctic seas and burning deserts. These stories present the human dimension of exploration, but they are not the whole truth, for the story of the physical journey is only the beginning. In reality European exploration, during what we may call its classic period between 1500 and 1900, is the story of the growth of knowledge, geographical knowledge that was recorded, centralized and used as never before. But discovery is a relative and misleading term, and perhaps the most persistent and subtle legend is that exploration and discovery are synonymous, whereas the lands or routes discovered were of course inhabited or known for centuries before Europeans arrived. 'Newly-discovered' routes across the Sahara, or through the Rockies invariably represented knowledge simply borrowed from native peoples. The discoverer of a certain land, or the route to it, may have been simply the first to record his discovery and incorporate it within the body of European knowledge. In order to do this he had obviously to find his way home again, therefore the first duty of an explorer was to survive; but the rivers and mountains which challenged his powers of endurance were already home to indigenous peoples, therefore the term Encounter is a more accurate one than Discovery.

Sometimes native knowledge was absolutely vital to the Europeans as they explored unknown territory. This was the case with the Aztec woman known as Dona Marina who served Cortes in the role of interpreter, or Sacagawea who was Lewis and Clark's ambassador to the Indians. The vital difference between the protagonists in these historic encounters was that knowledge once acquired by Europeans was recorded in map form and became part of a conscious world geography. Men in Seville, Amsterdam or London had access to knowledge of Mexico, India, Canada or Brazil, while the native peoples knew only their own immediate environment. The Europeans' true discovery was that all this knowledge could be merged into an accurate map of the world, which in turn became a vital tool of political power. The breakthrough which enabled them to achieve this synthesis was their mastery of the sea, for the great navigators linked the oceans and the continents in a way that was unprecedented in world history, and they arrived in their new-found lands as the possessors of unique skills and revolutionary knowledge. Historically, this explosion of knowledge must be seen in the context of the intellectual revolution which we call the Renaissance, but the immediate motives of the explorers were overwhelmingly worldly – rapacious, mercenary, military and imperial. The purely intellectual impact of the new discoveries was less than we might imagine: we search in vain for evidence that philosophers, artists, poets or theologians were quick to understand the importance of what was happening. Not until the later sixteenth century do writers such as Camões, Diaz, Montaigne and Marlowe reflect on a new world and the European ascendancy over it.

The history of exploration can be told in several ways: it can be told as a narrative of adventure and endurance, concentrating on the human drama in the exploratory journeys; there is the technical history of navigation, or that of the complex commercial networks which brought the world's goods to Europe; there is the political history of the overseas empires which the European powers built up in the wake of the explorers; each one of these is an enormous field of study. This book concentrates on the intellectual context of exploration: how did explorers and their patrons understand their expanding world and their place in it? What were they really seeking, and how did they believe they could achieve it? How did they balance the known and the unknown in their minds? Historical maps are vitally important in answering these questions, and this book attempts to display the geographical ideas of the explorers themselves, through the maps which they used or the new maps which they made. Many excellent books on exploration have been written using modern maps to trace the voyages and journeys, but this can be unsatisfactory for several reasons. First, modern maps obviously show a modern view of the world, clear, precise and complete, not the explorer's own view with its blank spaces and uncertainties. Second, we often do not know the exact routes of the early explorers, and the paths so clearly traced on the map may be misleading. And third, contemporary maps often show features which contemporaries believed were there – legendary cities, islands or straits – whose supposed existence was crucial to the explorers' whole course of action. Thus the maps of a given historical period serve as a revealing index to contemporary knowledge, belief and motivation.

This book briefly describes more than two hundred explorers and their achievements; but this number could easily be doubled or trebled, and a true account of any one of these journeys could fill a book in its own right. In the historiography of exploration the landmarks have been firmly established over many years, from the first printed editions of Marco Polo, the letters of Columbus and Cortes, the narratives collected by Ramusio and Hakluyt, the official records of Tasman or Cook, through to the personal accounts of later figures such as Livingstone or Nansen: all these enable us to reconstruct the historical events which lay behind the emerging world map. It is a striking fact that some of the most important explorers – Marco Polo, Columbus, Magellan – have left us no direct legacy of maps, and the historian must therefore examine the contemporary map record in order to trace the footprints or the seaways of the explorers.

This book is a highly compressed account, but I have tried always to set these journeys within their wider cultural context, for the geographical quest had always a motive and an aftermath, and it is impossible to avoid the larger perspectives opened by the study of exploration. The narrative of who first landed on a certain coast, or first passed through a certain strait, is only a beginning, not an end. We must ask why they were there, who sent them, what did they believe they had found, and above all, what was the impact of their journey? In short, I have tried to discern the spirit in which the European explorers set out on each new quest, and my central conclusion is that that spirit has evolved to reflect the various phases of European culture during the last five centuries. The European overseas adventure began as an aggressive search for wealth enforced by military power and rationalized as a crusade. This phase was succeeded by one in which the forging of trade networks was paramount, often leading to colonization; and finally by a phase of recognizably scientific exploration. The legacy of this process, for better or worse, has been to spread European culture, and especially European economic systems, throughout the world. By the year 1900, European power, direct or indirect, was dominant over eighty-five per cent of the earth's surface. Only the afterglow of this exploration culture now remains in the romantic search for escape and for wilderness, in which exploration has become a subjective, aesthetic experience.

The knowledge which the early navigators sought was hard-edged, mercenary and political in its application, and perhaps the greatest fallacy in writing the history of exploration would be to read back our post-romantic quest for the unknown into the lives of the ambitious expedition commanders of sixteenth-century Spain or England. Yet these ruthless, practical navigators and fighters brought about a revolution in knowledge. Did the motivation of the explorer really matter? What part did any individual really play in what was a global process? If da Gama had not sailed for India in 1497, or Magellan for the Pacific in 1519, another man would soon have done so, for exploration, perhaps like technology in our own time, had acquired a momentum of its own that was impersonal and unstoppable. But this does not make the history of exploration less important or less interesting, rather the reverse: it makes plain that exploration was a powerful expression of the European psyche. The task of understanding it is therefore as urgent as that of understanding the history of western science or religion, or warfare, indeed it shared with all these the potential for deeply destructive effects. Historical exploration, with the conflicts, the movement of peoples and the economic changes which it engendered, has had an incalculable impact on world history; the charting of a strait or the crossing of a mountain range cannot be isolated from its consequences, any more than the invention of the steam engine or the discovery of penicillin can be treated as technical matters, without consequences for the human race. The true history of exploration was often terrifying, almost too bad to be contemplated. Its blood has soaked into the fabric of our civilization and is all too easily forgotten. But without an understanding of the process of exploration, the world we now inhabit, its peoples, its economies and its conflicts, is barely comprehensible.

I have to thank several of the staff at The British Library for their parts in the genesis of this book: David Way for urging me to write it; Tony Campbell for criticizing and improving the text; and Kathy Houghton for the picture research. This is a brief history of a very large subject, and I have tried to render it coherent by not merely reciting events but by interpreting them clearly. To adapt what Poincaré said of science 'History is built up with facts, as a house is from stones; but a collection of facts is no more history than a heap of stones is a house.'

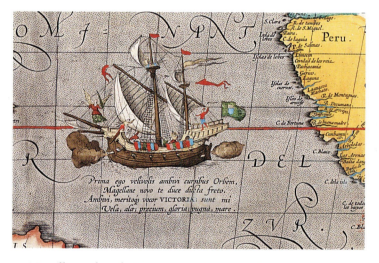

Magellan's ship the Victoria, *with its guardian angel, from Ortelius's map of the Pacific, 1589.*

The British Library Maps C.23.e.12.

CHAPTER ONE
EXPLORATION IN THE ANCIENT WORLD

THE MEDITERRANEAN FULCRUM

SOME TEN THOUSAND YEARS AGO, on the plains of Mesopotamia and in the hills of Anatolia, certain groups of men developed the arts of agriculture, metalworking and building, and used them to create the earliest civilizations. These people were descended from a far older race of men who long before had learned to use stone tools, to control fire, and to speak. Those first humans are believed to have emerged from East Africa perhaps 100,000 years earlier, and from that point of origin to have migrated across the entire world, entering America and Australasia via now-vanished land bridges. In a biological sense therefore, the entire world was man's home: as a species he had already travelled the earth. But this dispersal occurred before the beginning of human history, of man's collective memory. Each emergent civilization as it came to consciousness – in Mesopotamia, China or America – was aware only of its own immediate environment. For thousands of years of human history this pattern was maintained, of multiple civilizations developing in isolation and in ignorance of each other. This isolation was the natural product of physical geography, the impassable barriers of ocean, desert and mountain.

The history of exploration is the process by which this isolation has been broken down, the process by which the one world which mankind now inhabits was created. In this process it is not solely the act of travel that is decisive, but man's developing knowledge of the world, knowledge that becomes recorded, permanent, and above all centralized into one systematic view of the world. The European Age of Discovery remains all-important because of its scale and its completeness. It encompassed the entire world, drawing together for the first time a knowledge of Africa, Asia, the Americas and Europe, and of the oceans that now linked rather than divided them. For it was this power of ocean travel which distinguished the European explorers of the Renaissance from their predecessors: they were able to shape a new world order because they alone could range over the whole world. However great the geographical spread of earlier cultures – Roman, Arab, Mongol or Inca – vast areas of the world, indeed most of the world, had always remained unknown and inaccessible. It was the navigators of the sixteenth century who changed that forever: after Magellan, mankind was living, for better or worse, in a single world. In the Renaissance period the sudden explosion of geographical knowledge found its perfect expression in a newly-created icon: the map. For the monarch and the navigator, the merchant and the scholar, the map became a mirror of the world, both a symbol of knowledge and an instrument of power, and it now acquired an importance in European intellectual and political life which it had never enjoyed in any other culture. It became both a record of what was known, and a spur to probe the unknown. Its roots lay partly in science and partly in fable, and it promised both wealth and knowledge. The map was a meeting-place between the known and the unknown: only when the limits of geographical knowledge had been defined on a map could explorers set out in search of new lands, new routes and new knowledge.

After 1500 the history of exploration resolves itself into the history of European geographical knowledge, and it was in European maps that a decisive revolution in geography found its expression. There was a finality and irreversibility about these major discoveries – the circumnavigation of Africa, the crossing of the Atlantic and of the Pacific – for they created the modern world map, as surely as Copernicus created the modern cosmic map. In the years between 1480 and 1530, knowledge and power went hand in hand as intellectual, political and technical forces carried Europeans to Africa, Asia and America as traders or conquerors. The European culture of the later middle ages had not shown itself inherently greater or wiser or more powerful than the world of Islam or the Mongol empire; yet a few decades at the end of the fifteenth century saw a handful of radical ideas in geography and technology merge to create an explosive movement which enabled western Europe to outpace all rival cultures. The compass, the three-masted ship, the map and the gun – these were the weapons of the European explorers. Fifty years ago the Age of Discovery was chronicled in books with titles such as *The Conquest of the Earth*, or *Nine Against the Unknown*, or *Founders of Empire*, and so on. Such titles acknowledged the unique importance of these events, but today we are less triumphalist: we know that Columbus did not discover America, since there were some twenty million people living on the continent when he arrived. What he clearly did however, was to bring America into the sphere of European knowledge – with momentous consequences for the peoples of both continents. Furthermore he and the other great mariners of these early years inaugurated an era in which geographical knowledge – and the technical power to exploit it – acquired massive political importance.

Many earlier civilizations had been expansive in character: Greeks, Romans and Moslems had all pushed outwards from their historic centres, in pursuit of trade or conquest. These movements had been halted by natural obstacles, or by an opposing force strong enough to stop them. Certain other cultures, however highly developed, had remained fixed in their homeland; the Egyptians, the Maya, the Chinese (save for one short-lived experiment in the fifteenth century) were apparently not tempted intellectually or militarily to venture far beyond their own boundaries. On the eve of the European conquests, the Aztec and Inca civilizations had absolutely no mutual knowledge or contact. Later, when European ships thronged the harbours of the Atlantic, Pacific and Indian Oceans, no Indian or Chinese ship was ever seen in Seville, Amsterdam or London. Why certain cultures were geographically dynamic and others static can never be entirely explained, nor can the impulse to build experience into systematic knowledge, an impulse completely absent from some societies. Before the European Age of Discovery, the most dynamic culture in the world was that of the Polynesians, whose migrations carried them across millions of square miles of the Pacific. Yet, in that pre-literate and pre-scientific culture, these voyages were not built into a coherent body of geographical knowledge. Once the voyagers had settled a new group of distant islands, there was apparently no further contact with their place of origin, and each community then developed in isolation, nor was there any cartographic tradition among these remarkable seafarers.

The Polynesian experience is diametrically opposed to that of the ancient Hellenic people:

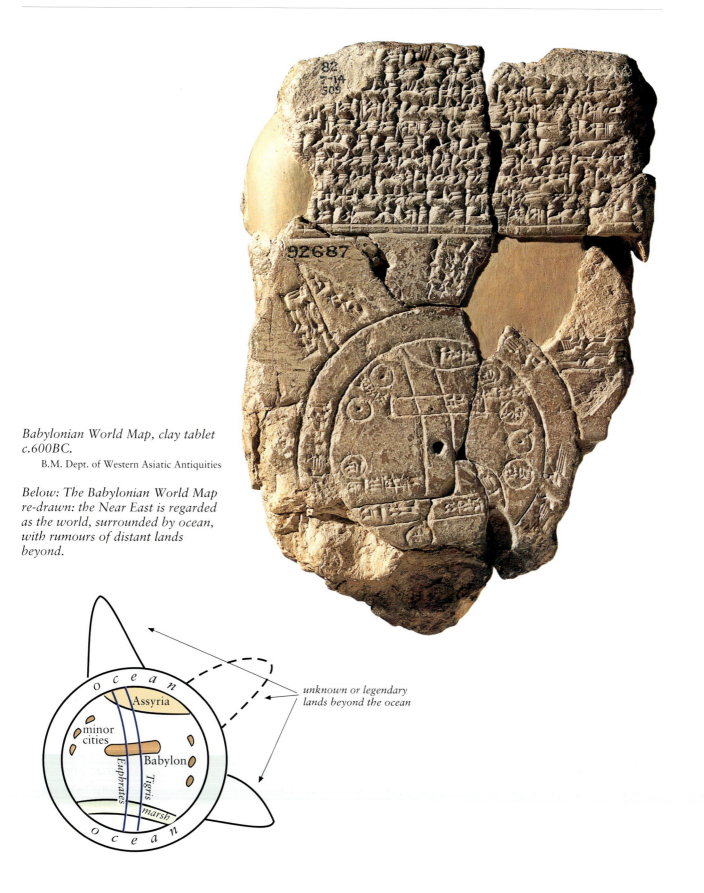

Babylonian World Map, clay tablet c.600BC.
B.M. Dept. of Western Asiatic Antiquities

Below: The Babylonian World Map re-drawn: the Near East is regarded as the world, surrounded by ocean, with rumours of distant lands beyond.

unknown or legendary lands beyond the ocean

ocean

Assyria

minor cities

Babylon

Euphrates

Tigris

marsh

ocean

Chinese World Map c.1500AD. China is shown as the Middle Kingdom, with the rest of the world at its edges. Note the structural similarity to the Homeric World Map opposite.

The British Library Maps 33.c.13.

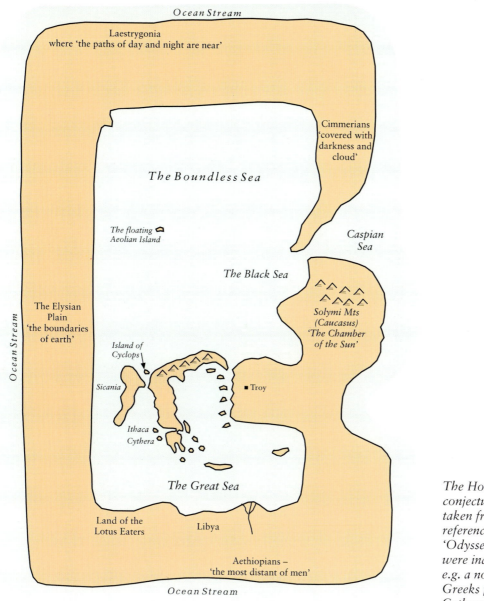

Ocean Stream

Laestrygonia
where 'the paths of day and night are near'

Cimmerians
'covered with
darkness and
cloud'

The Boundless Sea

*The floating
Aeolian Island*

*Caspian
Sea*

The Black Sea

*Solymi Mts
(Caucasus)
'The Chamber
of the Sun'*

The Elysian
Plain
'the boundaries
of earth'

Ocean Stream

*Island of
Cyclops*

Sicania

■ Troy

Ithaca
Cythera

The Great Sea

Land of the
Lotus Eaters

Libya

Aethiopians –
'the most distant of men'

Ocean Stream

*The Homeric World: a
conjectural reconstruction
taken from geographical
references in the 'Iliad' and the
'Odyssey'. Sometimes distances
were indicated by sailing times,
e.g. a north wind drove the
Greeks for ten days from
Cythera to the land of the
Lotus Eaters.*

although far more restricted geographically, they built up a body of objective geographical knowledge that was recorded and permanent. This tradition was eclipsed in the post-classical era, but was later to be rediscovered and became a decisive influence in shaping the geographical ideas of the Renaissance navigators. The most celebrated early Mediterranean seafarers, the Phoenicians, had, before 1000BC, sailed from their homeland in Canaan beyond the Pillars of Hercules, perhaps as far as Britain, and colonized the coasts of Spain and North Africa. Yet of their science, geography and chartmaking, if any, we know nothing. The secrets of their routes and their maritime knowledge were jealously guarded. They transmitted their skills through traditional, oral means, and as far we can tell formal cartography played no part in their maritime achievement. It was the Greeks who left the fullest record of the transformation of geographical experience into formal knowledge. Weaving together travel narratives, rational observation and scientific theory, Greek thinkers addressed the three most fundamental questions of geography: What is the form and magnitude of the earth? What are the shape and size of its land-masses and oceans? What is the nature and extent of human habitation on the earth? There is considerable fragmentary evidence that many ancient civilizations had regarded 'The World' as synonymous with 'Our World'. Egyptians, Baylonians, Indians and Chinese have all left 'World Maps' which are essentially maps of their own territory, surrounded by ocean. This was a natural concept, and the same thought is traceable in a number of ancient texts, such as the Homeric poems. These peoples plainly did not possess a world map – literally or psychologically – in which certain blank spaces were waiting to be filled; rather, what they knew filled the whole world. It was the achievement of certain Greek thinkers to break free from such subjective intuitions and to raise geography to the level of objective science.

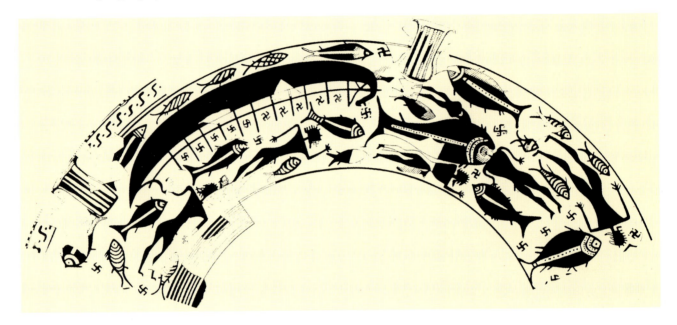

A shipwreck in the eighth century BC, drawn on a vase found on Ischia, near the Bay of Naples, site of the first Greek colony in the west.

By permission of Oxford University Press

The earliest documents of European history, the Homeric poems, display a pre-scientific geography. The known world was small and enclosed, for beyond the shores of the eastern Mediterranean were the regions of the Ethiopians, the Elysian plains, or the Cimmerian darkness, regions which were legendary yet which were traditionally assigned vague locations to the south, west or north of the Aegean heartland. The extensive Hellenic colonization of the Mediterranean and Black Sea coasts between 800BC and 400BC opened up this archaic world. Countless forgotten traders or warriors must have explored the hinterlands, dispelling uncertainty and legend. More distant lands became known through single, epic journeys, related by classical writers such as Herodotus, whose stories often exercised great influence on later explorers. Herodotus reports for example that five unnamed adventurers journeyed south-west from Libya across a vast desert until they reached a great river flowing from west to east. This was presumably the Niger, although Herodotus considered it was the Nile. Perhaps his most famous and intriguing story was of the Phoenicians who had sailed around the entire coast of Africa about the year 600BC. Equally celebrated was the great northern voyage of Pytheas from Marseilles to Britain and beyond. This journey, known to us through the later account

Below: Indian cosmic model, early nineteenth century.
Victoria & Albert Museum

Right: Indian cosmic model redrawn: the world is pictured as a lotus, with mountains at its sacred centre, surrounded by petal-continents, one of which is India. The British Library 434.e.8.

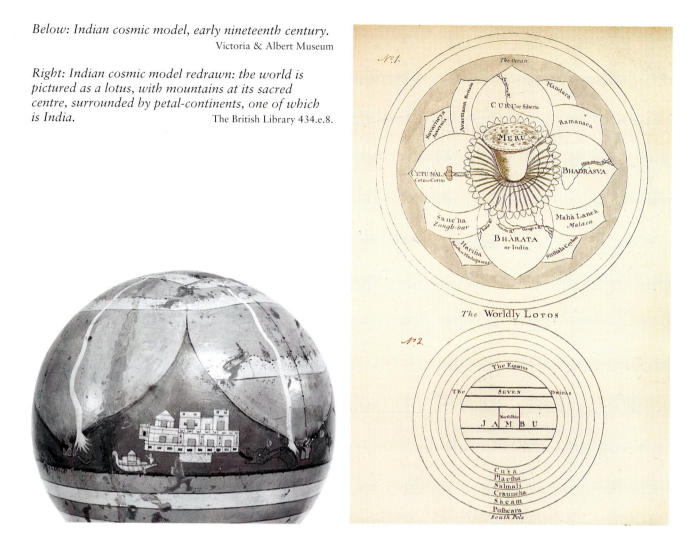

of Strabo, took place about 300BC, and was the source of all Greek and Roman knowledge of northern European geography until the time of Julius Caesar. Pytheas may have circumnavigated Britain, sailed the Baltic and the North Sea, and touched the coast of Norway or even Iceland. The identification of his 'Thule', the northerly limit of the world, is uncertain, but he reported that the midsummer day there lasted 24 hours, and that these lands at some 65 degrees north, were fully inhabited, contrary to the prevailing Greek belief that human settlement must stop short of this 'frigid zone'. To the east, around 510BC Darius, King of Persia, sent a Greek envoy, Scylax of Caryanda, to explore the Indus and beyond. Scylax travelled overland to the Kabul River and descended the Indus to the sea, before sailing westward to coast the Arabian Peninsula and ascend the Red Sea. He was the first known European to see India, and knowledge of his journey was the inspiration for that of Alexander the Great. Such journeys however were isolated and unrepeated, and the knowledge they brought remained uncertain, almost legendary. Yet their currency seems to show that classical thinkers were quite open to the possibility that the world was much larger than their own immediate environment.

This exploring activity was matched by intellectual innovation, as Hellenic philosophers began asking systematic questions about the world, and seeking rational rather than mythic answers. The Milesian philosophers of the fifth and fourth centuries BC – Thales, Anaximander and Hecataeus – were convinced that the earth was a sphere, and they are reported to be the first to have made globes

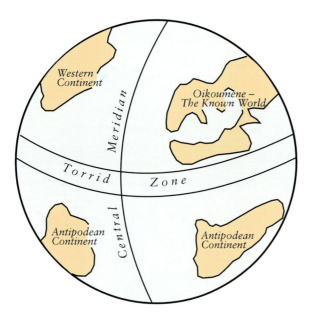
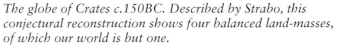

The globe of Crates c.150BC. Described by Strabo, this conjectural reconstruction shows four balanced land-masses, of which our world is but one.

and maps of the world. Spherical geometry and coordinate systems were first used by astronomers in relation to the heavenly sphere, and their subsequent transfer to terrestrial geography enabled estimates to be made of the size of the earth. The most famous of these, by Eratosthenes of Cyrene in the third century BC, was accurate to within 5% of its true value. The inescapable conclusion of such theoretical work was that the known, inhabited world – the Mediterranean and western Asia – represented only one small part of the globe; there remained vast areas of the world that were unknown and out of reach, and where other men and other civilizations might possibly exist. The Greek military and commercial experience served to confirm this. When Alexander led his armies through Persia into India he perpetually encountered new tribes, new cities and new cultures, apparently without end. Alexander's journeys were as important intellectually as they were politically, for they enlarged the classical world view. However it is clear that Alexander did not venture his vast army without a prior geographical plan. His aim was to reach the eastern ocean which Greeks considered must bound the Eurasian world. He took scholars and geographers to record his journey, and his political legacy meant that at his death the Hellenistic world was a known geographical realm which stretched from the Straits of Gibraltar to the Indus.

The use which Greeks made of maps is still very uncertain. Few Greek writers before Ptolemy explicitly describe a world map, nor has any contemporary world map survived from the entire classical period. Greek geographical ideas are recoverable only from texts, often secondary accounts by writers such as Strabo who around 10–20AD compiled a comprehensive history of geographical thought. Strabo describes for example the large globe made in Rome by Crates about the year 150BC, upon which Crates theorized that four continents existed, one in each quarter of the globe. They were symmetrically disposed on either side of the equator and of an Atlantic meridian. The three unknown continents could be very similar to our own, and inhabited by people like ourselves. This kind of theorizing seems to have appealed to the Greeks without driving them on to ask whether the unknown continents could be found and explored. In fact the classical doctrine of the earth's zones acted as a great barrier to distant exploration. All Greek thinkers seem to have considered that the earth was divided into five natural zones: an equatorial zone, two temperate zones and two frigid polar zones. Human habitation was possible only in the temperate zones, while heat and cold made it

Ptolemy's World Map, c.150AD, redrawn in the fifteenth century.

The British Library Harley MS 7182, ff. 58v–59.

impossible elsewhere, and presumably ruled out contacts between the four continents. It is noticeable that when Strabo describes countries and regions he does so in highly graphic terms: Sicily is said to be shaped like a triangle; Mesopotamia is like the profile of a boat, the Tigris forming the straight deck, the Euphrates the curved keel; the Nile mouth is like the Greek capital letter delta – Δ. These descriptions suggest strongly that Strabo was writing with a world map before him, but we cannot be certain.

It is from the second century AD that we possess a full and detailed statement of classical geography, in the work of Ptolemy of Alexandria. Drawing on every available source of travel and geography, Ptolemy compiled a world gazetteer, comprising over eight thousand place-names, from Scotland to Malaya. Ptolemy estimated their geographical coordinates as accurately as he could from his sources, longitude being measured eastwards from the Fortunate Islands, the western extremity of the known world. Whether Ptolemy himself drew the corresponding maps is uncertain, but it has been possible to translate his precise data into visual form and to produce a series of detailed maps of the world known in classical times. The context of Ptolemy's geography is that of Roman military power and the Roman economy, both of which had brought huge tracts of Europe, Asia and Northern Africa into the sphere of Greek knowledge. The legions patrolled from the North Sea coasts to the Caspian, while the Roman taste for luxuries supported trade routes between east and west, to bring silk, dyes, gems, spices and artefacts from as far away as China. Thus Ptolemy's world map

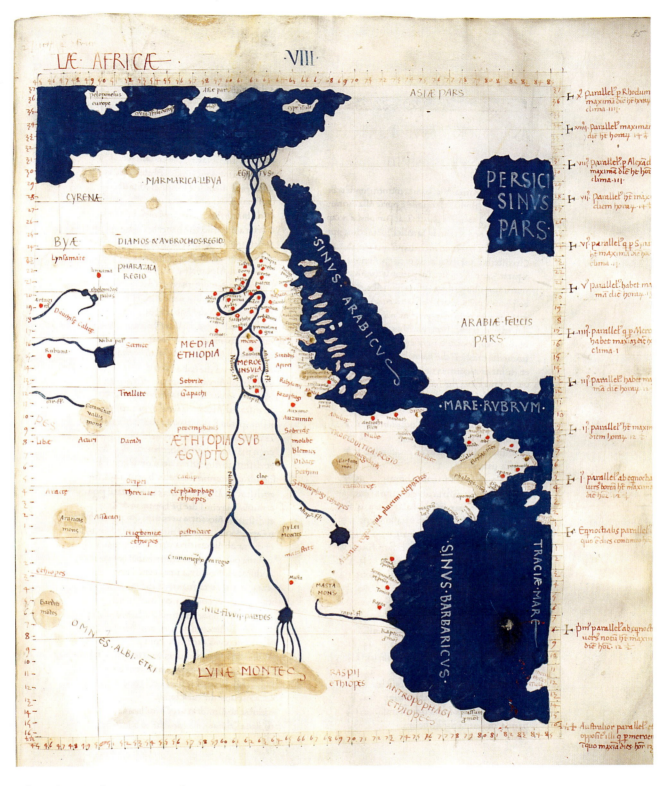

The Nile in Ptolemy's geography.

The British Library Harley MS 7182, ff. 84v–85.

extends north to the British Isles and Denmark, with the ancient region of Sarmatia – Poland and the Ukraine – as the remotest northern area mapped in any detail. His knowledge of East Africa extends some way south of the Horn of Africa, and the source of the Nile is fancifully traced to the 'Mountains of the Moon' lying in the African interior around 15 degrees south. The picture of western Africa is more confused, for the Fortunate Islands are placed much too far south at around 15 degrees north, and land detail is given for the coast here and for 'Libia Interior' for which Ptotemy can have had no authentic sources that we know of.

Not surprisingly, it is impossible to identify many of the places – cities, lakes, rivers, mountains – named by Ptolemy, and this serves to underline what the author himself explained, that his geography is collated and harmonized from many earlier sources, many of them of doubtful precision, and many quite unverifiable. Ptolemy's aims and methods were rigorous and scientific, but his materials were not equal to his demands on them. To establish longitude, for example, from a travel narrative where distances were given in days' journeys, was quite impossible. Nevertheless the extent of Ptolemy's world is impresssive, extending far beyond the Graeco-Roman heartland, into India, China and South-East Asia. Ptolemy plainly did not believe in the circumnavigation of Africa, although he was surely aware of the legend: his depiction of the Indian Ocean as an enclosed sea was pure theory. China is known as the source of the silk trade (its Latin name 'Serica Regio' meant simply 'silken kingdom'), but Ptolemy knows no sea east of the Malay peninsula: on the eastern ocean that bounds Eurasia, he does not care to speculate. With all their imperfections Ptolemy's maps of Asia are remarkable testimony to the trade routes that linked east and west, for we have no contemporary narrative accounts of them. They were not under Greek or Roman control, and this geographical data must have come through many traders, mariners and adventurers of whom we know nothing. Ptolemy's world map represents a geographic vision unmatched by any earlier civilization, and one that would not be superseded for fourteen centuries.

THE POST-CLASSICAL WORLD

The post-classical era witnessed a migration of peoples on a massive, unprecedented scale throughout Eurasia. Driven before the aggressive nomadic warriors from the Asian steppes, Saxons, Franks, Burgundians, Vandals, Goths, and Lombards migrated across Europe in their thousands. Roman power was the great casualty of the redrawing of the tribal, political map of Europe after 400AD. To speak of geographical knowledge in this context is difficult, yet a sense of geography must have underlain many of these events. The Saxons who sailed from northern Germany to seize large areas of Britain clearly knew where they going and what they were going to. The same is true of the Vandals who, having already migrated across Europe, crossed from Spain to North Africa, from where they launched seaborne raids on Italy, including Rome itself. What level of geographical knowledge, written or unwritten, influenced the movement of these peoples it is impossible to say.

The classical geography of Ptolemy was lost to the west and would remain so for many centuries. Yet the survival of his texts in eastern centres such as Alexandria, Antioch and Damascus meant that the first beneficiary of the Greek geographical system was Islam. By 750AD Islamic power had spread from its Arabian heartland west as far as Spain and east as far as India, and covered the larger part of the Ptolemaic world. Arab traders sailed to East Africa and to India and China, learning to master the monsoon winds that prevailed in the Indian Ocean. As remarkable as this maritime trade was the Islamic penetration of Africa, developing caravan routes across the Sahara, up the White and Blue Nile into Sudan and Ethiopia, and via the East coast trading ports. The twin demands of Islamic religious practice, the pilgrimage to Mecca and the observance of the sacred direction of prayer – the Qibla – fostered a strong sense of precise geography in Islamic

culture. When Arab scholars sought to construct a systematic geography of the known world, the Greek model was their principal guide. Even more than the Romans, the Islamic dominion over large regions of Asia, Africa and Europe provided both a context for travel and the data for a world map. The former is exemplified in the exotic figure of Ibn Battutah, who in the fourteenth century travelled from his birthplace in Tangier throughout North Africa and the Middle East, to Central Asia beyond the Caspian Sea, to Mombasa and Zanzibar on the East African coast, and eastwards to India, Sumatra and China. He cannot be called an explorer, for he travelled existing caravan and sea routes, mainly with fellow-Muslims, but for that very reason his travels hold up a mirror to the Islamic world of his day, and to the half-known, exotic lands that lay on its fringes, lands which become central in the fabulous tales of Sinbad.

The great cartographer of the Islamic world was al-Idrisi who worked under the patronage of the Norman king of Sicily, Roger II, during the years 1140–1155AD, where he constructed the most detailed and accurate world map of the era. Comprising seventy sectional maps, this work was accompanied by full textual descriptions of the countries, cities and peoples of each region. Al-Idrisi's world map bears a strong resemblance to that of Ptolemy; the most significant differences were that the Islamic scholar did not believe that the Indian Ocean was land-locked, and he clearly had definite knowledge of China's eastern coast. However he perpetuates a typical error of Islamic maps – the enormous eastward extension of Africa's east coast, and this was derived directly from Ptolemy. This is a puzzling feature, for Arab seafarers trading to Mombasa, Zanzibar and south as far as Sofala (near the mouth of the Zambesi) could surely have contradicted it. The effect is that the Indian Ocean is shown as an elongated sea with many large islands, resembling the Mediterranean. The huge peninsula of India escaped the mapmaker, as it had escaped Ptolemy. These errors are useful reminders of two things: first, whatever the scientific achievements of Islamic scientists in the fields of mathematics and astronomy, map-making and compass charting were technical and empirical skills that lay still in the future; and second, that the scholars who made the maps were not the same men who sailed to Malindi, Mombasa, Calicut or Ceylon. To the scholar the authority of his predecessors was often stronger than the reports of uneducated mariners. Al-Idrisi had to balance travel

South-East Asia from Ptolemy's geography.
The British Library Harley MS 7182, ff. 104v–105.

The World Map of Al-Idrisi, 1154AD (redrawn). South is at the top, but it clearly resembles Ptolemy's geography.

The British Library Maps 856 (6).

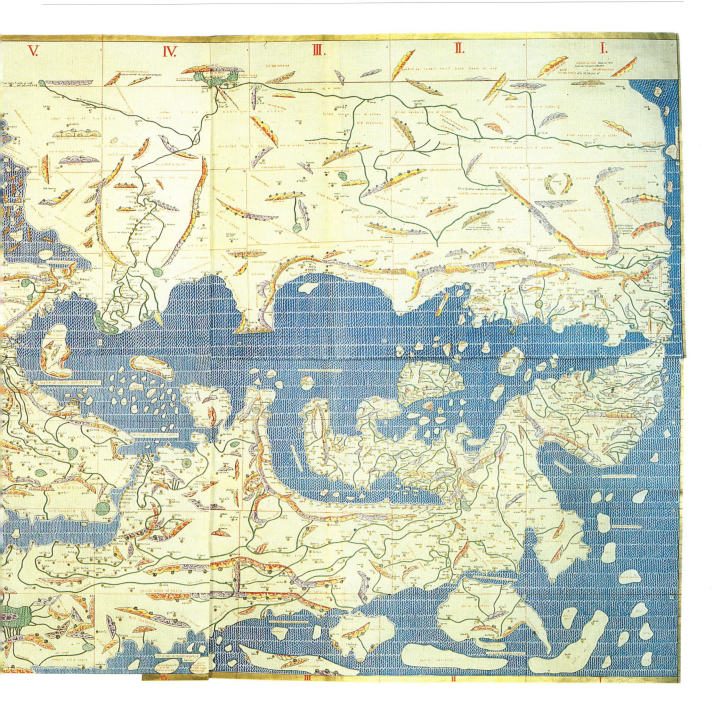

narratives against the geographical framework inherited from the great Ptolemy.

After its violent eruption into world history in the seventh and eighth centuries AD, the Islamic world remained relatively static, until the Ottoman era. In spite of their formidable scientific and military skills, no Islamic ship ever ventured out into the Atlantic, south along the East African coast beyond Sofala, or east beyond the Straits of Malacca. Had they done so, the most expansive culture in the world must surely have pre-empted the European era of discovery, and much of subsequent world history would have been radically different.

No other culture had shown such dynamic force as Islam. In the first century BC, Han China

Right: The Arabian Gulf by Al-Idrisi. South is at the top.

Bodleian Library, Pococke MS 375, ff. 132v–133.

Left: Roman coin of 64AD showing Ostia, the port of Rome, with its wharves, ships and statues.

B.M. Dept. of Coins and Medals

steadily extended its geographical power, south into Vietnam, north into Korea and east into the Tarim Basin. China's northern borders were always menaced by the presence of hostile tribes, and her relationship with other kingdoms in Asia was that of a dominant cultural influence, rather than an imperial power. The Chinese showed no great desire to explore beyond their own borders. An innate sense of self-confidence and superiority seems to have characterized Chinese civilization, so that China was the 'Middle Kingdom', the centre of the world, and all other nations were peripheral. The outstanding exceptions to this were certain journeys into India undertaken by Buddhists, both as factfinding missions and as pilgrimages. Between 399 and 414AD Fa Hsien journeyed across the Takla Makan desert, crossed the Hindu Kush, through Kashmir and down the Ganges, continuing by sea to Ceylon and Java. Two centuries later Hsuan Tsang traced the same course as far as the Ganges delta, from where he made an overland circuit of the subcontinent via Madras, Bombay and the Indus valley. Both men wrote full accounts of their travels, brought numerous artefacts and Buddhist texts back to China, and proved important eyewitnesses of ancient India. Hsuan Tsang saw temples and monasteries in north-west India that had been pillaged by Huns. Among the Buddhist concepts which they imported into China was a new form of world map, in which India, as the home of the Buddha, was the dominant feature, centred on Mount Sumeru, the mountain sacred to Hindus and Buddhists, which later came to be identified with Mount Kailas in Tibet. This form of world map became a Buddhist icon, and flourished especially in Japan, surviving into the nineteenth century. Thus, although these Buddhist pilgrimages added greatly to Chinese knowledge of the world beyond their own borders, they scarcely effected a revolution in geographical thought, while contacts between the two civilizations remained tenuous. Much later, between 1405 and 1435, the Chinese court sponsored a remarkable series of voyages in the China Sea and Indian Ocean, commanded by Cheng Ho. Fleets of Chinese ships visited Borneo, Java, Sumatra, South India, Ceylon, the Persian Gulf, the Arabian

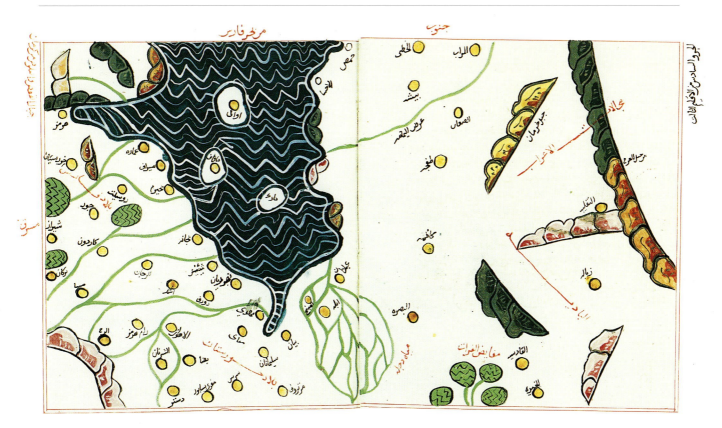

Coast and East Africa. The exact motive for these expeditions is unclear, and they established no permanent contacts or colonies. Had the Chinese desired to set up a powerful presence in South Asia, the experience of the Portuguese when they arrived in the region some seventy years later would surely have been very different.

Indian civilization was equally self-sufficient, showing neither the urge to explore nor an impulse towards systematic geography. Indian world maps were formalized and symbolic, sometimes taking the form of a lotus, having four petal-continents radiating from a sacred centre. The southern petal was identified with India itself, the others with the lands beyond the Himalayas, of which no individual geographical description was attempted. Another form of world map showed a single central continent representing the entire world of man, surrounded by water, then by further circular continents. The role of these maps was that of an icon, far removed from empirical geography. The strongly mystical element in the Indian intellect found satisfaction in such cosmic diagrams, nor were there any cultural or historical forces impelling Indians to explore or to migrate by land or by sea.

The civilizations of ancient America show some of the most striking effects of cultural dispersal and isolation. Entering America some 20,000 years ago from Siberia, the early settlers moved east and south and became fragmented into many tribes and nations. They became, in their different regions, arctic hunters, desert gatherers, maize farmers or jungle hunters. In some regions civilization developed with science, architecture, agriculture and metalwork, while elsewhere stone-age hunters flourished. Maritime activity was limited to fishing from rafts and canoes, and the contact between these groups, even between two contemporary civilizations such as the Aztecs and the Incas, was non-existent. Cultural development was startlingly uneven: mathematics, astronomy, architecture and engineering could flourish in the absence of writing and of basic tools such as the wheel. The vast Inca empire, 2,000 miles in extent, was linked through a series of well-engineered mountain roads, yet no maps were ever made of them. We know from the accounts of the conquistadors that the

A Norse Ship, from a tenth century manuscript.

The British Library, Cotton MS Tiberius B V pt 1, f.40v.

native peoples often had a clear geographical sense of their own region, but of the lands and peoples beyond their own borders they knew nothing.

The most dynamic phase of exploration between the fall of Rome and the Renaissance was the Norse voyages of the ninth and tenth centuries. The Norse journeys should be seen as part of the migrations of the post-Roman era. They pioneered trade routes across the Baltic and ascended the rivers to Novgorod and Kiev. Via the coasts of France and Spain they reached the Mediterranean. Their motives might be trade, pillage or colonization, the former often leading eventually to the latter, so that Norse dominions were founded in England, France and Sicily. Their voyages to Iceland from 870AD onwards and to Greenland from 980 onwards are more difficult to explain, for these lands were far less hospitable, nor can we say what originally led the Norse seamen to venture out into the forbidding waters of the North Atlantic. Some conscious impulse towards exploration and conquest there must have been, prompted perhaps by harsh living conditions at home and with sovereignty over any new lands as the possible reward. What geographical ideas lay behind these voyages it is impossible to say, for there are no contemporary records or maps, but the Norsemen had plainly developed formidable techniques of shipbuilding and navigation by around 800AD, superior to those of any other nations of the time. Some of their knowledge is preserved in the Norse Saga literature, although this took written form some three or four centuries after the events described. The

Landnamabok – the 'Book of Landtaking' – is a twelfth-century record of the Norse Atlantic settlements and includes many details of sailing times and means of estimating course and position. It is clear that they possessed an understanding of latitude, for Cape Farewell (the southern extremity of Greenland) is said to be reached by sailing due west from Norway's Hern Island (i.e. possibly South or North Hordland), and sighting the Shetlands to the south and the Faroes to the north: this describes the 61st parallel, which will indeed give a landfall at Cape Farewell. The significance of the altitude of the Sun and the Pole Star were understood and used in this form of latitude sailing, and the changing declination of the sun through the year must also have been tabulated.

Around the year 1000AD, Leif Ericsson sailed from the Greenland colony to investigate reports of land to the west. One of the key factors may have been that this land, said to have been sighted by Norse mariners blown off-course, was thickly wooded, for the absence of timber on Greenland was a great handicap. After a voyage no greater than from Norway to Shetland, he did indeed find land, but it was stony and barren; this may have been Baffin Island. Moving south, the explorers landed on the more hospitable beaches of a wooded country which Leif named *Markland* – Land of Forests – which was almost certainly the Labrador coast. Further south still, Leif described reaching a strait with a small island at its mouth and the mainland stretching out beyond it – surely the Strait of Belle Isle and Newfoundland. Going ashore, the Norsemen were impressed by the meadows and salmon streams they found, and decided to spend the winter there before sailing back to Greenland with news of their discovery. In the following ten to fifteen years there were further voyages and attempts to colonize the new lands; these attempts failed mainly through damaging encounters with hostile native peoples.

The single great enigma about the Norse discovery is Leif's statement that 'wild grapes' grew there in abundance, prompting him to bestow on it the name *Vinland*. Since wild grapes cannot possibly grow in northern Newfoundland, historians have been much exercised to locate Leif's settlement. It has been placed further south in Nova Scotia or Massachusetts, or it has been suggested that the grapes were really berries. The excavation in the 1960s of an ancient settlement on the northern tip of Newfoundland, clearly identified as Norse in character and dated to around the year 1000, has proved beyond doubt that the Norsemen reached North America; the mystery of the grapes remains unsolved. There is some slight evidence that the Greenland Norsemen made summer voyages to *Markland* (Labrador) for timber, and a few medieval writers make brief mention of the western discoveries, but there were no more expeditions to *Vinland*. Mainland Europe displayed no interest in the remote colonies on Iceland and Greenland, and no revolution in geographical knowledge flowed from the Norse achievement. The isolation of the American continent continued undisturbed for a further five centuries.

After the long centuries of migration, the Christian church acted as a powerful unifying intellectual force in medieval Europe, creating a sense of geographical identity among nations from Scandinavia to Spain, from Ireland to Greece. The religion of the Bible was of paramount importance in European culture, and the lands of the Bible – including Egypt and Mesopotamia – provided a field of intense interest and a fixed reference point to geography *beyond* Europe. By a curious historical paradox, Christianity had been displaced from its place of origin and was now centred in Rome and, more precariously in view of the Moslem threat, in Constantinople. The Crusades strongly reinforced the European sense of Christian identity over against the little-known but undoubtedly hostile world beyond Europe. These shadowy, barbarous realms, located far to the east and south, were now little more than exotic names – Ethiopia, the Indies, Persia or Arabia. Medieval maps developed a great richness of lore and imagery, and they showed considerable interest in Asia and Africa, but they show also a paucity of hard facts and an absence of a genuine geographical framework: European ideas about Asia and Africa were drawn largely from fable and legend, and true mapping was still some distance in the future.

The medieval *mappae mundi*, such as the celebrated Hereford map, show the three known

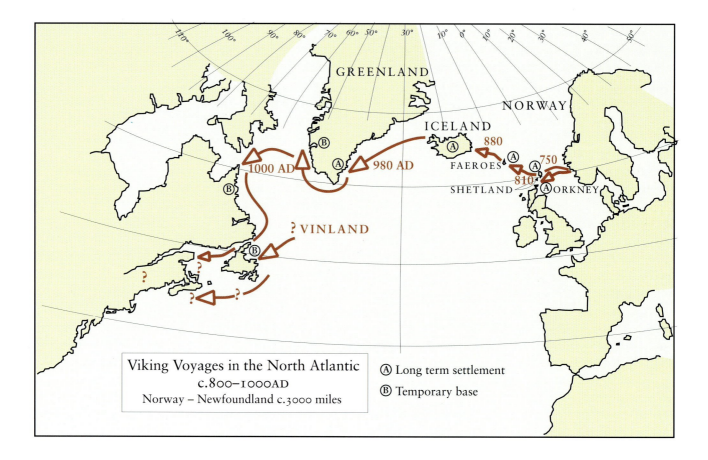

Viking Voyages in the North Atlantic
c.800–1000AD
Norway – Newfoundland c.3000 miles

Ⓐ Long term settlement
Ⓑ Temporary base

continents as roughly equal in size and forming one circular land-mass centred on the Holy Land. This form of world map has been used to support the view that the world was believed to be flat. However medieval thinkers at least after c.1150, were familiar with the Ptolemaic system of a spherical cosmos centred on a spherical earth. This view became universal and orthodox, and the circular disc-like earth of the *mappa mundi* should really be understood as no more than a graphic convention. The other well-known symbol of the earth, the ceremonial orb held by the monarch, was plainly a sphere, but the techniques necessary for representing the spherical earth on paper were quite unknown. By drawing on legend and tradition, the *mappa mundi* gave an impression of a breadth of geographical knowledge that was actually spurious: the names India, China and Africa appear on the map, but their geography and character are really quite unknown. European knowledge of the world really stopped at the Vistula, the Black Sea, the Syrian desert and the coastline of North Africa. In particular – and in spite of the Norse voyages – the Atlantic as the world's western boundary was absolute: beyond the Pillars of Hercules lay only the mythical lands or the islands of legend – Atlantis, the Hesperides, St. Brendan's Isle, Avalon or Lyonesse.

If we survey man's knowledge of his world at the close of the first millenium AD, around the time of the *Vinland* discovery, the overriding impression is of peoples inhabiting island-civilizations isolated from each other, whether by ocean and desert, or by mutual indifference and hostility. Christian Europe and the Islamic world confronted each other across the waters of the Mediterranean, their mutual enmity acting as a barrier to exploration and knowledge. Of these two dominions, the latter was by far the greater, stretching from the Pillars of Hercules to the regions that were mere names in Europe: Arabia, Persia, India. While the Islamic peoples traded with India, China and South-East Asia, the isolation of western Europe was acute, and the achievements of its only explorers – the Norsemen ignored. In India a long period of conflict between rival kingdoms had not prevented a cultural flowering in literature, temple-building and especially science (with mathematics probably more advanced than anywhere in the world), yet any movement to explore the wider world by land or sea was totally absent. The brilliance of the Sung period made China technically the most advanced civilization of its time, but one consciously confined within its own borders, with no curiosity about the barbarians beyond. The American peoples were isolated not only from the rest of the world but from each other, their ethnic identity having fragmented into a myriad of tribes and nations. The same is true of African and Polynesian peoples, whose pre-literate culture prevented the emergence of any formal geographic sense. In all of these cultures there was no escape from the perception that 'The World' was 'Our World'. To cross over from one world to another – if that were physically possible – would mean to be at the mercy of barbarians, or to face the hostile sea. And of course it was equally impossible intellectually, for no man could set out explore regions of the world of whose very existence he was ignorant. The crucial motive for exploration was missing, which is a distinct sense of the known and the unknown, and the challenge of bridging those two realms. It is precisely that sense which is mirrored in the map, displaying the borderland between the known and unknown regions of the world. In the post-classical era, this kind of cartographic awareness was absent: there was no conceptual model of a world map awaiting completion. The age of the great European voyages, when it dawned was characterized by motives that were unmistakably worldly and political. Yet these political goals came into focus only as part of an intellectual revolution, which included the discovery of Ptolemy's geography and the techniques of navigation. The challenges consciously accepted by the protagonists of the Age of Discovery could only be understood in geographical terms. A knowledge or at least a theory of world geography was essential as they defined their aims, and essential to the means they used to achieve them.

CHAPTER TWO

THE LURE OF THE EAST

'I give you my word that I have seen in this city fully 5,000 ships at once, all afloat on this river . . . I assure you that the river flows through more than sixteen provinces and there are on its banks more than 200 cities, all having more ships than this . . . fully 200,000 craft pass upstream every year and a like number return . . . The interior of the Khan's palace is gold and silver and decorated with pictures, the ceilings similarly adorned. No man could imagine any improvement in design and execution. The roof is all ablaze with scarlet and green and blue and yellow, and all the colours are so brilliantly varnished that it glitters like crystal . . . the sparkle can be seen from far away.'

– The Book of Ser Marco Polo

CATHAY REVEALED

IF ONE HAD TO NAME the most influential book in European history written between say 1200 and 1600, the choice might well fall not on the works of Aquinas or Dante, of Machiavelli or even of Copernicus, but on Marco Polo's narrative of his journey to China. By unveiling Chinese civilization to Europe – its social magnificence, its technical inventiveness, its great cities and its fabulous wealth – Marco Polo created the motivation for the Age of Discovery, and all the consequences that flowed from it. When they turned their eyes beyond the shores of Europe, the navigators of the fifteenth century and their patrons were not seeking new *lands*: they were seeking new *routes* to countries already known by report and reputation, and the most enthralling of these reports was that of Marco Polo, whose own eastern journey became the most powerful single inspiration for the European era of exploration.

The journey took place during the years 1271 – 1295 and was the fortuitous result of a complex set of historical events. By the first century AD, tenuous trade-links had been established between Rome and China, with silk the mysterious and highly-prized import to the west. The route by which the silk, together with other commodities such as jade and spices, reached the west, was the famous

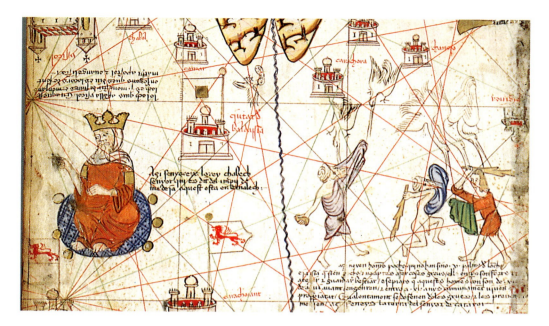

Cathay from the Catalan Atlas, 1375. The Great Khan is shown in the city of Chanbalech.

Bibliothèque Nationale, Paris

Below: Travellers crossing the desert, from the Catalan Atlas, 1375.

Bibliothèque Nationale, Paris

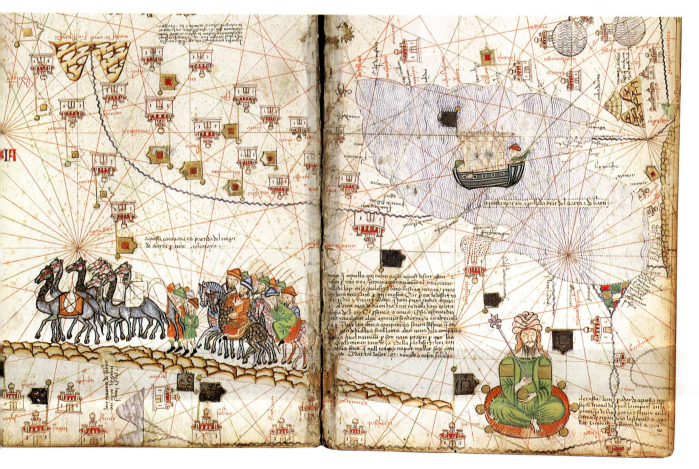

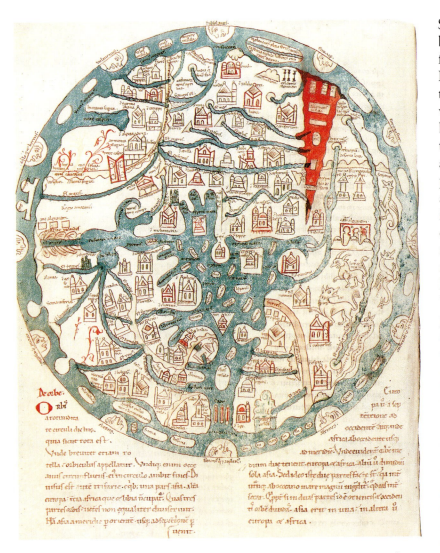

An eleventh-century world map, showing schematically Europe, North Africa and part of Asia.

Bayerische Staatsbibliothek, Munich

Silk Road, actually not one road but a network of possible routes from the western rim of the Gobi Desert, crossing Central Asia and the Near East. This trade survived into the post-classical era, but these routes crossed the territory of numerous independent and warlike peoples. Goods passed through many hands and at each stage their price increased. Then in the seventh century the western sector of this route fell under Moslem control, making travel there for Europeans all but impossible. This situation, and the entire political geography of Asia, were revolutionized by the coming of the Mongols, or Tartars. By around the year 1200 Genghis Khan had united the tribes of fierce, nomadic steppe-dwellers into a single nation of formidable military strength. They attacked Sung China, piercing the Great Wall and taking Cambaluc (Beijing) in 1215. From there Genghis Khan and his successors swept invincibly westward across China, Turkestan, Persia, Russia and into Eastern Europe, conquering and destroying everything in their path. It is generally accepted that only the death of the Khan Ogedei in Hungary in 1241, and the long succession procedure that followed, saved a terrified Europe from being overwhelmed. When the Mongols returned to the attack under the new Khan Möngke in 1256, the Islamic territories were their target: Baghdad was sacked in 1258, before the Mameluke Turks at last turned the tide at the battle of Ain Jalut, near Nazareth in 1260. Thereafter Mongol power stabilized, separated into four Khanates with the rivers Euphrates and Dnestr marking its western limits. Thus for the first time in history a single authority held sway in Asia, from the Pacific coast to the Black Sea, and it was in this context that the opportunity for contact between Europe and China was first opened.

The Europeans had several motives for this approach to a nation that had formerly inspired them with terror. First there was the desire to pre-empt if possible any further westward expansion by forming some kind of alliance or understanding with them. Second, the Mongols were not known to possess any clear religion of their own, therefore it seemed possible they might be converted to Christianity, and become an ally to outflank the Moslem world, a hope that was encouraged by the

Portrait of Marco Polo, from the first printed edition of his book, 1477.

The British Library G.6787.

Mongols' ruthless campaign against the Islamic World during 1256–1260. And third was the perennial lure of trade. The secret of the manufacture of silk had in fact reached the west in the sixth century AD (according to tradition, silkworms were smuggled west in hollowed bamboo canes by spies employed by the Emperor Justinian). But now the great attraction was the spices that were so highly prized in enriching the grim, monotonous diet of western Europe, – pepper, cloves, cinnamon, mace and ginger.

When the initial terror of the Mongols had thus turned to slender political hope, the first known Europeans to make the great journey to the east were Papal envoys charged with persuading the Khan and his followers to 'give up their bloody slaughter of mankind and receive the Christian faith'. Two Francisan friars, Giovanni Carpini in 1245 and Willem van Rubruck in 1253, travelled the northern caravan routes, skirting the Caspian and Aral Seas and the Tien Shan mountains then crossing the Gobi Desert. In the face of great privations, though not apparently of danger, they both succeeded in reaching the court of the Khan at Karakoram, west of present-day Ulan-Bator. They both noted the harshness of steppe life, and the customs by which the Mongols had adapted to it, not the least of which was the plunder from as far away as Hungary with which they enriched their court. It was Rubruck who observed the presence of luxurious silks, and made the connection between this Cathay and the land of the 'Seres', by which classical and medieval writers alluded to the silk-producers of the east. Carpini and Rubruck brought a frosty and dismissive message from the Great Khan to his European suitors, but at least they were permitted to return safely to deliver it, retracing their outward route. They had not reached Cathay itself, but had been informed at length about it, and their accounts stand as the first witness to this alien civilization, and their experiences attracted wide interest.

Whether in direct response we do not know, but in 1255 two Venetian brothers, the jewel-merchants Nicolo and Maffeo Polo, set out on the first European trading journey to China. After crossing the desert and the steppe, they entered Cathay itself and reached the imperial city of Cambaluc (near modern Beijing). They were well received by Kublai Khan and asked to return bringing more scholars and ambassadors. It was fortuitous that the Polos' arrival coincided with the reign of Kublai Khan, the most enlightened of the Mongol rulers, who had no desire for further conquest. Their first trip occupied fourteen years yet just two years later they embarked again, this time taking

Left: West Africa from Fra Mauro's map of c.1450. The rivers of West Africa and the Gulf of Guinea are clearly visible, and the entire continent is believed to be navigable. South is at the top.

Right: Cathay from Fra Mauro's map of c.1450. The place-names and descriptive texts are derived from Marco Polo, but the architecture is that of Renaissance Italy. South is at the top.

not scholars and ambassadors but Niccolo's son Marco, a youth of seventeen whose subsequent experiences and recollections form the all-important opening chapter in the European exploration of the world.

The Polos took a southern route through Persia to Hormuz, before turning north-east through Afghanistan to cross the Pamirs and make the 2,000 mile journey through desert and steppe to Cambaluc. For seventeen years the Polos remained in China, and Marco travelled extensively through the Khan's dominions in the service of the Emperor. It was not unusual for foreigners to be given such political appointments, for they were felt to be immune from the intrigues and corruption of the Chinese themselves. Marco's subsequent narrative of his travels established the geography of 'Cathay' as it was understood by Europeans for the next three centuries: the great cities of Cambaluc and Quinsay where silk and gold were traded in fabulous quantities; the sea-port of Zaiton whence huge ships left for Champa (Vietnam), Malaya, Java and India; the eastern ocean containing 7,448 islands, the most enticing of them Zipanga (Japan) whose wealth in gold and jewels was inexhaustible. He visited Java, Sumatra, Ceylon and the islands of Andaman and Nicobar, the savagery of whose inhabitants contrasted so strongly with the civilized Chinese; the image of 'men with heads like dogs and teeth and eyes likewise, who eat everybody they can catch' would appear for centuries on European maps of south-east Asia. In 1292 the Polos finally prepared to return to Venice by sea. Sailing from Zaiton via the Straits of Malacca, they crossed the Indian Ocean to Seilan (Ceylon), coasting thence to Gujarat and Hormuz. It was some five years after his return that Marco set down his story, dictated while imprisoned by the rival Genoese to a fellow-prisoner Rusticello, a writer of romances and fables. In time the book became probably the most popular secular work of the later middle ages; today some 140 extant manuscripts are known, suggesting that during the fifteenth century it circulated in its thousands.

Marco's narrative is colourful and engaging, yet in some respects it is also vague and unsatisfactory, for we cannot always be sure what his exact routes were, what precisely he was doing in the service of the Emperor, which places he visited and which he merely heard described. His tendency to exaggeration was legendary, so that everything in Cathay was on a colossal, fabulous scale: any city must have thousands of bridges, any harbour must contain thousands of vessels, any palace must accomodate tens of thousands of men, and so on. These characteristics of his writing have been attributed by some to Rusticello's imaginative editing, but by others they have been used to argue that Marco Polo never went to China at all, that he picked up the materials for his colourful descriptions from travellers in Constantinople or the Black Sea ports. This argument is strengthened by some mysterious omissions in his narrative: despite spending seventeen years in China, he never mentions the Great Wall, the habit of drinking tea, the Chinese script, and many other characteristics of Chinese culture. Whatever the truth may be, there is no doubt that Marco's text shaped the European conception of China for the next three centuries and became the greatest single spur to the European age of exploration. A printed copy was owned by Columbus, who studied and annotated it carefully – in the course of his own voyages he sought to identify many locations in the Caribbean with places decribed by Marco, imagining himself to be among the islands of the eastern sea.

To modern eyes one of the greatest curiosities about the Polo tradition is that none of the manuscripts (or later printed copies) were ever illustrated with maps. We can only conjecture that when the original manuscript took shape around the year 1300, neither Marco himself nor Rusticello nor any copyist was aware of any cartographic forms or models which could have served as a framework to his narrative. The mechanics of scribal copying made it highly unlikely that any map would be added at a later date. Thus it is that the earliest and most important record of European exploration is a text and not a map. Nevertheless the geography of Marco Polo found its expression 50 years after the great traveller's death in 1324, in one of the monuments of medieval cartography, the Catalan Atlas of 1375. This map was drawn by a Mallorcan artist, Abraham Cresques, and presented to King Charles V of France. In some ways the Catalan Atlas is still a medieval *mappa mundi*, for the world it shows comprises only Europe, North Africa and Asia, and it retains many of the legends and fables of medieval geography. But the author of the Catalan Atlas had taken over certain important innovations from contemporary sea-charts: it is orientated to the north, it shows compass-lines, and its accurate depiction of the Mediterranean coasts is that of the early sea-charts. The geography of Asia in the Catalan Atlas is vague and imprecise (the whole of the South-East Asian peninsula is omitted), but the texts and place-names are new in medieval mapmaking, for they are drawn almost entirely from Marco Polo. North-East of the Caspian Sea is a vivid miniature of a mounted caravan of camels and horses crossing the desert. The adjacent text describes the town of Lop (thought to be Ruoqiang, south of Lop Nor) where provisions should be bought for the seven-month desert journey into Cathay. In Cathay itself is a portrait of the Emperor 'Holubeim' (Kublai Khan) with a reverential note proclaiming him to he the wealthiest monarch 'in the whole world, habitually guarded by

The Viladestes Chart of 1413, southern portion. The 'River of Gold' is shown as crossing the whole of West Africa and joining the Nile.

Bibliothèque Nationale, Paris

[28]

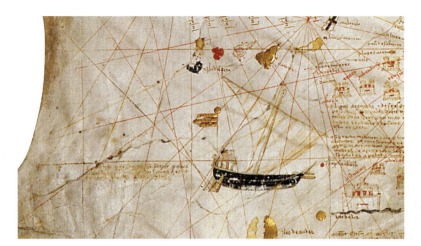

Left: A Portuguese ship, a falua, *from the Viladestes chart.*

Right: The Portuguese seafarer seen through African eyes: a Benin ivory.
B.M. Dept. of Ethnography

12,000 horsemen'. The cities made famous by Marco Polo, including 'Chambalech', 'Cansay' and 'Zayton' are all marked, while the eastern sea is filled with the myriad islands said to number 7,448. The largest island is named 'Trapobana', the name Ptolemy applied to Ceylon, while the island in Ceylon's place is named 'Jana', presumably meant for Java, mentioned by Marco. He had in fact spoken of two Javas, the Lesser and the Greater, and he called Ceylon 'Seilan'. The confusion between the names of these large islands, compounded by the first reports of Sumatra around 1450, shows itself on all maps of the fifteenth and sixteenth centuries.

The Polos were followed into China by more Franciscan missionaries, but not by any merchants whose names have come down to us. Giovanni da Montecorvino arrived in China in 1294 and remained until 1328, acquiring the title of Archbishop of Peking in 1307. He travelled by the sea-route from Hormuz via Ceylon and Malacca to Canton, and it was Montecorvino who first reported the cycle of the monsoons, which it was essential to understand in planning the sea-route to India. He was followed by a fellow Franciscan in 1318, Odoric of Pordenone, whose lively memoirs of Asian travel supplement those of Marco Polo. Odoric returned overland in 1328–30, becoming the first European to enter Tibet and reach the capital Lhasa, 'abode of the chief of all idolators', the Grand Lama. He describes the Tibetans as living in black felt tents, practising cannibalism, and drinking from the skulls of their ancestors. He explained the concept of the 'sky-burial', where the dead are left in the open to be eaten by birds of prey, whom the Tibetans regarded as angels carrying the souls of the dead to heaven. Pordenone, like the other early Asian pioneers, left memorable descriptions of what he saw, but no maps.

In 1335 a Mongol mission to Christendom arrived at the Papal court in Avignon, making friendly overtures towards the west, and suggesting increased trade and cultural contacts. In response the Florentine Franciscan John Marignolli took the overland route to Peking, and has left us a description of the last years of Mongol rule under the emperor Togon Temur, to whom he presented gifts in 1342. This is the only one of these western missions that can be traced in Chinese historical records, and it caused a great stir in the imperial court. Yet it was to be the last such contact for many centuries: Mongol rule in China was crumbling, and even as the Catalan Atlas was being drawn, their successors were retreating once more into isolationism. The 'Pax Mongolica' had lasted almost exactly one hundred years and had bequeathed to Europe a number of seminal works of exploration literature. Their hold on the imagination of Europe was heightened by their popular imitators, principally the miraculous travel fictions of Sir John Mandeville, penned in the 1350s. It was through Mandeville that certain geographical ideas became widely known and exercised great influence on explorers and mapmakers: the legend of Gog and Magog, the apocalyptic or demonic figures

imprisoned by Alexander the Great in the Caspian Mountains, appears on the Catalan Atlas; while the figure known as Prester John, ruler of a mysterious Christian kingdom in the east, would be discussed and sought by generations of European explorers. These motifs appeared again and again on maps from the thirteenth to the sixteenth century, shaping the European vision of the world.

As Mongol power weakened in the the east, the rise of the Ottoman dynasty in the west threw up a new barrier to European trade and exploration. The Venetians and the Genoese secured trading rights to collect goods at the ports of the eastern Mediterranean and the Black Sea, and they were the great beneficiaries of a very restricted system of travel. Marco Polo's China remained an isolated vision whose influence grew and tantalized the other nations of Europe. Yet if contact with the great civilization to the east was ever to be renewed, it was clear that new ways must be found to reach it. Moslem occupation of the entire Near East raised the question whether it was possible to reach the east by sea. The Polos' Journey to China had been an isolated personal adventure, and it had been overland. A sea route from Europe raised scientific and technical questions that were unanswerable in the year of Marco Polo's death, 1324, but which a century later began to appear capable of solution. In the intervening years the compass and the portolan chart had been developed by Mediterranean seafarers, and they had ventured out into the Atlantic to explore the Canary Islands, Madeira and Azores. The typical chart of Europe around the year 1450 distinctly showed that Africa had an Atlantic coast and a Red Sea coast: was it possible that the two might be connected? How far south did Africa extend? To answer these questions required a conscious sense of geography and a financial investment in ships and men that only royal patronage could provide, and such patronage would in turn imply political aims and motives.

THE PASSAGE TO INDIA

The Iberian peninsula in the early years of the fifteenth century provided the setting where these motives and capabilities merged. The reconquest from the occupying Islamic forces was complete (save in the Moslem kingdom of Granada) and this process had shaped a culture in which a warlike, crusading ethos was dominant. In 1415 the struggle against Islam was carried into North Africa, with the Portuguese conquest of Ceuta, led in person by King John I, assisted by his son Prince Henry, later appointed governor of Ceuta. This miniature crusade was, according to Henry's enthusiastic chronicler, Gomes Eanes de Zurara, the starting-point of a programme of exploration and expansion that was partly economic and partly religious. At this period much of the gold entering Europe originated in West Africa and was carried by Moslem traders across Saharan caravan routes, through the celebrated oasis towns of Timbuktu and Tamanrasset to ports such as Algiers and Tunis. Ivory, slaves and salt were also traded, and there were rumours of rivers running over beds of gold. The important Viladestes map of 1413 clearly shows this 'Riu de lor' linked to the Nile, and fed by many streams running down from 'montanies dellor'. The Portuguese prince, known to posterity as Henry the Navigator, may have conceived the plan of diverting this trade to Portugal via a sea route along the coast of Africa, of subverting or possibly attacking Islamic territory from the rear, and of searching for the legendary Christian king to be his ally. In the early stages it is unlikely that the Portuguese were considering a seaway to the Indies, but within a few decades that had emerged as the overriding aim. As early as 1418 Henry sponsored voyages of reconaissance to Madeira, and in the following year at Sagres, on the extreme south-westerly point of Portugal's coast, he established a small court to which he attracted scientists, navigators, mapmakers and ship-builders to further his enterprise.

How deliberate this enterprise was, and what knowledge and motives Henry brought to it, are controversial. It has become obligatory to point out that the title 'the Navigator' is quite undeserved, and recent historians have, inevitably, sought to demythologize Henry, to brand the 'Academy of Sagres' a fable, and to argue that one cannot set out deliberately to discover what is unknown. The latter is a simplistic argument, and one wonders how it can account for the careers of Copernicus or Magellan or Newton or Darwin. That the history of European exploration always begins with Prince Henry is undoubtedly due to Gomes's adulatory chronicle which commemorates the events of his career, but clearly there had to be something to commemorate, and the historical record speaks for itself. By 1431 the Azores and Madeira had been explored (the Canaries had been settled by the Spanish) and their colonization began a decade later. By 1434 Cape Juby and Cape Bojador, on the African coast some 500 miles south of Tangier, were passed by Gil Eanes. The latter was a considerable milestone, despite its apparent insignificance on today's map: it was the most southerly point on the map of Europe at that time, a place of frequent fogs and strong currents, known as the limit of the world. Indeed because of the current from the north-west that runs between Fuertaventura and the African coast, the return by that route was considered impossible, and this may have been responsible for the superstitious belief that ships could fall off 'the edge of the world.'

The Portuguese sailors were clearly being directed in a conscious programme: by 1443 Cape Blanco was passed by Nuño Tristão, and the following year Dinis Dias had progressed as far as the mouth of the Senegal River 'which men say comes from the Nile, being one of the most glorious rivers on earth, flowing from the Garden of Eden and the earthly paradise.' The arid Saharan coast was at last left behind and replaced by tropical forest. Cape Verde and the Gambia River followed in 1446, more than a 1,500 miles distant from Portugal. Alvise Cadamosto explored the Cape Verde Islands in 1456, and by the year of Prince Henry's death in 1460, the Portuguese had probed south as far as Sierra Leone. During this time their principal aim had been to find a navigable river that would lead to the African interior and the gold which they knew was there. They were also landing where possible and exploring the hinterland, making contact with native peoples, sometimes trading with them, sometimes fighting, and taking their first slaves. As early as 1448 a fort was built on the island in Arguin Bay, the first European overseas trading-post, and soon the gold they sought began making its way back to Portugal: the first gold coin minted in Portugal in modern times appeared in 1457, called symbolically the *cruzado* – the 'crossbearer'. Of more scientific importance was the navigational experience which the Portuguese sailors were accumulating, especially the art of estimating latitude from the altitude of celestial bodies. At the mouth of the Gambia, Cadamosto recorded that the Pole Star 'sank so low it seemed to touch the sea', while a new, unknown group of stars in the

Right: Cape Verde to Cape Rosso, with the Gambia River, from the Benincasa chart of 1473.

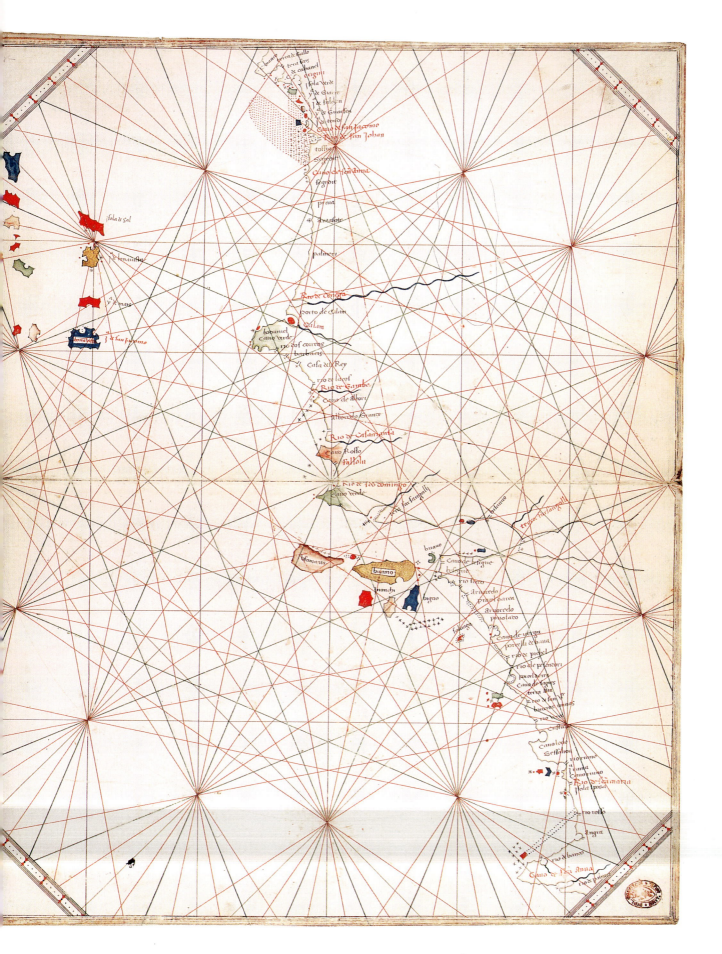

terra de Gallo
terra das de camel
origini
Jsola verde
A de Salcen
de Guardes
de Verde
Cauo Nsan Jacomo
Rio X san Johan
tolfin
Senega
Cauo de sea Anna
segout
praia
Antalote
palmeri
Rio de cologa
porto de Salun
Salun
Johaniel
Cauo verde
rio dos conuos
barbacas
Casa dell Rey
rio de lacos
Rio de Gambe
Cauo de alturi
Altorodo Grande
Rio de Casamania
Cauo Rosso
falfolu
Rio de sco dominho
Cauo verde
tre de sta sangalli
tre de sta sangalli
biliano
bugauo
sicamania
buamo
Cauo de besreque
besquia
rio treto
Aruoredo
prita barca
Aruoredo
puoulado
tuonchu
Cauo de yerua
porcesli debama
rio de peseadori
jancelaria
Cauo de lagris
terra alta
Rio de bun
lancos danas
rio
cristal
Cauo todo
Sessiluou
moruno
a sina
Cauo ruuno
Rio de samaria
Jsola tposul
rio tollo
Engra
rio dabano
Cauo de sta Anna
dos pina

isola de Sal
J de Jonauilla
J de Anais
J de Sanfuismo
Sona Vista

[33]

shape of a cross appeared in the southern sky. Longitude was a far more difficult matter, for there were no physical markers from which it could be derived. Yet it was correctly understood to be a function of time, and it was estimated from the ship's speed and the distance covered. The careful monitoring of the ship's course from the moment of its initial departure was the basis of the method known as dead reckoning, but an accumulation of errors was inevitable.

How scientific were these voyages, and how innovative were the Portuguese sailors? Although the African coast was a fixed point, the prevailing winds and currents were north-westerly, making the return voyage full of difficulties and the danger of the lee shore. To deal with this they learned to sail out into the Atlantic west of the Cape Verde Islands and north of the Azores until, on the parallel of Lisbon they picked up the westerly winds that would take them home. They could only do this when they had mastered the art of latitude-finding by sighting the sun or the Pole Star, first by fairly crude vertical measurement on a staff, and later by means of the mariner's astrolabe. They could remain out of sight of land for many days with reasonable confidence. Thus compass bearings and latitude-finding were the two key skills they must master; they had a scientific basis, but they could be learned empirically, and in the few decades covering these voyages a body of knowledge could be built up that would accumulate and carry them on to the next goal. Of course there was danger and of course they had courage, but they were not perhaps probing the unknown in quite the way that Columbus and Magellan were later to do. As for their ship-building, the Portuguese like the other European nations began with a fishing fleet, whose simple vessels were progressively adapted to the new demands placed on them. Technically they were neither better nor worse equipped at the outset than the English, the French or the Dutch. The typical Portuguese *falua* is beautifully illustrated in the Viladestes chart of 1413. It was deckless, had one or two masts, was lateen-rigged, carried steering boards on the bows, and it was small enough to be rowed. A process of gradual modification saw this design evolve into the larger *caravel*, which was at least partly decked, and partly square rigged, and with small sterncastles. This in turn was succeeded by the *carrack*, which was larger still with castles fore and aft. It is difficult to be precise about when these changes occured; for example it is usually stated that da Gama's vessels were carracks, yet the Cosa chart of 1500 shows Portuguese ships approaching India which are rather small, lateen-rigged caravels. This evolution in ship design was dictated by the unique experience gained on voyages longer than those made by any other nation at this time.

If the Portuguese had been recording their discoveries on sea-charts, they have, through some unknown historical accident, failed to survive. We would naturally suppose that great secrecy would be maintained around what were after all maritime gold-routes. Yet by the 1460s the leading Italian chartmakers such as Grazioso Benincasa were drawing charts of the African coast which embodied the Portuguese discoveries, and from the middle years of the fifteenth century we have two extremely important Italian world maps which reflect the Portuguese achievement and set it within the context of world geography: the Fra Mauro map of c.1450 and the Genoese map of 1457. The Fra Mauro map at first sight appears to be in the ecclesiastical tradition of circular medieval world maps, but in fact it embodies navigational information from both Mediterranean and Arab seafarers, and like the Catalan Atlas draws heavily on Marco Polo for its concept of Asia. On the coast of Africa, Cape Verde and Cape Rosso are marked, as are two prominent rivers, the Senegal and the Gambia, before the coast trends east into the 'Gulf of Ethiopia', where a note states that the Portuguese had reached as far east as the meridian of Tunis, that is the eastern end of the Gulf of Guinea. Below this gulf the

Right: West Africa between Cape Lopez and Cape Santa Maria, from a chart of c.1490. The River Congo is central, and the crosses are those set up by Diego Cão in the 1480s.

The British Library Egerton MS 73, f.33.

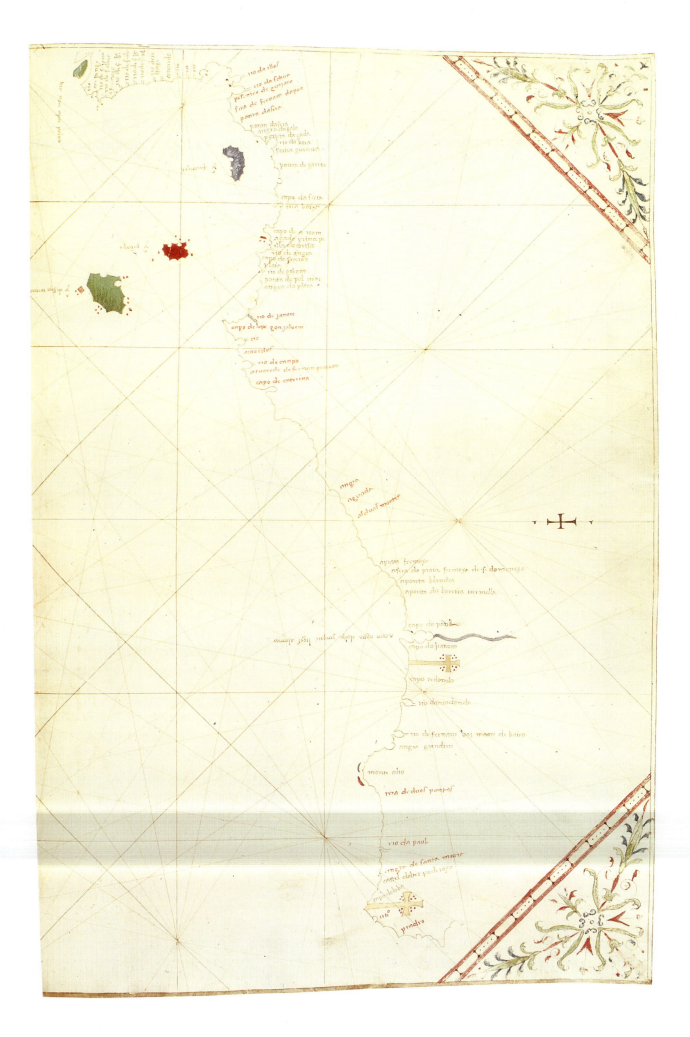

coast resumes its southward course for a great distance. This is puzzling, for although the eastern end of the Gulf of Guinea is certainly on the meridian of Tunis, all the historical records show that the Portuguese had not penetrated beyond Sierra Leone when this map was drawn, and even if they had, the accurate measurement of longitude was not possible – it had merely to be estimated by dead reckoning. On the East African coast, Fra Mauro names the ports of Zanzibar, Kilwa, Mombasa and Sofala, all centres of Arab trade on a coast where Moslems had been active for centuries. It is entirely possible that Fra Mauro working in Venice had access to Arab geographical sources, and it is significant that the map is drawn with south at the top, unlike all other western world maps, but following the pattern of Islamic mapmakers. This depiction of Africa as a whole is intriguing since it clearly expresses the belief that the continent is navigable, and it can only have encouraged the Portuguese to continue in their enterprise. Equally striking and prophetic is the text which confesses that the map must necessarily be imperfect since the full extent of the world was unknown. The Fra Mauro map is known to have been commissioned by the Portuguese court and to have used Portuguese charts among its sources. The exact date of its composition is uncertain and it is disputed whether it had any direct connection with Prince Henry. It was almost certainly drawn between 1448 and 1458.

In the Asian sector of the Fra Mauro map, Marco Polo is the most important single source, and the densely-drawn cities with their golden domes and spires do ample justice to the Venetian writer's dazzling textual descriptions. In the Genoese map of 1457, the great Marco has been supplemented by the narrative of a later Venetian observer, Niccolo Conti, who travelled in India and south-east Asia, though not China, between 1420 and 1440. The author of the Genoese map and the circumstances of its production are unknown. It is at once more recognisably modern than Fra Mauro, drawn with north at the top and having the proportions of the three continents and the Indian Ocean approximately correct. It may well have been drawn on the Ptolemaic model, since the Ptolemaic world map was familiar to scholars by this time, although it lacks the scientific apparatus of Ptolemy. Less intricate and inclusive than the Fra Mauro map, it embodies the outstanding landmarks of fifteenth century geography: the great Khan ruling in China; Prester John in his African kingdom; the islands of the Indian Ocean, Xilam (Ceylon) and Syamutha (Sumatra); Africa with its navigable coast, and an open Indian Ocean, where, in a prophetic image, a three-masted European ship is sailing. A statement taken directly from Conti appears in a text in the Indian Ocean: 'In this sea they navigate by a southern pole star, the northern having vanished'. The mermaids and dragons are the conventional space-fillers of the mapmaker's studio; the map's clear message is that the seaway from Europe to the east exists.

The deliberateness of what the Portuguese were doing during these years is attested by a remarkable document, the Papal bull *Pontifex Romanus* of 1455. It is effectively the charter of Portuguese imperialism, granting them a monopoly of navigation and trade between Cape Bojador and the Indies. The church decreed that those who died in the course of these voyages would be regarded as having died in the course of a crusade and therefore receive a plenary indulgence for their sins. The aims of winning land and trade from the Moslems and linking with Prester John were kept constantly in view. This nationalistic, military culture of crusade and conquest is eloquently expressed in Portugal's great epic poem *The Lusiads* of Camões, which gives the clearest possible insight into the psychology of the European Age of Discovery. The language of *The Lusiads* is one of destiny: the poem glorifies a historical process in which the Christian faith, seafaring skills and military courage, all focussed in the Portuguese nation, are destined to open a new era in world history. Nor did Henry's death bring this movement to an end, for its rewards thus far had convinced the Portuguese

Right: India and the vital Straits of Malacca, from a Portuguese chart of c.1518.

Part of the Martellus World Map of c.1490, showing Dias's voyage around the Cape.

The British Library Add. MS 15760, ff. 68v–69.

Right: The Cape of Good Hope, the first great gateway to the east, from Joan Martines chart of c.1578.

The British Library Harley MS 3450, f.8.

of its enormous potential. Through the 1470s the African coast was found to stretch steadily east-ward, and the hope was born that the seaway to the Indies might be opening before them. This was the coast of gold, ivory and slaves, and here the first fortunes of the Age of Discovery were made. After Prince Henry's death the Portuguese tried the novel experiment of leasing exploration rights to a private agency. Fernão Gomes was authorized to explore 400 miles of West African coast per year, and it proved highly successful for him. Passing Cape Palmas in 1470, the trading post of El Mina was founded in 1471. The island of Fernando Po was explored in 1472, and in the following year the equator was first crossed by European ships at Cape Lopez. The islands of São Tome and Principe were reconnoitred in 1474. By this time it had become clear that the coast was trending directly south again, but for how far no one knew. The rewards of exploration must be now have been consider-able, for for Gomes's contract was not renewed after 1474, and the process of exploration was taken back into royal hands. After a pause of several years caused by the war with Spain, the new king, John II, selected Diego Cão to push forward the next phase of exploration. In 1482 Cão passed the mouth of the River Congo, and in a second voyage in 1485–6 he reached Walvis Bay, a mere 500 miles north of the Cape. It was Cão who erected the stone columns – *padrões* – marking the Portuguese progress along the coast, which became an eloquent symbol on the contemporary maps, and some of which survive today. Cão's ultimate fate is a mystery, for he never returned from this voyage. He may have died on the coast, or he may have returned to the Congo and attempted to ascend it, for eighty miles upstream a stone was found years later inscribed with his name and others', and stating that ships sent by the king of Portugal came to that place.

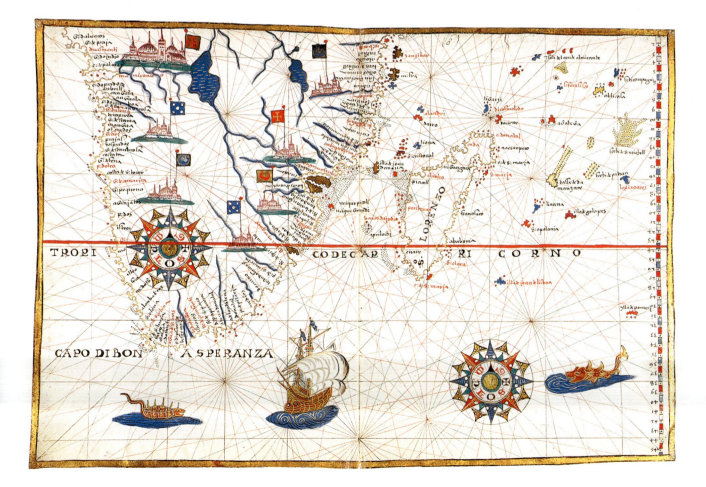

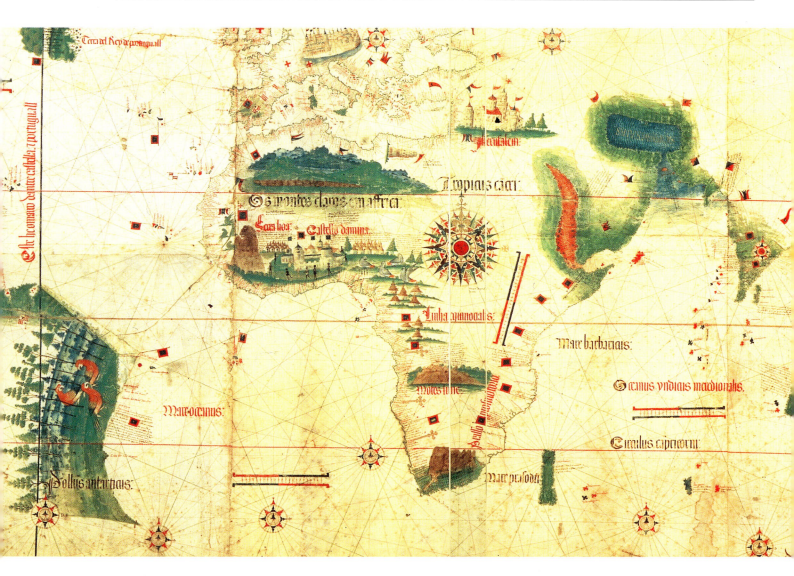

Part of the Cantino World Map, 1502. The Brazilian coast and the whole of Africa are shown following the voyages of da Gama and Cabral.

Biblioteca Estense, Modena

By now the avowed aim of the Portuguese was the sea passage to India. So confident were they that in 1484 they dismissed the alternative plan for a western route which Columbus presented to them, 'seeing that King John II has ordered the coast of Africa to be explored with the intention of going by that route to India'. This geographical reconnaissance was given a radical new twist in 1487 with the dispatch of a Portuguese spy, Pedro da Covilhão, charged with the dangerous task of following a land route to the east and gathering information about the Indian Ocean. Travelling in disguise through Egypt and sailing the Red Sea to Aden, Covilhão took ship to Calicut, and returned via Hormuz to Egypt. Here he reported to his king what he had learned – that it was indeed possible to gain access to India by sea. Covilhão then carried out his most dangerous exploit of visiting the holy city of Mecca, before proceeding down the East African coast. He either settled or was detained in Abyssinia, for he never travelled again, and was still living there in 1520.

In the same year that Covilhão set out, the ship of Bartolomeu Dias's, the latest Portuguese

Asia and the Indian Ocean from the Genoese World Map of 1457.

Biblioteca Nazionale, Florence

navigator, progressed beyond Cão's last known position. Encountering fierce storms, he was driven westward out into the Atlantic. When he was able to turn eastwards at an estimated 40 degrees south, he found no coast. Shaping a course north by north-east, he made land on a sandy beach running east-west. Dias had rounded the southernmost cape of Africa without seeing it. Continuing eastwards for some 200 miles, he was satisfied that the coast was now trending north-east, and that the long-sought seaway to India now lay open. On the return voyage he saw the Cape with its cliffs and peaks, which he first named Cape of Storms, but which King John II renamed Cape of Good Hope.

Dias returned triumphantly to Lisbon in December 1488 having established the latitude of the Cape and with the certain knowledge that India was within reach. Yet a further nine years were to pass before a fleet was dispatched to reap the reward of half a century of tenacious progress. The reason for this long delay is unknown, as is the process by which this new geographical knowledge spread through Europe. Once again there are no Portuguese charts, but manuscript maps of the new discoveries were being drawn in Italy. The most eloquent is a world map by the German scholar Henricus Martellus, in which the classical Ptolemaic world outline is radically transformed by the remapping of Africa, in which the array of place-names terminates abruptly at the point where Dias turned back. Five years after Dias's return, the news arrived of Columbus's western voyage. No doubt the Portuguese waited anxiously for confirmation that the Spanish had forestalled them in the quest for the Indies. But the reports from the west ocean were deeply puzzling: neither the Spice Islands nor

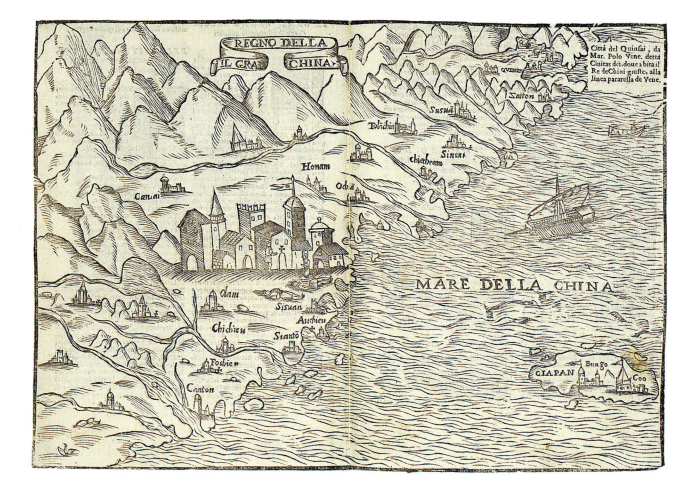

the great cities of Cathay were found. Meanwhile some understanding had to be reached between Portugal and her Spanish neighbour about their overseas activities. The Treaty of Tordesillas in 1494 agreed that a line be drawn in the Atlantic 370 leagues (about 1,200 miles) west of the Cape Verde Islands. Land discovered to the west of this line would be in the Spanish sphere, those to the east in the Portuguese. The intention was clearly to secure to Portugal the African route to India, while reserving to Spain the routes or discoveries in the western sea. This agreement was later ratified by Papal Bull, but the problem of its continuation on the opposite meridian of the globe could not be foreseen at this stage.

The new king, Manuel I, now moved to prepare a definitive expedition to India by the Cape route. New, larger ships were built, armed and fitted out, and a gentleman of the royal household, Vasco da Gama, was selected not only as the fleet commander but as an ambassador to the eastern kingdoms, with the aim of securing treaties and monopolies. The fleet of four vessels and 120 men left Lisbon in July 1497. Accompanied part-way by Dias, da Gama took a bold but calculated course from the Cape Verde Islands, sweeping far out to the south-west to avoid the adverse currents of the Guinea coast. He was confident of locating the Cape by latitude observation, which he did after 96 days at sea, probably the longest European voyage to date out of sight of land. In fact they made the coast at St. Helena Bay, just 1.5 degrees north of the Cape. Passing the Cape, da Gama now coasted steadily northwards, entering the Moslem sphere of influence, finally anchoring at Malindi, where an Arab pilot who knew the passage to India was taken on board. Tradition has it that this pilot was Ibn

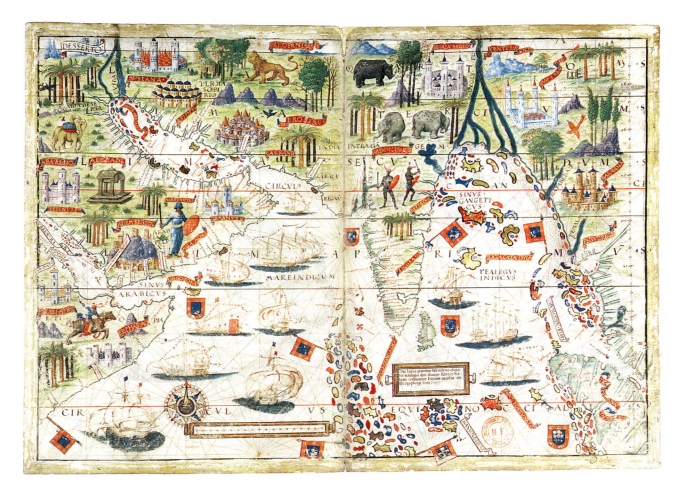

Left: *China from Mendoza's 'History of China', printed in Rome in 1585, still deriving its geography from Marco Polo – the text quotes Marco's description of Quinsai as the 'City of God'.*
The British Library C.114.d.9.

Above: *The Indian Ocean from a Portuguese atlas of c.1519. Beneath the riot of imagery, the coastal geography is now strikingly accurate.*
Bibliothèque Nationale, Paris

Right: *The all-important Strait of Malacca, the gateway to the Spice Islands, from a Portuguese atlas of c.1519.*
Bibliothèque Nationale, Paris

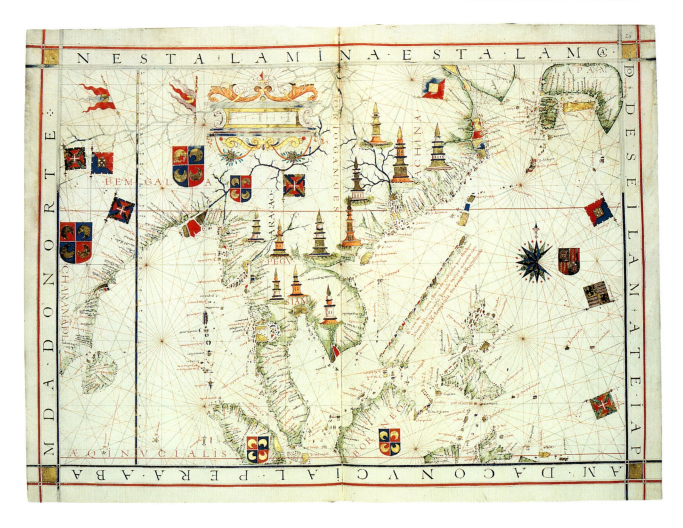

China and Japan from the Vaz Dourado atlas of 1573. The pagodas lend an authentic feel to this map, but the geography of the major rivers, the Korean Peninsula and Japan is confused; within a few years Jesuits would provide much better information.

The British Library Add. MS 31317 f.25v–26.

Majid, a celebrated navigator and author of a pilot guide to the Indian Ocean. Whether by chance or not, da Gama had arrived as the favourable south-west monsoon was beginning, and just 23 days out from Malindi the western Ghats were sighted. The Portuguese anchored at Calicut on May 20 1498, the first European ship to sail these waters since those of Alexander the Great, after a maritime achievement arguably as great as that of Columbus. Yet it began badly for the Portuguese. The hostility of the Arab merchants who had been established in India for centuries was understandable, but the trumpery merchandise the Europeans brought – beads, hats and cheap knives, which had been thought suitable for the African trade – were laughed at by the Indians. Failing to impress his hosts or negotiate any treaties, da Gama had no choice but to leave, and after a much more arduous homeward voyage, bedevilled by adverse winds and disease which killed half his crew, he entered Lisbon nonetheless triumphantly in September 1499. King Manuel shared his triumph, assuming the title 'Lord of the conquest, navigation, and commerce of India, Ethiopia, Arabia and Persia'.

This time there was no delay in following up da Gama's achievement. Barely six months elapsed before the departure from Lisbon of a strong fleet of thirteen ships under the command of Pedro

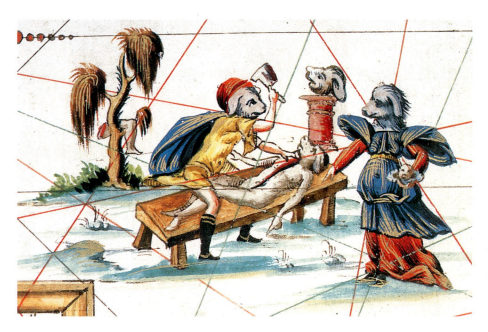

*Left: The dog-headed
cannibals said by Marco Polo
to inhabit the Andaman
Islands, from the Desceliers
World Map.*
The British Library Add. MS 24065.

Cabral. Their south-westerly sweep was so deep on this occasion that Cabral touched the coast of Brazil on April 22 and took possession of it in the name of Portugal, calling it 'The Land of the True Cross' – later amended to 'Holy Cross'. The terms of the Treaty of Tordesillas had given Portugal her claim to this land in the west, quite unintentionally since no one had then known how far east the American coast extended. Pressing on to India, the fleet was battered by storms off the Cape which destroyed four ships and claimed the life of Bartolomeu Dias. In Calicut violent conflicts arose with both Moslem traders and the inhabitants, and Cabral removed his ships further south to Cochin where he was able to trade for spices, filling six ships with merchandise for the return to Portugal.

Once again there is, strangely, no Portuguese map commemorating these historic voyages. But the celebrated Cantino chart of 1502 was drawn directly from Portuguese sources, indeed it is known to have been smuggled out of Portugal by an Italian diplomat, Alberto Cantino, and presented to the Duke of Ferrara. In Italy it was seen by scholars and navigators and exercised enormous influence on mapmakers for many decades. It is a landmark of geographical knowledge in several respects: the Indian peninsula is now shown unmistakably; Cabral's Brazilian coast dominated the western section; Newfoundland appears in the north Atlantic; above all the coast of Africa is mapped with startling accuracy. The only major fault here is that the depth of the Gulf of Guinea is exaggerated by about 10 degrees, so that São Tome and Principe are on the meridian of Benghazi instead of that of Tunis. But longitude was the bane of the navigator, and could only be estimated by dead reckoning. The Cantino chart is a celebration of Portuguese Africa, with the Portuguese flags defending its coast, and the fort of El Mina pictured like a huge Renaissance city dominating Guinea.

On the Cabral expedition and still more on the subsequent one commanded again by da Gama in 1502–3, the velvet glove was removed to display the iron hand of Portuguese intentions: intimidation, violence and massacre took the place of diplomacy in showing the Arab traders and their Indian allies that the Europeans were determined to seize the trade routes of south Asia. We must assume that the Portuguese had no precise knowledge of where the long sought-for spices originated, how they were cultivated or how they reached ports like Cochin and Calicut. Within a dozen years they obtained this information, and created by ruthless force of arms a trading empire that stretched some 10,000 miles from Lisbon. In 1505 Francisco de Almeida was sent in command of a new force with a new strategy. Attacking and subduing the East African ports of Kilwa and Mombasa en route,

Almeida established himself with a permanent garrison in Cochin, proclaiming himself governor of India. His son Lourenço was sent to explore Ceylon and the Maldives and to gather information on the sources of the spice trade. Superior Portuguese fire-power ravaged the Moslem shipping and bases, and finally in the Battle of Diu Island, off Rajkot, Almeida routed a great Moslem fleet and broke their power in the region. His successor, Alfonso de Albuquerque, ruthless, bloodthirsty and entirely successful, made Goa his headquarters after bitter fighting with the Moslems. In 1511 he led the fleet which seized Malacca, straddling the vital sea-lane to China, Japan and all the islands of south-east Asia. From Malacca in 1513 Francisco Serrão explored Java, Timor and finally the Moluccas themselves, the 'Spice Islands', where the fabled plants grew in abundance, and where Serrão was able to negotiate treaties and establish Portuguese bases. In 1515 Albuquerque seized the port of Hormuz, sealing off the Gulf route and completing the Portuguese monopoly. The extent of Portuguese success may be gauged from the fact that by 1515 pepper was being sold in Lisbon at one fifth of the price it commanded in Venice. In 1514–15 trade was opened with China itself via the port of Canton, and the growth of Macao on the Pearl River estuary began soon afterwards. Japan was reached in 1542, but by accident rather than design, when a Portuguese ship was wrecked on the south coast of Kyushu. The Europeans including Francisco Zeimoto returned safely, and western interest in Japan was greatly stimulated, leading to the Jesuit mission of Francis Xavier, who landed in Japan in 1549.

The mapping of the Indian Ocean and South-East Asia did not proceed in steady progression and the islands in particular were not definitively fixed on European maps for many decades. The Portuguese must have possessed a full chart base for their activities, but much of it has perished. The situation is further complicated because major islands such as Japan and Java were known as names and were placed on maps long before any European ever visited them or was able to locate them correctly. The confusion over the two Javas, Taproban, Seilan and Sumatra persisted into the 1560s, half a century after the Portuguese arrived there. The earliest maps to depict the all-important Strait of Malacca date from around 1519 or 1520. The clearest of these is contained in a highly-finished atlas made for presentation to the king of Portugal by Lopo Homem. Malacca is mysteriously shown twice, both as fortified cities, and to their north the celebrated Burmese city of Pegu. Homem has adhered to the tradition that Sumatra is Taproban. To the east are the two Javas and 'Candin' which may be Timor. Two unnamed islands to the north representing Borneo and Sulawesi are well-placed, as are the all-important Moluccas, but the large island to their east which should be Papua is confusingly named 'Seilam'. The scores of smaller islands scattered like autumn leaves are generalized artistic images, but they do reflect the complexity of the island-groups in this region. Two large three-masted Christian ships and five smaller Moslem vessels commemorate the political rivalry for the spice trade.

After 1540, following the voyages of Magellan and his successors, the Philippines appear, but very imperfectly mapped, but then Jesuit contacts with Japan a decade later resulted in its improved location. While the manuscript maps of the period 1520–1550, such as those of Ribero and Reinel, showed the increasingly complex geography of south-east Asia, publishers of printed maps were purveying a noticeably outdated picture. The highly popular maps of Sebastian Münster's *Cosmographia* are particularly faulty in this respect. Naturally map-publishers in Venice, Nuremberg or Paris had no access to the charts of Portuguese or Spanish navigators, and this serves merely to highlight the extraordinary public 'escape' of the map of Africa forty years earlier in the Cantino Chart. Mercator in his world map of 1538 and his globe of 1541 was better informed, showing the

Right: The mysterious southern land-mass named as Java on the Rotz world map of 1542.

The British Library Royal MS 20.E.IX.

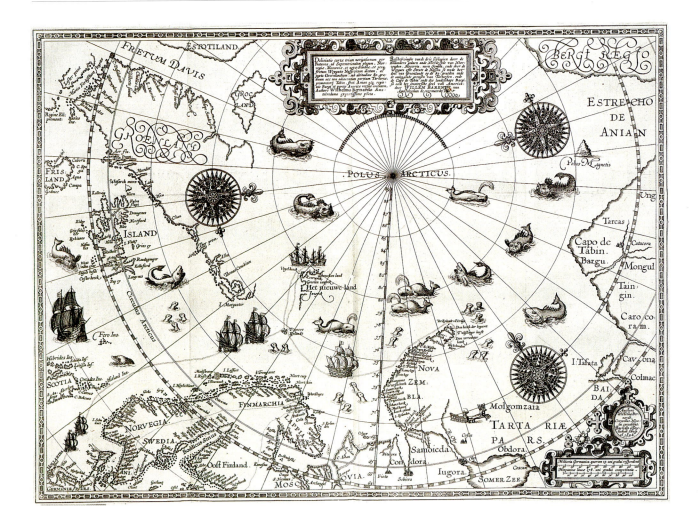

The North Polar Regions, 1598, printed from the charts of Willem Barentsz. The polar continent has now vanished from the map. Dutch ships are seen off Spitsbergen – 'Het nieuwe land', while the magnetic pole has been placed above the Strait of Anian.

The British Library G.7006.

all-important Strait of Malacca, and showing the Spice Islands clearly to the east. But the literary basis of geography was far from being displaced by rigorous respect for empirical discovery, and the shadow of Marco Polo still fell over the maps of the sixteenth century. The first post-medieval European account of China, Gonzalez de Mendoza's *History of the Great and Mighty Kingdom of China*, 1585, drew its geography still from Marco Polo, quoting on his map the Venetian's phrase about Quinsai – 'The City of Heaven'. More important, both Venetian and Flemish map publishers from the 1560s onwards drew large continental landmasses south of Java on which they marked placenames from Marco. Mercator himself in his great world map of 1569, names three kingdoms described but never visited by Marco: Beach, Lucach and Maletur. For a further century these names continued to be shuffled like jokers in the mapmaker's pack, even co-existing with the Dutch discoveries on the coast of Australia in the 1620s. By the mid-sixteenth century certain charts derived from Portuguese sources, such as those of the French chartmaker Jean Rotz, display an extensive coastline south of the Spice Islands, named as 'Java la Grande'. This has given rise to much speculation concerning a possible Portuguese discovery of Australia, and this land in some of the Rotz charts does indeed bear Portuguese names. However, there is no independent corroboration of any Portuguese landfalls on the southern continent at this period; and if there had been, it is hard to see why they should have been concealed. This is one of the unresolved enigmas in the history of exploration.

For a full century after Bartolomeu Dias, no non-Portuguese ship rounded the Cape and crossed the Indian Ocean eastwards. The other European nations took many years to understand what the Portuguese had done, and to gather the will and the techniques to emulate them. Moreover there was an accepted doctrine of sovereignty and monopoly attaching to these new sea-routes, a doctrine that was enforced by Papal authority, regarded as arbitrator among Christian monarchs. The African coast and the Indies were regarded as belonging by right to the Portuguese, while Mexico and the Caribbean were now Spanish. This question of sovereignty over new lands was a vitally important one, and it explains why royal patronage was essential; an individual explorer could make no claim to sovereignty in his own right, nor would he be able to defend his discoveries against rivals without the authority of a ruling monarch. The Reformation, with its rejection of Papal authority, encouraged the breaching of these monopolies, yet a respect for the first-comer's rights survived, and it was the major factor in the continuing search for new sea-routes. The convention was challenged in dramatic fashion when a Dutch fleet left Amsterdam in 1595 and made its way via the Cape to Java and Bali, where they bought spices. Significantly the Dutch were political and religious enemies of the Portuguese and the Spanish, and they were taking advantage of Portuguese weakness, their empire having become over-extended. In 1580 Philip II of Spain had annexed the vacant throne of Portugal, and Spain's European enemies seized the opportunity to attack her overseas. The Dutch were the principal beneficiaries as Portugal's empire crumbled.

THE WAY OF THE NORTH

Before the Dutch challenged the Portuguese monopoly, another possibility had attracted the English, in which the lure of the east was still paramount: to find an entirely new *northerly* route to Cathay, India and 'the Spicerie'. It was plain that sailing northward near the pole must offer a much shorter route to the east than those followed by the Portuguese or the Spanish. Moreover the established monopolies would not be breached, and England would indeed create her own . 'There is one way to discover, which is into the north', wrote Robert Thorne in 1527, 'for out of Spain they have discovered all the Indies and seas occidental, and out of Portingall all the Indies and seas oriental.' Traditional beliefs about the geography of the North Pole show a continental land-mass clearly separated by sea from northern Russia. This picture was accepted by Mercator for example, and he wrote in 1580 that the voyage to Cathay by the east 'is doubtless very easy and short'. Roger Barlowe, author of the *Briefe Summe of Geographie* 1541, wrote that 'the shortest route, the northern, has been reserved by Divine Providence for England', and in 1553 the Muscovy company was formed with Sebastian Cabot at its head. In May of that year the first expedition left Deptford, carrying a letter from King Edward VI to the 'Kings, Princes and other Potentates inhabiting the North-East parts of the world, toward that mighty empire of Cathay'. Sixty years after Dias rounded the Cape and Columbus arrived in America, the northernmost coasts of Europe were still untravelled.

The confidence of Sir Hugh Willoughby and Richard Chancellor was matched only by their total inexperience of the arctic environment. The ships became separated towards the north of Norway, and Willoughby's fate later became known through the report of some Russian fishermen who found his ship and her dead crew frozen into the ice of the Kola Peninsula. Chancellor succeeded in rounding the whole Peninsula, where 'He found no night at all, but a continual light and brightness of the Sun shining clearly upon the huge and mighty sea'. He reached Archangel, from where he travelled

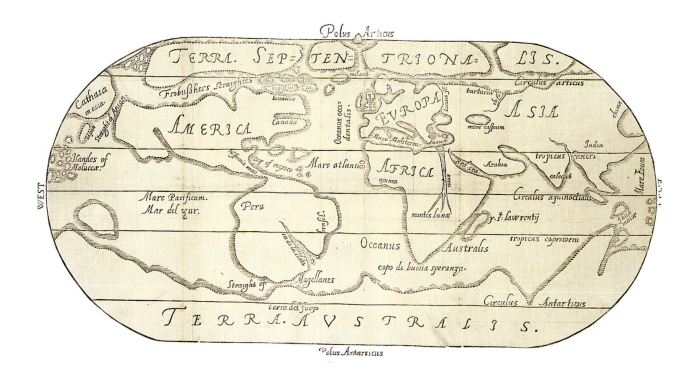

overland to Moscow and met Ivan the Terrible. He returned safely bringing valuable information about this virtually unknown region, but a second voyage in 1556 claimed his life too. A further significant voyage was made by Stephen Burrough, who had sailed with Chancellor, in 1556–7. Passing the North Cape and the White Sea he seems to have reached the southern parts of Novaya Zemlya. On his return he survived an overwintering on the Kola Peninsula, and his voyage served to reveal the unimagined harshness of travel in these latitudes. Perhaps as a consequence, some years elapsed before the next venture in June 1580 when Arthur Pet and Charles Jackman were given a command to penetrate the strait between Novaya Zemlya and the mainland 'Eastward to the countries or dominions of the mighty Prince, the Emperor of Cathay . . . and the cities of Cambaluc and Quinsay'. They did indeed pass the strait north of Vaygach Island, but soon found their progress blocked by ice. Pet's ship made it safely back to London by late September. Jackman was reported in Norway that winter but on his return voyage the ship was lost with all hands. These English sailors had no charts to these unmapped waters, save those they made themselves, their entire navigational technique being based on the compass and dead-reckoning.

The Dutch now manifested the same interest in the North-East Passage as the English. They had already established overland trade with Moscow, and one of them, Olivier Brunel, had made coasting voyages as far as the mouth of the river Ob. Between 1594 and 1597, Willem Barentsz led three expeditions in the sea that now bears his name. The most successful in new discoveries was the third, for he landed on Bear Island, explored a large new group which we now know as Spitsbergen, and reached the northernmost point of Novaya Zemlya. But these achievements cost Barentsz his life, for winter overtook them on the north-east coast of Novaya Zemlya. The men spent eight months in a hut built from driftwood, and lived by trapping bears and arctic foxes for food. In June 1597 they prepared their boats and committed themselves to the sea. Weakened and despairing, Barentsz himself died at sea, but the survivors somehow succeeded in reaching Kola where they found food and shelter, and in November they landed in Amsterdam.

Even now the quest was not over, for Henry Hudson was commissioned by the Muscovy

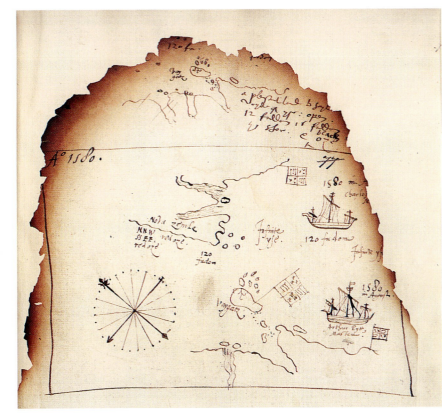

Right: The ships of Pet and Jackman in the Kara Sea, 1580. Sketched by one of the expedition, Hugh Smyth. Note the English standards on Vaygach and Novaya Zemlya.
The British Library Cotton MS Otho E.viii, f.38.

Left: World Map by George Best, 1578, showing both the North-East and the North-West Passages.
The British Library G.6527.

World Ocean Currents. The winds and currents of the world's oceans were a major obstacle to navigators: they needed to know that, having reached their destinations, they could also return safely. From the late fifteenth century onwards, decades of trial and error were required before reliable ocean routes were found, especially in the Pacific.

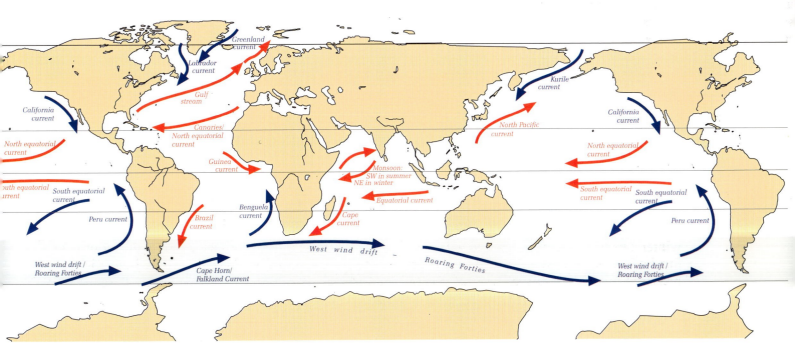

The imagined North Polar Continent from Mercator's 1569 world map.

Maritime Museum, Rotterdam

Company in 1607 to attempt a *northwest* route to Asia, to which Hudson responded with the novel plan of seeking a passage between the east coast of Greenland and the newly-discovered Spitsbergen, thinking 'to have made my return by the north of Greenland, to Davis his Straight'. He reached the very high latitude of 80 degrees before being forced to retreat from the ice. Hudson was subsequently employed by the Dutch East India Company to search for the North-East Passage, but this and several more voyages English, Dutch and Danish, down to the 1620s failed always to penetrate far into the Kara Sea. Spitsbergen became better known and whaling developed in the Barentsz Sea. Linschoten's 1598 chart of the Polar regions placed thousands of square miles of arctic coastline on the map. But failure in the search for the 'Passage to Cathay' was inevitable, indeed we can only marvel at the courage and endurance shown by these mariners who were ill-equipped to face the rigours of the arctic seas, but who returned year after year in the conviction that 'no sea was unnavigable'; so strong was the lure of the east, and the spell of Marco Polo's narrative, written three centuries before, and now drawing English and Dutch mariners into the waters of the Arctic.

CHAPTER THREE
THE NEW WORLD
1490–1550

The Madonna of the Navigators.

Patrimonio Nacional, Madrid

'From a very small age I went sailing upon the sea, which occupation inclines all who follow it to wish to learn the secrets of this world.'

– Columbus, 1501

'Our world hath of late discovered another, no less large, fully-peopled, all-things-yielding, and mighty in strength than our own.'

– Montaigne, 1580

ACROSS THE WESTERN OCEAN

IN CLASSICAL AND MEDIEVAL geography, the Pillars of Hercules stood symbolically for the edge of the known world. By the time the Portuguese maritime experiment was beginning, this symbol had lost touch with maritime reality. The deeds of the Norsemen were all but forgotten, and indeed the Greenland colony in the fifteenth century was dying for lack of contact with Europe, but Venetians vessels coasted regularly around Spain and France to their markets in Flanders, whalers and fishermen from Britain and Scandinavia were active around Iceland, the Canaries were settled as early as the fourteenth century by the Spanish, the Madeira archipelago by the Portuguese around 1420, and the Azores by 1440. The exact sequence of exploration in these Atlantic islands is disputed, and their appearance on charts before c.1440 is often equivocal. This uncertainty is heightened by the legendary islands which imagination and false sightings placed in the Atlantic, including Hy-Brasil and Antilia. The former has no connection with Brazil, but was the 'Isle of the Blest' in Gaelic folklore, while the latter was merely a vague term meaning 'Opposite Island', and it became

Above: Columbus arrives in Hispaniola.

The British Library IA 37918.

elaborated into the fanciful 'Island of Seven Cities'. Any imperfect sighting of land in the Atlantic, a cloudbank or a reef, might be associated with such islands. The hold that these legends had on the imagination is simply a function of the fact that much of the world was still unexplored: man was not master of his environment, and the unknown was as real as the known. Documented voyages were undertaken in search of these islands, from Bristol for example before Cabot's expedition, while in the 1460s and 1470s there were many Portuguese commissions to 'search and find' Antilia, and they haunted mapmakers long after the Age of Discovery. These voyages had the effect of increasing mariners' familiarity with the North Atlantic, and the discovery of the Azores was taken as proof that the ocean was far from empty. But this was very different from setting out to penetrate this untravelled realm, to test it to its limits: for such a wild undertaking there was no motive and no logic.

Or was there? 'If the immensity of the Atlantic Sea did not prevent it, we could sail from Iberia to India along the same parallel,' wrote Eratosthenes in the third century BC. This concept became available to the west in a printed Latin translation of Strabo's *Geography* in 1469, at exactly the same time as Ptolemy's maps. Unlike the geography of the ecclesiastical *mappa mundi* or of the Mediterranean sea-chart, Ptolemy's measured world had an unmistakably spherical form. The known, inhabited world occupied slightly more than half of the globe, just over 180 longitude degrees. In the awakening maritime age, surely it was only a matter of time before someone asked: What of the other half? And once again the motive for such a question was to hand in the image of the East, the wealth and civilization of another world, cut off from Europe by the hostile forces of Islam, or by a sea voyage of 8,000 miles. 'In the carrying out of this Enterprise of the Indies', wrote Columbus in 1501, 'neither reason nor mathematics nor maps were any use to me'. In one sense this was completely untrue, but Columbus said it for dramatic effect, to emphasise the inspired leap of imagination which he was required to make as he worked out his geographical ideas during the 1470s and 1480s. Thanks to the survival of certain books from Columbus's library, annotated in his own hand, we know a good deal about the sources of these ideas. He read Marco Polo, Ptolemy, Strabo and the *Imago Mundi* of Pierre D'Ailly – in which the size and sphericity of the earth are fully discussed. From these sources Columbus distilled three fundamental ideas, one true, the others completely false: that the earth is round, and that therefore any part is theoretically accessible from any other part; that the extent of the Eurasian land-mass was approximately 280 longitude degrees; that the diameter of the world was of the order of 20,000 miles, and

Contarini World Map, 1506, the first printed map to show any part of the New World. The mapmaker did not share Columbus's own view of his discoveries: Cuba and Hispaniola are placed some 3,000 miles east of the coast of Cathay, with Japan midway between them. South America is 'Terra Crucis', the name given to it by Cabral.

that therefore the value of a meridional degree was $55\frac{1}{2}$ miles. Using these quite erroneous estimates, Columbus convinced himself that a sea voyage of 4,500 miles west from Spain would bring him to the coast of Cathay. This figure was still daunting, but it could be reduced by accepting Marco Polo's statement, utterly unsupported though it was, that the great island of Zipangri (Japan) lay 1,500 miles east of Cathay. Given fair winds, a ship could easily average 100 miles per day; thus Columbus arrived at the conviction that a voyage of scarcely more than thirty days would carry him west across the Atlantic to Japan then Cathay and 'the Indies'. This theory of a 'small Atlantic' was also put forward by the Florentine cosmographer Paolo Toscanelli, with whom Columbus is reported to have corresponded, and it is precisely this world picture which appears on the globe of Martin Behaim, made in Nuremberg in 1492, on which the Atlantic covers slightly more than a quarter of the earth's longitude.

But to translate such a theory into an open-sea voyage far longer than any ever undertaken before required energy and vision amounting to an obsession, and Columbus's personality included all three qualities. After almost eight years spent in seeking royal patronage in Portugal and Spain, Ferdinand and Isabella at last agreed to Columbus's demanding terms for honour and fortune if the scheme were successful, and provided him with a small fleet of three ships and a commission to reach

Detail from Waldseemüller's World Map, 1507. Vespucci is honoured as the discoverer of the New World, counterbalancing Ptolemy, the geographer of the Old World. The ocean west of the Americas had never been seen by any European at this date.

Schloss Wolfegg

Right: Part of the World Map by Johannes Ruysch, 1507. The peninsula on the extreme eastern coast of Asia is named 'Terra Nova' a direct equivalent of Cabot's 'New Found Land'. Ruysch adds the words 'Ins. Baccalaurus' – the island of codfish. Greenland is depicted as a promontory of Asia, while Japan is not shown at all.

The British Library Maps C.1.d.6.

'the lands of India and of a prince called Great Khan . . . by way of the west'. On 3 August 1492, Columbus sailed from the small town of Palos on the first and most important of his four Atlantic voyages. After taking on supplies in the Canaries, the fleet awaited an easterly wind before setting out into the unknown on September 6. The voyage lasted just 36 days and had favourable winds, but in that time both Columbus and his crew were in constant fear and tension as they sailed where no men had ever sailed before. For thirty days with repeated altitude observations of the sun and stars, they resolutely followed a course along the latitude of 28 degrees north, for Columbus was convinced that this would lead them to the coast of Asia. But on October 7 his resolve wavered. Flights of birds could now be seen making for the south-west, and Columbus's second in command, Alonso Pinzon, argued that Zipangri lay further to the south. Columbus altered course to the south-west, and in the night of October 12 the outline of land, now at 24 degrees north, was unmistakably discerned. At dawn a green and fertile country revealed itself, clearly an island but clearly inhabited. Columbus and a small party carried the royal banner of Spain ashore, gave thanks to God, and took possession of the land in the name of Ferdinand and Isabella. This act, performed on the day he touched land, without any attempt at reconnaissance, presents the crux of the geographical problem Columbus had created for himself, for his contemporaries and for historians: where did he conceive that he was? If he had reached Cathay, or even an island close to it, how dared he take possession of the territory belonging to the 'Great Khan'? But if his calculations were wrong and he was not in eastern Asia, where was he? The inhabitants were friendly, but they were 'naked', which in fifteenth-century terms meant that they were savages, and nothing that Columbus was to see in this region in the next twelve years bore the slightest resemblance to the image of Cathay which he had formed from Marco Polo. If that course-alteration had not been made, he would have reached the sand and marsh of the Florida coast, near Cape Canaveral, and he would surely have formed no different view of his location then. The exact identification of Columbus's first landfall has long been the subject of

controversy; it might have anywhere in the Bahamas or Turks and Caicos. Its indigenous name was Guanahani, and modern research identifies it with San Salvador, the name later given to it by the Spaniards.

For some weeks he cruised among the Bahamian islands before pressing on south-west to arrive off Cuba, where he explored some three hundred miles of the northern coast trying to convince himself that this was Japan. Sailing east, he then discovered Hispaniola, the most impressive island so far, with signs of a certain degree of civilization and natural wealth. Columbus's eager eye for colonial opportunities again forces us to wonder if he truly believed he was in Zipangri, or Cathay. He later reported to his royal patrons:

> 'All the islands are so utterly at your Highnesses' command that it only remains to establish a Spanish presence and order them to perform your will. For I could traverse all these islands in arms without meeting opposition . . . so that they are yours to command and make them work, sow seed and do whatever else is necessary, and build a town and teach them to wear clothes and adopt our customs.'

On Christmas Day 1492, disaster struck when his flagship the *Santa Maria* ran aground on the north-west coast of Hispaniola. Thirty-eight men were forced to remain in a settlement which the Spaniards named 'la Navidad', while the two remaining smaller ships set sail for Spain on 4 January 1493. It was a long, stormy and difficult voyage, during which Columbus was tormented by the fear that he would not reach Spain with news of his achievement. Touching the Azores on 18 February, the wild weather persisted and forced him to land in Portugal on 4 March, before he finally anchored again in Palos on 15 March 1493.

He was royally received at court, and within months a second voyage was in preparation. Yet the high-point of his life was undoubtedly that spring of 1493; thereafter his career was one of failure, intellectual, political and personal. He made three further expeditions to the Caribbean, in which he explored the Leeward Islands and Puerto Rico, reconnoitred the mainland coast of Venezuela and also from Yucatan to Panama. But he never found Cathay or the Indies, or a route that would take him to them. He resolutely maintained his belief that this was the coast of Asia, yet he devoted enormous energy to establishing colonies there, principally on Hispaniola. His contract with Ferdinand and Isabella had been to find a new route to the eastern kingdoms, not to find new islands in the Atlantic, so an admission of geographical uncertainty would have endangered his fortune and his entire authority: was this a factor in his avowed position? The settlement he had left behind on Hispaniola in January 1493 had been wiped out, and all his subsequent colonial schemes were disastrous failures, rent by internal divisions, conflicts with the inhabitants and challenges to his autocratic rule. During his third voyage he touched Trinidad and the coast of South America, where the vast outflow of the Orinoco River compelled him for a time to revise his geographical ideas, acknowledging that this must be a continental land-mass. He made several statements suggesting a conversion to the belief that this was 'another world', and prophesied to his royal patrons that they would one day possess these territories. But he later recanted, and insisted again that this was Asia. His final voyage was a desperate attempt to break through the barrier of Central America with its savage inhabitants, and find the cities, the civilization and the wealth of Cathay. He was driven deeper and deeper into a religious mania, into the belief that his was a Messianic role to unite the scattered peoples of the world in a new era of Christian faith.

To his contemporaries in Europe the problem was equally puzzling. We have few direct written comments on Columbus's discovery, but Pietro Martyr, who would later write the first history of the western discoveries, stated clearly his belief that Columbus had found Atlantic islands previously unknown, and the Majorcan geographer Jaume Ferrer agreed that Columbus's faulty estimates of the size of Asia and of the Atlantic made it impossible for him to have reached Cathay. The political

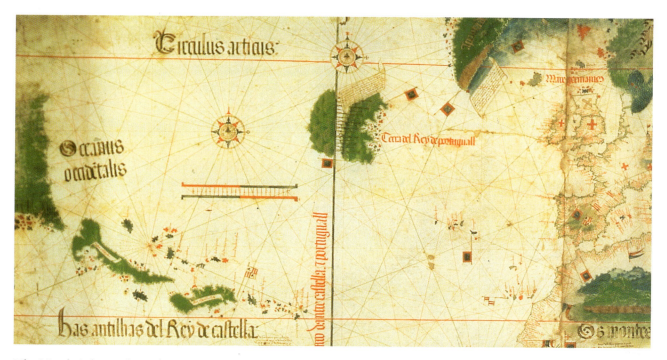

The North Atlantic from the Cantino World Map, 1502. The Tordesillas line of demarcation between Spain and Portugal is emphatically shown. In Newfoundland, the legend 'Land of the King of Portugal' is a direct reference to the voyages of the Corte-Reals, who described it as the huge wooded island depicted here.

Biblioteca Estense, Modena

decisions which the Spanish court had to reach were ambiguous: on the one hand they rewarded Columbus according to their contract, while on the other they set in train a plan to colonize the newly-claimed islands. Columbus himself notoriously failed to produce the definitive map of his voyages which he was always promising, and other European mapmakers were equally hesitant. The first known printed map to show the new islands, that of Giovanni Contarini, did not appear until 1506. Its geography is essentially that of the Behaim Globe with the addition of a large blank landmass in the south Atlantic (which, following Pedro Cabral is named 'Terra Crucis') and the islands of Cuba, Hispaniola and the Leewards. The western edge of Cuba lies barely fifteen degrees from Japan, while the coast of Cathay is a further thirty degrees west. This map would surely not have pleased Columbus, for it sited his discoveries some 3,000 miles from the Asian coast. We have no way of knowing what manuscript maps may have circulated in Spain, Italy or elsewhere between 1493 and 1506, but the map which is accepted as the first to show any part of the new world is the chart of the Spanish navigator Juan de la Cosa, which is dated 1500. This chart can be interpreted as reflecting Columbus's own beliefs, for the Caribbean Islands are placed very near a huge coast stretching north and south; although the chartmaker refrains from identifying this as Cathay, it would naturally be assumed that the continents on the eastern and western edges of the map are one and the same. This map pre-dates Columbus's last voyage, in which he followed some 800 miles of central American coast vainly seeking a passage west, but this part of the map is tantalizingly obscured by an image of St. Christopher – surely a tribute to Columbus himself. The Cosa chart contains an obvious puzzle concerning its dating: it shows Cuba as a completely navigable island, which was not achieved by Columbus, or by any other mariner until 1508. It is possible that this map is a revised copy which has retained the date of the original.

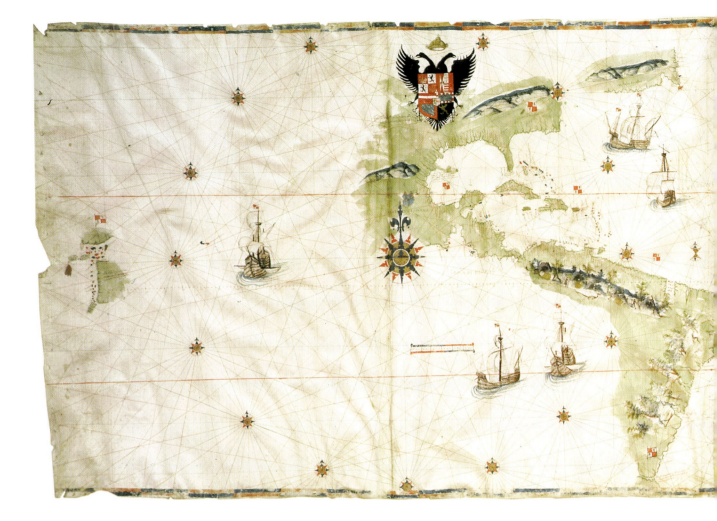

THE SUCCESSORS OF COLUMBUS

Both the Cosa chart and the Contarini map had the opportunity of incorporating the results of the first post-Columbian voyages, those of Cabot, Corte-Real and Vespucci, but the way that they did so reveals the continuing uncertainty about the western discoveries. These three mariners undertook the earliest 'follow-up' voyages after Columbus, on behalf of England, Portugal and Spain, not in the Caribbean, but exploring to the north and the south, attempting to place Columbus's discoveries on the incomplete map of the western Atlantic.

The career of John Cabot, a Venetian or Genoese, is surrounded by obscurity. He was probably in Spain in the early 1490s, and if so he must have been well aware of Columbus's achievements. He travelled to England in 1495 and succeeded in gaining the approval, although not the financial backing, of King Henry VII for a western voyage of exploration. Cathay and the Indies are not specifically mentioned in the royal patent granted to Cabot in March 1496, but he was given leave to 'sail to all parts, countries and seas of the east, of the west and of the north under our banners and ensigns . . . to seek out, discover and find whatsoever isles, countries, regions and provinces of the heathen and infidels . . . which before this time have been unknown to all Christians.' This leaves open the possibility that Cabot was seeking new islands, new fishing-grounds or new trade of any kind, as well as new routes to 'the Spicerie'. Finding support from a syndicate of Bristol merchants, Cabot sailed in a single square-rigged ship of fifty tons, the *Mathew*, in May 1497. We have few details of his plans or his voyage, but it seems that he aimed to make a shorter northerly crossing and kept to latitude 51 north. He passed Dursey Head on May 22, and exactly one month later land was sighted, a sizeable

Juan Vespucci's World Chart of 1526 shows the world divided between Portugal and Spain: Africa and the Indian Ocean belong to the former, while the ships and the eagle of Spain surround the New World.

Hispanic Society of America, New York

Portrait of Vespucci, from de Bry's America.
The British Library, 10003.e.19.

island separated by perhaps fifteen miles of sea from what they took to be a rocky mainland. At between 51 and 52 degrees north, this landfall has always been identified as Belle Isle and northern Newfoundland. Remarkably, this was only a few miles from the spot where Leif Ericsson made his settlement at L'Anse aux Meadows in the year 1000.

Cabot landed and took possession of the territory in the name of the king of England. He found no people, but he did find signs of habitation, snares and worked pieces of wood. Perhaps in fear he never went ashore again, but coasted the 400 miles southwards to Cape Race, where he turned, retraced to Belle Isle, and was back in Bristol on 8 August 1497. The land he discovered became known as 'The New Isle', which by 1502 had become 'The New Found Land', so Cabot clearly did not imagine he had touched Cathay, indeed to claim it for England as he did, and as it was gratefully accepted by Henry VII, it had to be 'New Found'. Cabot's account dwelt on its wealth in timber and especially fish – the huge codfish in their thousands which soon attracted fishermen from England, France and Portugal to the waters off Newfoundland, (although there is some slight evidence that Bristol fishermen had visited the Grand Banks before Cabot's voyage). Like Columbus, Cabot left no map, but it seems likely that that he promoted his 'New Isle' as offering a new route to the east, since a new syndicate was formed, this time with a measure of direct royal investment, to find 'the region where all the spices in the world have their origin, as well as the jewells.' In May 1498 with five ships, Cabot sailed once more from Bristol. One ship had to return almost immediately for repairs; the other four were never seen again. John Cabot vanished from history as mysteriously as he appeared. The Cosa chart shows the coast of North America adorned with several English flags and with the note *Mar descubierta por Inglese* – 'sea discovered by the English.' Some historians have related this to Cabot's second voyage, deducing that he coasted far to the south from Newfoundland, and that somehow Cosa had access to an account of Cabot's lost fleet. Even if the Cosa chart is actually dated after 1508, its detail of the North American coast never has been, and probably never will be, satisfactorily explained, for aside from the possibility of John Cabot's second voyage, the only reported English venture along the American coast at this time is that of Cabot's son Sebastian in 1508–09. This voyage is ill-documented, and what it achieved is uncertain; many historians have rejected it as spurious.

The Contarini map makes no overt reference to Cabot, but the extreme tip of Cathay shows a peninsula which is annotated 'This land was discovered by navigators of the King of Portugal'. This refers unmistakably to the voyages of Gaspar Corte-Real who, in 1500 and 1501, mounted two expeditions from the Azores to explore the North-West Atlantic. On the second voyage his ship was lost, and in 1502 his brother Miguel retraced his route in search of him. Gaspar had found a huge, wooded island whose waters abounded with codfish. He called it *Terra Verde* but it was undoubtedly not Greenland but Newfoundland. Although it was unclear on which side of the Tordesillas line this land was located, the Spanish had no interest in these remote, northern territories, and conceded to Portugal the right to sail and fish there. A year later than the Contarini map, the world map of Johannes Ruysch shows a peninsula on the east of Cathay which is reasonably similar in shape to Newfoundland. This time it is named *Terra Nova* – a direct translation of Henry VII's 'New Found Land' – but with the gloss *Insula Baccalauras* – 'Island of Codfish'. The Portuguese built up a large fish-curing industry on Newfoundland, but the crown displayed no official interest in the territory, occupied with its vast seaborne empire in the east, and England was able to reassert its claim through Sir Humphrey Gilbert in 1583.

Of greater significance than either Cabot or Corte-Real were the voyages and the subsequent reports of Amerigo Vespucci. A Florentine, socially well-connected, Vespucci entered the employ of the Medici and in 1491 he was in Seville as their banking agent. He was involved in funding the ships of Columbus's second and third expeditions, and became personally acquainted with Columbus, perhaps even a close personal friend since he witnessed Columbus's will. Vespucci wrote several

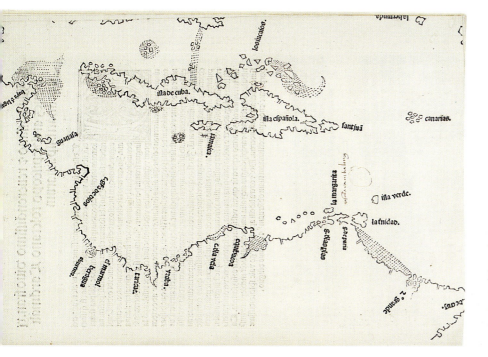

The Caribbean, 1511, from Pietro Martyr's Decade of the New World. *Bermuda appears for the first time on any map, and landfalls on the Mexican coast to the west are indicated, probably those of Vincent Pinzon and Diaz de Solis.*

The British Library G.6811.

accounts, published and unpublished, of four separate Atlantic voyages, accounts which are brief, vague and occasionally contradictory – modern navigational experts distrust many of his claimed latitude positions. It is generally considered that only two of his voyages are authentic. Between May 1499 and June 1500 he was navigator aboard a ship which touched the coast of modern Guyana and then coasted to latitude 6 degrees south. He wrote that his intention was 'to turn a headland which Ptolemy call the Cape of Cattigara . . . in my opinion we were not a great distance from it'. Cattigara is the last, the most easterly named point in Ptolemy's description of the world. Vespucci at this time had no reason not to share Columbus's belief that he was following an island or peninsula off southeast Asia. Failing to find an open sea leading west, Vespucci turned back, and passed the mouth of the Amazon and the Orinoco before sailing back to Spain. If thisvoyage is genuine, Vespucci discovered the coast of Brazil a year before Cabral, although Columbus on his third voyage had spent time on the Venezuelan coast. There seems no reason to doubt the southern limit of this voyage since Vespucci noted that the North Star was lost altogether at six degrees south.

Still with the aim of penetrating to India and Cathay, Vespucci planned a further expedition, but was unable to secure Spanish backing and transferred his services to Portugal. On 13 May 1501 he sailed from Lisbon direct to Cape São Roque in Brazil, and spent the following nine months exploring the coast southwards, passing and naming Rio de Janeiro (mistaking the inlet for a river-mouth) and the Rio de la Plata. Vespucci claims to have continued to latitude 50 degrees south, into near-Antarctic waters before turning northwards again. If this latitude is authentic, it entitles Vespucci to a high place among the explorers of South America. By the time he anchored in Lisbon again in July 1502, he had become convinced by the extent of the South American coast that this had to be recognized as a 'new world', a view he publicized in his pamphlet *Mundus Novus*, 1505. In the same year he returned to Spain and was appointed chief navigator in the famous *Casa de la Contratacion de las Indias* – the House of Commerce, a highly important post in which Vespucci had to examine all incoming mariners' reports and maintain the official charts of the Spanish lands and routes to the west. Vespucci's critics and detractors, who argue that he was liar, an incompetent navigator and a

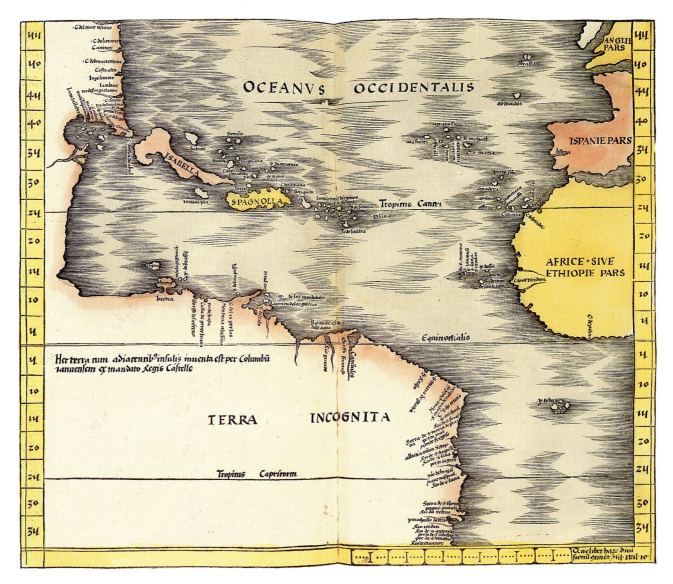

The Atlantic from Waldseemüller's edition of Ptolemy, 1513. The introduction to this map states that it was based on information from 'The Admiral', presumably Columbus; the map thus reflects Columbus's failure on his final voyage to find any strait leading to the west.

The British Library Maps C.1.d.9.

usurper of other men's discoveries, have never explained how he came to be entrusted with such an important position in the Spanish government. It may be that Vespucci's position in the *Casa* prevented him from publishing maps of his own, but his experiences and his geographical ideas found their full and magnificent expression in the world map published in 1507 by Martin Waldseemüller.

Waldseemüller, a humanist scholar and cosmographer in St. Dié, at the court of the Duke of Lorraine, had read and been entirely convinced by Vespucci's narratives. He conceived a new world map which would combine the 'Old World' of Ptolemy, updated by the Portuguese map of Africa, with the 'New World' now revealed by Vespucci. It was Vespucci's insight in this respect which contrasted so strongly with Columbus's impatience with the new western lands as mere impediments on the route to Asia, and which secured Vespucci his immortality. Waldseemüller placed the name America on his great map of 1507, and in an accompanying text, entitled *Cosmographiae Introductio*, he explains: 'Now the continents have been investigated more comprehensively, and a fourth has been discovered by Americus Vesputius. I do not know why anyone should object to naming this continent Amerige or America after its discoverer, a man of resource and intellect . . . Its location and the customs of its people can easily be gathered from the two journeys Americus made. . .' The status of the 'New World' is given the clearest possible form on the map by its depiction as a separate continent, removed from Cathay by some 90 degrees of longitude. It is difficult not to believe that this reflects Vespucci's own conclusions; it seems inconceivable that Waldseemüller would have planned and published this map without the prior knowledge and co-operation of the man who inspired it. It seems likely that the two men corresponded or even met between 1505 and 1507, and that Vespucci provided Waldseemüller with sketches showing his voyages, and his interpretation of the status of South America. This is conjectural, but it is entirely consistent with Waldseemüller's celebration, almost apotheosis, of Vespucci as the geographer of the New World, matching the greatness of Ptolemy as the geographer of the Old World. Waldseemüller's map of the Old World has a Ptolemaic basis, but its updating of Africa and India resembles the Cosa chart of 1500 rather than the more accurate Cantino chart of 1502. This again suggests the possibility that Waldseemüller was in Seville around the year 1506, and had the opportunity of studying the Cosa map (the Cantino map was in Ferrara at this date). In addition to its other claims to importance, Waldseemüller's map contains a considerable mystery in that it depicts North America also a continent, plainly separated from Asia, and having a mountainous western coast. In 1507 there was no basis that we know of for such a picture of America, for no European had penetrated the northern mainland or sailed its western coast. The sea to the west is not named, but is nonetheless mysterious, for this was six years years before Balboa's famous first sight of the Pacific. All this was either an extraordinarily prophetic guess, or Waldseemüller had somehow obtained access to some now-lost description of North America. The story of Vespucci and Waldseemüller, the voyage of the one and the map of the other, is one of the most intriguing and enigmatic in the history of cartography.

PROBING THE NEW WORLD

How should we sum up European knowledge of the New World in 1507, the year of Waldseemüller's prophetic map, a year after Columbus's death and fifteen years after his first voyage? The Caribbean Islands had become a Spanish colonial domain with attention centred on Hispaniola. Some thousands of Spaniards, and no doubt a few mariners of other nationalities, had now made the journey across the Atlantic, lured by the prospect of frontier fortunes. Trade was sufficient for the Spanish monarch to set up the *Casa de la Contratacion* – the House of Commerce – as a department of state to regulate trade from the Indies. The volume of this trade may be gauged from the Caribbean storm of June 1502, in which nineteen Spanish ships were lost, with more than 500 men aboard, together with the largest shipment of gold yet dispatched for Spain (most of the records of Columbus's administration of the Hispaniola colony also went down with this fleet). To the south of this colonial archipelago, a vast continental coast had been encountered which was known to extend some 2,000 miles to the east and then to trend south for at least a further 2,000 miles. Non-Spanish voyages from Europe had also made western landfalls far to the north, but whether the northern coastline was continuous was still unknown. So the great question of the status of the Caribbean Islands remained unanswered, in particular no one had yet sailed directly west from Cuba across the north of the Yucatan Peninsula to find the shores of Mexico and the huge arc of the coast of North America. Nor of course was there any awareness of the civilizations of Mexico and Peru, so different from the island cultures so far

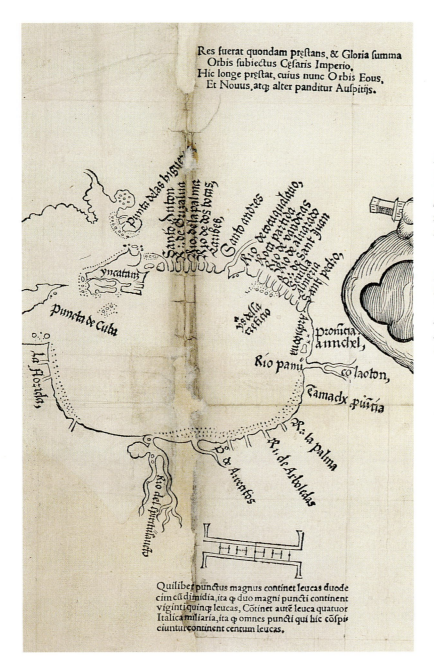

Res fuerat quondam preſtans, & Gloria ſumma
Orbis ſubieċtus Ceſaris Imperio.
Hic longe preſtat, cuius nunc Orbis Eous,
Et Nouus, atcɜ alter panditur Auſpitijs.

Quiliber punċtus magnus continet leucas duode
cim cū dimidia, ita cɜ duo magni punċti continent
viginti quincɜ leucas, Cōtinet autē leuca quatuor
Italica miliaria, ita cɜ omnes punċti qui hic cōſpi
ciunturcontinent centum leucas.

Left: The Gulf of Mexico, printed in 1524 with Cortes's second letter. Yucatan had been visited in 1517, but is here shown as an island, and Florida is named for the first time. South is at the top.

The British Library C.20.e.26.

Right: Mexico City from Cortes's second letter, 1524. This map of the lake city of Tenochtitlan, emphasizing the human sacrifices in its temples, became the standard European image of the Aztec capital.

The British Library C.20.e.26.

encountered. On a pragmatic level, these western lands were being treated as *de facto* a 'New World', open to European domination; they were 'the Indies', but not India and not Cathay. The possibility of a strait leading to the west was still very much alive, but it clearly must be sought north of the latitude of Cuba, while the Spaniards crowding into Hispaniola were eager for new territory to exploit. From these twin motives the map of the North American coast, with the exception of the north-west above California, was completed in a series of steps during the next forty years. This may seem like slow progress; to modern eyes a single voyage from Florida to Newfoundland could have settled the matter in two months. But this ignores the physical uncertainties of surveying unknown coasts: any one of the large inlets – Pamlico Sound, Chesapeake Bay, Delaware Bay, Long Island Sound and so on –

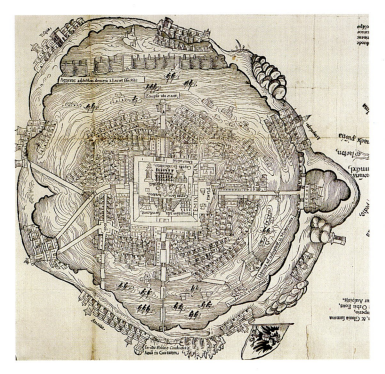

might be the desired strait, and therefore must be explored. Mariners had a constant and understandable fear of unknown coasts, of striking reefs in uncharted waters which meant almost certain death far from any possible help: therefore they stood far out from unexplored coasts, even though this often meant missing vital features. It also ignores the political will and the financial support which must be secured before each fresh expedition could be launched: Spain and Portugal were sufficiently occupied, while neither England nor France was yet ready to pursue wholeheartedly an overseas enterprise where the demands in courage, skills and money were great, and the rewards uncertain.

Spanish ventures into the central American mainland (setting aside Columbus's fourth expedition) may have begun with an ill-documented voyage in 1505–6 by Vincent Pinzon and Diaz de Solis, which may have coasted Yucatan and the Gulf of Campeche. In 1509 Alonso de Ojeda was granted leave to found a colony at Uraba (the extreme north-west of modern Colombia). It failed through dissension, hunger and disease, but on the advice of Vasco Nuñez de Balboa, the survivors moved across the Gulf of Darien (into modern Panama) and recommenced bartering with the inhabitants and gold-hunting. Balboa made himself the head of the colony, and his policy of brutality to the Indians reached new depths of cruelty. It was here that rumours first emerged of a kingdom far to the south rich in gold and silver, and of a great ocean that lay to the west. Balboa set out to cross the isthmus towards the Gulf of Panama, and in September 1513 standing 'silent upon a peak in Darien' became the first European to see the Pacific, into which he waded some days later to take possession of it for Spain. Even Keats' celebrated confusion of Balboa with Cortes was unable to tarnish the fame of this event, one of the legendary moments in the history of exploration. Balboa was afire to explore the 'Southern Sea', and in 1517 by dint of colossal efforts he had prefabricated boats dragged across the isthmus and launched in the Bay of San Miguel. Rivalry in the colony cost Balboa his life in 1519, but one of his companions on the 1513 journey fulfilled his ambition of finding the gold-rich kingdom – Francisco Pizarro.

Hispaniola was the starting-point from which a number of important reconnaissance voyages left to explore the Gulf of Mexico. Puerto Rico was colonized in 1508–9, and it was from here in 1513 that Juan Ponce de Leon set out north-west to find the island of Bimini, reported by the Indians, about which a legend resembling that of the Fountain of Youth had gathered. In April of that year he landed on a coast to which he gave the name 'Florida' because of its luxuriant vegetation. His landfall was near the modern St. Augustine, from where he coasted south around the Keys, imagining however that this was the island of Bimini. In 1517 an expedition under Hernandes de Cordova made the first landing on Yucatan, where they found signs of a civilization higher than any previously encountered in the region. Cordova reported 'A thickly-peopled country, with stone-built houses, and people who covered their persons and went about clothed in cotton garments, and who possessed gold and who cultivated maize fields.' These were the descendants of the Maya, and these reports

World Chart by Juan de la Cosa, 1500. The Caribbean Islands are located between two continental coasts, but the crucial area to the west is obscured by the image of St. Christopher.

Museo Naval, Madrid

excited great interest among the Spaniards, and the following year a second force under Juan de Grijalva obtained gold and jewelled artefacts and was told of a magnificent kingdom in the interior, whose power and wealth were the greatest in the region. The Aztec nation had been found and the stage was set for the most violent clash of cultures yet witnessed in the age of European exploration. To speak of Cortes, or Pizarro, as explorers is like describing them as reformers of indigenous governments. Their motive was conquest and plunder, which they achieved with ruthless success, but in the process they gained, incidentally, a place in the history of exploration. The Caribbean as an enclosed sea had first appeared recognisably in the map drawn for Pietro Martyr's *Do Orbe Novo* of 1511, the first published 'history' of the new world, but after Cortes, Mexico as an entity with its western coast appears on European maps from 1526 as *Nueva España*. It was through information supplied by the indigenous Mexicans rather than through exploration that Cortes knew the Gulf of Mexico to be enclosed on the north, and he revealed this in the map published in 1524 with his letter to the

Part of the Verrazano World Map, 1529. In 1524 the Verrazano brothers believed they had seen the Pacific Ocean across the Outer Banks of North Carolina. This 'Sea of Verrazano' was convincing enough for mapmakers to copy it for the next fifty years.

Biblioteca Apostolica, Vatican

Emperor Charles V. It would be a further ten years before the Spaniards began to push to the north and north-west of their new kingdom. Meanwhile the problem of the east coast of North America remained, and the question of a possible strait to the lands of the East.

Estevão Gomez, a Portuguese who had deserted Magellan in the dangerous strait to the Pacific in 1520, had entered the service of Spain, and was dispatched from Corunna in 1524 to reconnoitre the coast from Newfoundland to Florida. Gomez had secured his release from the prison where his desertion had placed him by arguing that he could find an easier route than Magellan's, to the north of New Spain. During June and July Gomez explored the eastern seaboard, finding neither the strait nor any alluring natural resources, but his voyage left its clear mark on the Spanish charts of the time, such as the great world map of Diego Ribero. A Spanish fleet under Luis Vasquez de Ayllon left Hispaniola in 1526 to colonize the Carolina coast. Their chosen site is uncertain, but it may have been near Cape Fear, a malarial terrain where the colony was rapidly broken down by disease and

The Americas from the World Map by Sebastian Cabot, 1544. This map is among the earliest to show the Amazon, descended by Orellana in 1541, and the Gulf of California which Ulloa had explored in the previous year.

Bibliothèque Nationale, Paris

hunger. Yet in the same year in Spain itself Panfilo de Narvaez received a royal commission to conquer Florida, and sailed from Sanlucar with a large fleet in June 1527, in what was destined to be an epic failure. Landing on the west coast of Florida near Tampa Bay, they marched west but lost touch with their ships. In improvised boats they struggled along the Texan coast, becoming separated from each other, until the few survivors gathered on the 'Island of Misfortune', perhaps Galveston Island, where they were reduced to a dozen survivors. In Spain the fleet was given up for lost and after this experiment and the reconnaissance of Gomez, Spain effectively lost interest in northern exploration, and concentrated on South America. Yet a small group of men had escaped the Island of Misfortune, and were engaged in an epic struggle for survival. Cabeza de Vaca and his companions reached the coast of Texas and trekked inland, trading with and learning survival from the Indians. They found the Rio Grande and followed it northwards then struck west through the Sierra Madre. Cabeza either claimed or possessed great sanctity and powers of healing, and he gathered a following of nomadic Indians. He descended to the Gulf of California and arrived in Spanish territory at Compostella in April 1536, after his six-year journey.

Exactly contemporary with the voyages of Gomez and Ayllon was that of Giovanni da Verrazano, an Italian navigator who was employed as the first French emissary to the new world, sent by King Francois I in the hope of entering the race for the east; perhaps the king's famous and bitter rivalry with the Spanish Emperor Charles V was the spur. In 1524 Verrazano sailed Gomez's route in reverse, from approximately Cape Fear to Maine and Nova Scotia. The most remarkable legacy of his voyage was his interpretation of what he saw around Cape Hatteras, for he convinced himself that the water of Pamlico Sound was the long-sought western sea which would led to Cathay. The map later drawn by his brother Gerolomo shows North America narrowing to an isthmus at this point, and the 'Sea of Verrazano' was born, a cartographic myth which persisted for at least fifty years. The land north of the isthmus he called hopefully 'Nova Gallia' and considered it Arcadian; this word was shifted by later mapmakers steadily north-east until it came to rest in French Nova Scotia. Verrazano somehow missed sighting either the Chesapeake Bay or the Delaware Bay, but was the first to enter what later became New York Bay.

The crises of Francois I's reign after 1525 prevented him from giving further thought to exploration until 1534. By this time a considerable French school of navigation and boatbuilding had begun to flourish in Normandy, and the king was able to appoint a Frenchman, Jacques Cartier, to lead a new Atlantic venture. Commissioned to sail to 'the New Lands to find a route to Asia', Cartier's two ships departed from Saint-Malo in April 1534. Entering the Strait of Belle Isle he emerged into the Gulf of St. Lawrence and during June and July he reconnoitred Prince Edward Island, the Gaspé Peninsula and Anticosti Island before turning back for France. His modestly successful voyage left open the possibility that the Gulf might indeed lead to the eastern strait. The king was sufficiently encouraged to commission a second voyage in the following year. This time with three ships Cartier sailed up the St. Lawrence as far as the site of Quebec and established a base near an Iroquois village, from where he pushed on by boat to the rapids below Montreal. Here he learned from the Indians, or thought that he did, of lands to the west bearing gold, silver and copper. The party spent a miserable winter at their base, racked with disease and cold and earning the hostility of the Indians. As soon as the river was free of ice, they set sail in May 1536 for France. Once more the attention of the embattled Francois I was elsewhere for some years. In 1541 however a more ambitious fleet was prepared with Cartier as second-in-command to Sieur de Roberval, whose task was to settle several hundred colonists in what the king hoped would become the French 'Terre Neuve'. All these early attempts at colonization failed because they were ahead of their time, lacking essential survival experience, or the alternative of regular support from the homeland. Cartier sailed first, retracing his route to Quebec and Montreal, and this time finding what were thought to be gold and gems. After another grim winter, Cartier encountered Roberval and the colonists at Newfoundland but deserted

Above: Canada from the Desceliers World Map, 1550. Cartier's three voyages between 1534 and 1542 explored the St. Lawrence as a potential gateway to the American interior and to the western ocean. Cartier is seen here approaching some Indians.

The British Library Add. MS 24065.

Right: The Americas by Diogo Homem, 1558. From California to Chile, Spanish flags dominate the New World.

The British Library Add. MS 5415, ff. 69v–70.

them and returned to France, convinced that their enterprise would fail. Roberval took possession of the territory for France, the basis of all later French claims, and set up the fortified base of France-Roy on the banks of the St. Lawrence, but one winter was sufficient to confirm Cartier's prediction. The survivors struggled home, and no Frenchman returned to Canada for fifty years, for Cartier's gold was found to be dross. Nevertheless Cartier had survived three Atlantic adventures and had discovered the main artery into North America from the east. This made a great impact on mapmakers, especially the French school, who showed the French nobles in their forest base parleying with the natives of 'La Nouvelle France', and the Huron-Iroquois names 'Hochelaga' (on the site of the modern Montreal) and 'Saguenay' and of course 'Canada' itself, meaning simply 'village' or 'settlement'. Yet in practice the crowns of both France and Spain had now lost interest in America north of Florida.

Yet the ambitious conquistadors of Mexico and Hispaniola never ceased to dream of further conquests, and the reports of Cabeza de Vaca when he returned to his compatriots in 1536 re-awoke these ambitions, for he spoke of 'pearls and great riches on the coast of the south sea, and the best

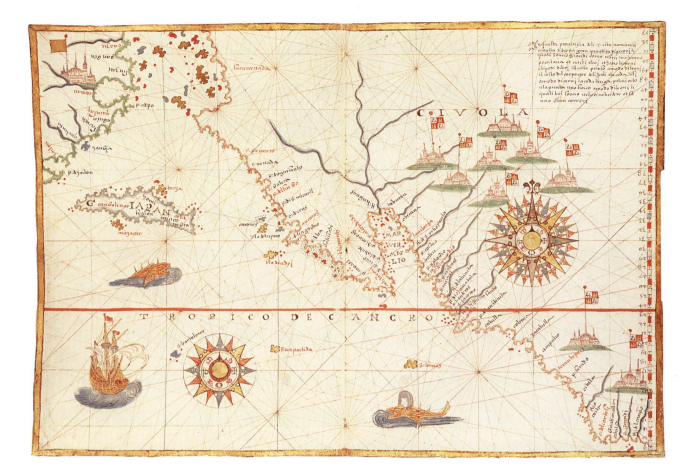

and most opulent countries are near there.' His sources for these statements are unknown; had he genuinely heard such legends among the Yaqui Indians of Sonora, or was it the self-glorification of a heroic survivor? Significantly de Vaca himself never returned to northern Mexico, but turned his attention to South America while others pursued the mirages he had created. Hernando de Soto had been with Balboa in Darien, but in 1539 he revived the project of conquering Florida. Landing near Tampa, de Soto's force marched for nearly three years through much of the south-east of the modern United States, discovering the Mississippi, where de Soto himself died. They found no gold, established no trade and built no settlement. What they left behind was a memory of the Europeans' consuming greed and their hideous cruelty to the Indians they encountered. The men of de Soto's expedition suffered terrible privations in their 2,000 mile march, and their rage at the hostile terrain and their failure to find gold was evidently directed against the native inhabitants. The same was marginally less true of the other important overland expedition, that of Francisco de Coronado in 1540–41.

This expedition was inspired by the return to New Spain of a Franciscan priest claiming to have seen the legendary 'Seven Cities of Cibola' while journeying in the mountainous country of north-western Mexico. Cibola had originally been sited on the fabulous island of Antilia, and had now migrated, like many of those stubborn legends that were periodically revived to fill the unknown spaces of the world. Its wealth was now reported to rival that of Tenochtitlan when first seen by Cortes, and the Viceroy of New Spain, Antonio de Mendoza, immediately commissioned Coronado to lead a small army of three hundred men to find it. Coronado's route took him along the west coast of Mexico from Compostella as far north as the San Juan Mountains, and east to the Arkansas River,

Left: North America by Joan Martines, c.1578. The territory north of New Spain is still dominated by the mythical seven cities of Cibola. Asia is still imagined to be extremely close to the American coast.

The British Library Harley MS 3450, Map no. 10.

Right: Virginia by John White, 1585. Based on surveys by Thomas Harriot, this graceful and accurate map is a record of the first English colonies in Roanoke, sponsored by Sir Walter Raleigh.

B.M. Dept. of Prints and Drawings

Virginia by John Ferrar, 1651. The breadth of North America is greatly underestimated, so that 'The Sea of China and the Indies' is little more than one hundred miles from Chesapeake Bay!

The British Library K.278.a.3.

Left: North America from Gastaldi's World Map, 1546. The Gulf of California was explored during Spanish voyages after 1540; the island California myth arose much later. The imagined seven cities of Cibola are placed in modern Arizona.

The British Library Maps K.Top.IV.6.

and he was the first European to see the Grand Canyon. But the only cities he found were the pueblos of the Zuni Indians. Coronado's force was supported by ships under Hernando de Alarcon, who penetrated the Gulf of California to its head and the mouth of the Colorado River. He had however been preceded in the discovery of the California peninsula by Francisco de Ulloa who had sailed the Gulf a year earlier, and who subsequently rounded Cape Falso to follow the west coast north perhaps as far as Cedros Island. This coast was explored further in 1543 by Juan Cabrillo, whose ships surveyed the land as far north as Oregon, although Cabrillo himself died before completing the voyage. The Peninsula of California appeared decisively on maps from 1544 onwards, until it was overtaken by strange myth of 'Island California' in the 1620s. This illusion had its origin in a voyage of Sebastian Vizcaino in 1602, who claimed to have sailed north out of the Gulf of California into the Pacific; his chart recording this imagined feat later fell into Dutch hands and was widely publicized and believed. Taken together, the importance of these probing journeys north from Mexico – those of de Vaca, de Soto, Coronado, Alarcon and Cabrillo – was to demonstrate the immensity of North America, that it was undoubtedly continental. If a strait to the western sea existed, or if there was a land-link with Asia, it must be far to the north. They had also established that this vast territory was, from the Spanish viewpoint, barren and unrewarding: it contained no gold, no other identifiable natural resources, no civilizations worth plundering. Exactly the reverse was true in the Spanish expansion from Mexico southwards.

Maps of the 1520s show the land of Central America narrowing at Panama, the east coast running towards Brazil and well-mapped, but the west coast is blank, or takes the form of a purely theoretical line running south. In 1513 Balboa, on his celebrated crossing of Panama to the Pacific, had heard rumours of wealthy, civilized kingdoms to the south. Francisco Pizarro participated in that expedition, and was subsequently mayor of the new city of Panama. A stern, silent man, illiterate and apparently unambitious, he was almost fifty years old, considerably older than most of the Spanish adventurers, when he embarked on a plan to explore the southern coast and pursue the source of these rumours. Between 1524 and 1528 Pizarro twice ventured down the coast of Colombia and Ecuador, sighting the Andes and meeting small native craft, some of which carried enticing artefacts from the interior, and whose crews gave distinct reports of an Indian empire, evidently comparable with that of the Aztecs. In 1528 Pizarro sailed to Spain to obtain from Charles V a mandate to explore and conquer, as Cortes had done. He convinced his sovereign and was created Governor of 'New Castile', which should extend some 600 miles south of Panama. Pizarro returned to Panama and by January 1531 was ready to embark, with fewer than 200 men and 37 horses, for Peru. The events of the 1530s – the capture of the Inca cities of Cajamarca and Cuzco, the murder of the Inca king, the massacres, the destruction of Inca culture – belong outside the history of exploration. It is the apparent invincibility of the Europeans in these conflicts, the superiority that was both physical and pyschological, that goes to the heart of the exploration-culture of the sixteenth and seventeenth centuries, and this will be returned to later. What happened in Peru was a prelude to the penetration of much of South America by the Spanish and Portuguese, which was accomplished more swiftly and deliberately than in North America, not for any geographical reasons, but entirely because the thirst for gold and conquest drove it forward.

THE NORTH-WEST PASSAGE

The quest for a northern route to Cathay and the west ceased to interest the Spanish, but was taken up by the English, just as they had embraced the idea of a North-East Passage. Once again armchair geographers convinced themselves that a North-West Passage existed, that it was far shorter than any Spanish or Portuguese route, and that its success would be attended with a new English monopoly and with great profit. Sir Humphrey Gilbert's *Discourse of a Discoverie for a New Passage to Cataia* was published in 1576 accompanied by a map on which what is evidently the Gulf of St. Lawrence reaches open sea leading to the Pacific. The newly founded Company of Cathay sponsored Martin Frobisher's three successive voyages in 1576, 77 and 78, in the course of which he reached the Hudson Strait and the southern part of Baffin Island. Here on his first voyage he sighted 'a foreland, with a great gut, bay or passage, dividing as it were two mainlands or continents assunder'. The excited Frobisher believed he had found the magical strait to the west, but was in fact in the bay which now bears his name, little more than 100 miles long. He was turned back by ice, and its enclosed northern end was not definitively mapped until around 1860. In his bay Frobisher and his

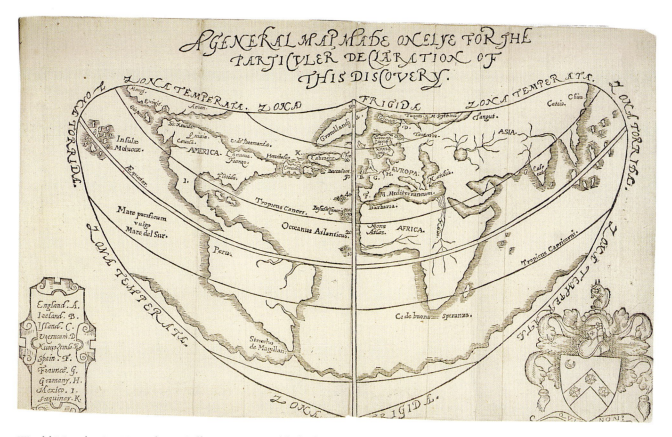

World Map by Sir Humphrey Gilbert, 1576. Published to promote the search for the North-West Passage, this map confidently predicts a clear passage from the Labrador coast through the Strait of Anian to Japan and Moluccas.

The British Library C.32.b.29.

men sighted some strange objects floating far from the ship which he supposed to be 'porposes or seales or some kind of strange fish'. They were in fact Eskimos in their kayaks, the first to be encountered by Europeans, and their Asiatic appearance greatly excited the English, taking them for 'strange men of Cathay'. Frobisher became totally distracted from his goal by the discovery on a small island of some heavy black rock streaked with what appeared to be veins of gold. Hurrying back to London, the gold was assessed as genuine, and Frobisher received the intoxicating title 'High Admiral of all seas and waters, countries, lands and isles, as well of Cathay as of all other countries and places of new discovery'. In two further voyages Frobisher explored the mouth of the Hudson Strait, with its dangerous currents and ice-floes which Frobisher was glad to escape, naming it the 'Mistaken Strait'. He landed teams of men and extracted more than one thousand tons of rock, which were however destined to repair the streets of London and Bristol, for no ounce of true gold ever emerged from it: it was 'iron pyrites, or 'Fool's Gold'. On their final return journey in 1578, some of the men of Frobisher's fleet contributed a small chapter to the history of cartography. Somewhere south-east of Cape Farewell, Greenland, the crew of the buss *Emmanuell*, known as the 'Busse of Bridgwater' (a buss was a type of large fishing-boat) sighted a considerable island, with several harbours, full of woods and meadows. The 'Island of Buss' was added to those phantom Atlantic islands of a much earlier generation such as Brasil and Antilia, and it haunted maps throughout the seventeenth century.

Frobisher's backers were incensed by the fiasco of the Fool's Gold, but they did not lose faith in the North-West Passage, and a new syndicate chose John Davis to lead three voyages in 1585, 86 and

The North Atlantic, c.1594 by Jan van Doetecum. Although recording the early phase of the quest for the North-West Passage, this map perpetuates a number of Atlantic-Island myths: Frisland was a duplicate Iceland, Brazil and St. Bernaldo were medieval survivals, while Bus was a contemporary illusion.

The British Library Maps C.2.a.3.

87. Davis was an expert navigator, and had redesigned the backstaff, a quadrant which enabled the mariner to measure the sun's altitude without facing it, by means of shadows on a graduated staff. Davis sailed past Frobisher's position, to latitude 73 degrees north in the Davis Strait. On returning from each voyage he reported optimistically that the North-West Passage was 'a matter nothing doubtful, but at any time almost to be passed, the sea navigable', or again 'the Passage is most probable, the execution easy'. Davis had indeed discovered the beginning of the route by which the Passage would finally be achieved, but although the map of the Canadian Arctic was taking shape, success lay more than three centuries in the future, and certainly the advocates of the Passage paused to take stock for more than a decade.

Henry Hudson was the only navigator to test both the North-East and the North-West Passages. In 1609 he made a voyage in the service of the Dutch East India Company along the eastern seaboard of North America, one of whose results was discovery of the Hudson River, which was the basis of later Dutch claims to what became the New England region. In 1610 Hudson was commissioned by a London syndicate to try again for the Passage. Hudson directed his efforts to Frobisher's 'Mistaken Strait' which he found 'a great and whirling sea' so deep that no bottom was sounded at one hundred

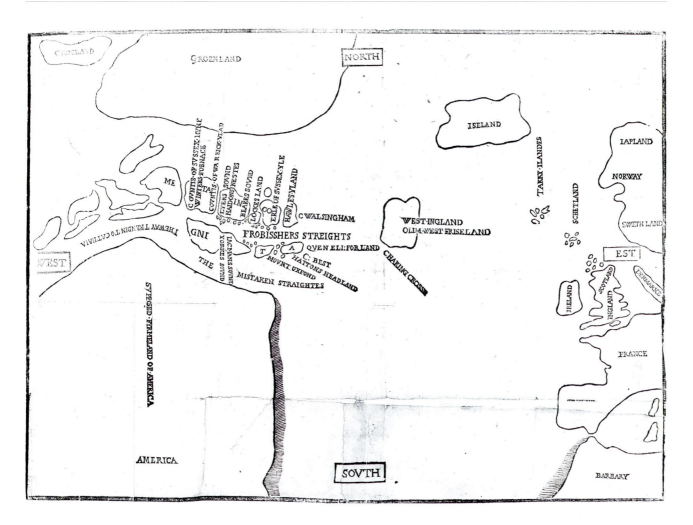

Above: The North-West Passage as conceived after Frobisher's voyages, 1578. 'The way trendin to Cathaia' is confidently marked, even though Frobisher's Strait was in fact merely an inlet in Baffin Island, while the 'mistaken' strait was the far more important Hudson Strait.

The British Library G.6527.

fathoms. Turning south-west he entered 'into a spacious sea, confidently proud that he had won the passage'. But large though this sea was, it was to prove a fatal prison for Hudson. The ship became frozen in in November at James Bay and survived with difficulty. In the spring the ice began to break up and they prepared to escape northwards. But the crew found, or later claimed to have found, that Hudson had cheated in his allocation of rations: they mutinied and cast Hudson, his son and seven others adrift in a small boat, while they sailed away northwards for home. Hudson was never seen again, and those directly responsible for the mutiny were killed in a fight with Eskimos during the return voyage. The survivors of the crew struggled home, bringing Hudson's log and eyewitness accounts of his fate. The famous Victorian painting of Hudson's boat drifting hopelessly among icebergs has made his story one of the best-remembered landmarks in the history of exploration, comparable to Balboa's journey.

The survivors could not confirm whether Hudson's Bay was indeed open to the west, and a voyage under Captain Thomas Button was initiated in 1612 to investigate. Hopes were high, and one observer wrote ' we do not think that we shall hear anything about them before they return from East

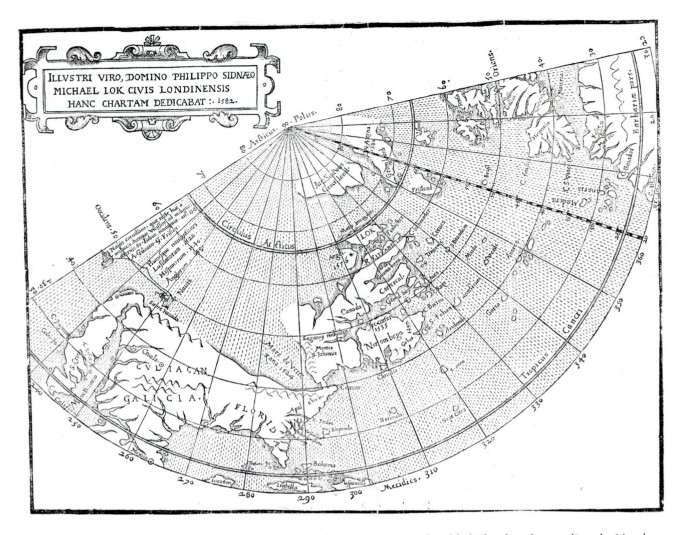

North America published by Hakluyt in 1582. A map illustrating geographical belief rather than reality: the North-West Passage leads easily to the Sea of Verrazano, which in turn opens into the Pacific.

The British Library C.21.b.35.

India or China or Japan'. Button's revelation of the western shore of Hudson's Bay did not deter further attempts. In 1616 William Baffin and Robert Bylot sailed far to the north in the Davis Strait, to the entrances of Smith Sound, Jones Sound and Lancaster Sound, the last of these being indeed the true opening of the Passage. But in these very high latitudes reconnaissance was always dangerous and highly dubious because of ice, and none of these sounds appeared to promise success. The North-West Company displayed a tenacity equal to that of its navigators however, and in 1631 two further expeditions sailed for the Passage under Captains Luke Foxe and Thomas James, who this time returned to seek a westerly exit from Hudson's Bay. Foxe's famous cry of greeting to James when they met in Hudson's Bay – 'You are out of the way to Japan, for this is not it!' – perhaps expresses the wry disillusionment which finally ended this impossible quest. The western Arctic had been explored however, and whalers and fur-hunters entered the history of Canada, while the search for the Passage languished for more than a hundred years. Both James and Foxe wrote memorable

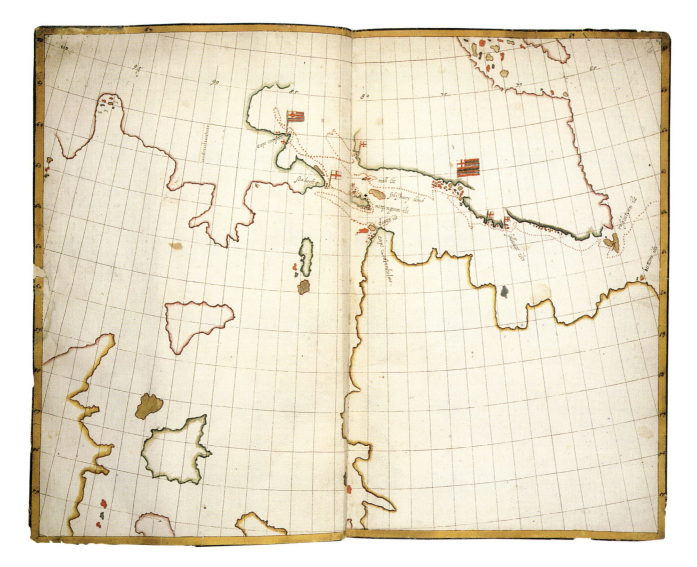

William Baffin's chart of the Hudson Strait, 1615. His route is marked by the dotted line, and the crosses mark the places where he landed to observe the tides. The apparent absence of tides led him to the correct conclusion that the Strait offered no passage to the west.

The British Library Add. MS 12206.

accounts of their voyages, and James's description of navigating through ice-filled seas has been identified as one of the sources of Coleridge's 'Rhyme of the Ancient Mariner'.

Perhaps the most significant question about the North-West Passage is why all its devotees consistently underestimated the distance to be overcome. Almost any westerly opening from Davis Strait or Hudson Bay was likely to be hailed as leading within a few days' sail to the northern Pacific. It is true that mariners at this date had no practical means of gauging longitude, but more than this, it is evident that their estimates of the circumference of the globe were fundamentally wrong. They had no intuition that even from the head of Davis Strait, some 2,000 miles of arctic sea lay between them and the Pacific, and a further 2,000 before Japan could be reached to the south. Despite all their advances, sixteenth-century geographers had been unable to arrive at any more certain values for the earth's circumference than their Greek predecessors 1,500 years earlier. Plainly they were prepared to brave the hostility of the arctic environment in the belief that the way was short; had they possessed the knowledge of its true length, surely the attempts on the North-West Passage, or indeed the North-East, would never have taken place.

By the time that hopes of northern sea passages were fading, English ambitions were turning in a new direction – to the settlement of eastern North America. The most influential propagandist for this scheme was the historian of discoveries Richard Hakluyt, who saw English colonies as acting as 'a great bridle to the Indies of the King of Spain', as an outlet for goods and surplus population, and as a base for that apparently imperishable dream, the passage to Cathay, which might be 'searched out as well by river and overland as by sea'. Like the voyages of discovery, such colonies might be financed in a variety of ways, but royal approval was essential to secure a title to any newly-claimed lands. Sir Humphrey Gilbert's brief summer visit to Newfoundland in 1583 can claim to be the first English colony in North America, and it has been held to mark the birth of the British Empire, since he proclaimed there the sovereignty of Queen Elizabeth I and promulgated English law, rather to the indifference of the many Portuguese and French fishermen camped there. But England's claims were greater than that, for on the strength of Cabot's voyage of 1497, and of the second voyage in which he vanished without trace, 'that part of North America which is from Florida to 67 degrees northward', was deemed by Hakluyt to be English.

This northern limit at 67 degrees north is the Arctic Circle, midway in the Davis Strait, but English eyes were turned much further south, and Sir Walter Raleigh received a patent from the Queen to finance and settle a colony on the coast of present-day North Carolina, although Raleigh himself never participated in person. Here on Roanoake Island just over 100 English settlers under the com-

The North Atlantic, c.1628 by Hessel Gerritsz. This chart by the official Dutch hydrographer summarises the position after fifty years' endeavour to find the North-West Passage: Baffin Bay and Hudson Bay had been repeatedly probed, without result, and no real advance would be made for a further two centuries.

Bibliothèque Nationale, Paris

[84]

Left: The Island of Buss, by John Seller, 1678. This charming map shows the phantom island 'discovered' somewhere south of Greenland by Frobisher's fleet in 1578.

The British Library Maps C.22.d.2.

Right: North America, 1566 by Bolognini Zaltieri. One of the earliest depictions of the Strait of Anian, the undiscovered but imagined strait separating America from Asia.

The British Library Maps C.7.e.1.

mand of Ralph Lane maintained themselves from July 1585 until June 1586, when they were evacuated by Sir Francis Drake. It had been a familiar story of unpreparedness, lack of survival skills, internal dissension and uneasy relations with the Indians. Perhaps the colony would be scarcely better-known than that of Newfoundland had not one of its members, John White, made dozens of fine drawings and water-colours of the inhabitants and environment of Roanoke. Many of these pictures were later printed and were highly influential in forming the European perception of North America and its people, while White also drew several maps from the surveys of Thomas Hariot, which rank as the most accurate maps of any part of the North American coast drawn in the sixteenth century; they were widely copied by European map-publishers. Raleigh tried again in 1587 with a second Roanoke Colony of which White was now appointed governor, although he was compelled to return to England later in the same year. This colony was left unsupported for almost three years, and when it was finally revisited in 1590 the settlers had vanished. Their fate became a mysterious *cause célèbre* for there were no signs of violence and no message was left except the one word 'Croatoan', carved on a post. Croatoan is the name of an adjacent island, but the relieving force was prevented by storms from investigating, and no English ship visited the region for several more years. White's grand-daughter, Virginia Dare, the first English child born in North America, was among those who vanished so mysteriously. The first successful English colony was at last established at Jamestown 100 miles north of Roanoke in 1607. The permanent colonization of North America would naturally lead to a new era in exploration of the interior, but this was accomplished very slowly, while the concept of America as a bridge to Asia survived tenaciously. In 1651 a map of

Virginia portrays the region as an isthmus less than 200 miles broad, beyond which lies the 'Sea of China and the Indies'.

But if, in the second half of the sixteenth century, the geography of America remained deeply uncertain, its identity as a separate continent was at last clear. No European explorer had found anything corresponding to Marco Polo's description of Cathay, and the penetration of the Pacific from 1520 onwards (see Chapter Four) revealed the vast tract of sea dividing America from Asia. This separation of the Old World from the New was given symbolic form by mapmakers long before it was finally established on the ground. In 1560 in the extreme north of the Pacific, where Asia and America had formerly been shown to be joined, a strait appeared with a name drawn from Marco Polo's geography of the north of Cathay: 'The Strait of Anian'. It was first shown in the world map by Giacomo Gastaldi of 1560, and was swiftly copied by the other Italian mapmakers, Forlani and Camocio, and by Ortelius and Mercator. Although it is situated where we now know the Bering Strait to be, it was not based on any discovery, for in 1560 no European had sailed within 2,000 miles of the Bering Strait. Its origin was literary, and its appearance at this time must be taken as marking the recognition of the separate identity of America, in a sense completing the revolution in geographical thought initiated by Columbus's landing on a tiny offshore island which he imagined to be on the verge of Cathay.

As we attempt to sum up this revolution, our deepest impression must be of the massive and arrogant display of power with which Europeans surveyed and confronted the world. Any intellectual sense of wonder created by the discovery of a new world was apparently overwhelmed by the military and economic drive to possess it. This sense of pride, that Europe was queen among nations, was expressed by the French polemicist. Louis Le Roy:

> 'I who in the past hundred years have made so many new discoveries, even of things unknown to the ancients – new seas, new lands, new species of men, new constellations; with Spanish help I have found and conquered what amounts to a new world. . . Do but listen to the sacred voice of Europe.'

The history of exploration is a mere curiosity if it cannot progress beyond lists of names and dates, for it raises unavoidable questions about human culture and human conflict which are far more urgent than who first rounded this cape, or who first set foot on that shore. Why did Europeans believe from the outset that the world beyond Europe was theirs to take and to rule? There seem to be two obvious answers: technology and religion. It was Europeans who travelled to America, not Americans to Europe: only Europeans possessed the knowledge and the skills to cross the oceans, therefore they entered the New World as superiors, on their own terms. They possessed ocean-going ships, maps, instruments, guns, armour and military discipline with which to overawe the peoples they encountered. Their global ambitions were graphically expressed by the imposition on the map of the names 'New Spain', 'New France', or 'New England'. Charles V created Pizarro governor of 'New Castile' when it existed as merely an idea upon a map; its several million inhabitants were of no greater importance than the trees in its forests or the stones on its shores. There was no check, physical or moral to such an arrogation of power, for the legality of Spain's rule in the Indies had been established by Papal decree. If the dominance of the natural world was an idea that typifies the Renaissance, what clearer expression could there be of it than to re-map the surface of the world, and place the stamp of Europe upon it? Historians have advanced the theory that the urge towards discovery and the seeds of imperialism must be seen in military terms, as expressing the pyschology of crusade and conquest of a military class; these navigators and expedition commanders, whether Portuguese, Italian, Spanish or English, were overwhelmingly fighting men, not scholars or merchants.

Psychologically more profound than any technical advantage may have been the sense of religious superiority. 'European' was synonymous with 'Christian': when Spain and Portugal initiated the era of exploration they chose to present their conquests as new crusades against the non-Christian world. Christians were favoured with access to a truth and salvation that was unknown to, or rejected by, other cultures, and this gave them by natural right dominion over other peoples. The most radical argument used to justify the brutality shown towards native populations was that they were not human, but some lower form of life, perhaps even lacking souls. The new imperialism was defended by the theologian Juan de Sepulveda:

> 'War against these barbarians can he justified not only on the basis of their paganism but even more so because of their abominable licentiousness, their prodigious sacrifice of human victims. . . their horrible banquets of human flesh and the impious cult of their idols. . . For these numerous and grave reasons these barbarians are obliged to accept the rule of the Spaniards by natural law. . .'

How significant it is that when Pizarro planned the judicial murder of the Inca king Atahualpa, it was on a charge of heresy that he was tried and condemned to death.

Such arguments were countered by other theologians, such as Bartolomé de las Casas, who argued that the Spanish owed a duty of pastoral care and education towards the Indians. Others, like José de Acosta, were led to speculate on the means by which human and animal life reached America, and the implications of the new discoveries for traditional teachings about the physical world. This intellectual response to the New World was slow in developing however, and the culture of exploration that existed in the sixteenth century had overwhelmingly an economic and military drive. The princes of Europe saw only new sources of wealth, their soldiers saw new fields of conquest, their navigators new avenues of employment; and the cost in human terms was terrifying. This is not simply a modern perspective, for thinkers such as Montaigne were far from blind to what was happening in the New World:

> 'So many goodly cities ransacked and razed; so many nations destroyed and made desolate; so infinite millions of harmless people of all sexes, states and ages massacred, ravaged and put to the sword; and the richest, the fairest and best part of the world topsiturvied, ruined and defaced for the traffic of pearls and pepper. . . oh base conquest.'

But such views were those of a minority, without political power and greatly outnumbered by those who profited from the new discoveries. As for the conquistadors, they were men of another time, inured to cruelty, and as pitiless towards themselves as towards others. The great paradox of the history of exploration is that the courage, skill and endurance of the navigators, which we cannot fail to admire, was often the prelude to conquests whose conduct has degraded them and their achievements forever.

Columbus and the Indians: the historic encounter
between two worlds and two cultures, from de Bry's
America.

CHAPTER FOUR
THE PACIFIC AND AUSTRALIA

We sailed about 4,000 leagues during those three month and twenty days through the open Pacific Sea. In truth it is very pacific, for during that time we did not suffer any storm. We saw no land except two desert islets, where we found nothing but birds and trees, for which we called them Isolle Infortunate. . . Had not God and his blessed Mother given us so good weather we would have all died of hunger in that exceeding vast sea. Of a verity, I believe no such voyage will ever be made again.'

– Antonio Pigafetta (companion of Magellan), 1522.

MAGELLAN AND HIS LEGACY

T HE PORTUGUESE WITH THEIR EASTERN sea-routes and the Spanish with their conquests in the west had apparently divided the maritime world between them. In the year 1515, when spices from the Moluccas were being unladen in Lisbon and gold from Hispaniola was arriving in Seville, this division must have appeared absolute. Yet these two competing empires were of course but two sectors of the same world, and through the vast unexplored waters of the Pacific, they were linked. The man who forged that link between the two realms, the two hemispheres, was a Portuguese in the service of Spain, Fernão de Magalhães – Ferdinand Magellan – arguably the most single-minded and

Mactan in the Philippines, from Pigafetta's narrative. This tiny island was the scene of Magellan's death, and the legend reads 'Here the great Captain died'.
Beinecke Rare Book and Manuscript Library, Yale University

tenacious of the early navigators. The existence of an ocean beyond the Americas was deduced as soon as it became clear that the lands discovered in the west were not Cathay. Yet when Balboa waded thigh-deep into the sea south of Panama in 1513 to take possession of it for Spain, neither he nor any European could have conceived that this was the greatest body of water in the world, and that almost 10,000 miles of ocean lay between him and the coasts of Asia; the unfolding of the geography of the Pacific was to occupy a further three centuries.

Magellan had served under Almeida and Albuquerque, learning the arts of war and navigation. He was present at the decisive Battle of Diu in 1509 and at the taking of Malacca in 1511. Between 1513 and 1516 he was in Morocco, but somehow he forfeited royal favour and in 1517, wounded and embittered, he travelled to Spain, renounced his Portuguese nationality and offered his services to King Charles I (the later Emperor Charles V). In Seville, Magellan joined the Portuguese cosmographer Rui Faleiro in planning what amounted to a radical attack on Portugal's trading empire. The demarcation between the Portuguese and Spanish maritime realms, the one taking Africa and the East, the other the Atlantic, had seemed satisfactory in 1494, but of course it left open the question where the line of demarcation would fall on the opposite side of the globe. By 1515 the Portuguese had identified the Moluccan Islands as the richest of all the spice-growing regions – for example the small volcanic island of Ternate was found to be the source of all clove cultivation. The distance to the Moluccas was great – it was estimated to be around 10,000 miles east of the Tordesillas demarcation line – but the measurement of longitude was impossible, and no one could demonstrate the precise position of the islands. Magellan and Faleiro set out to prove that they lay so far east that they were actually within the Spanish sphere, and that they could be reached by a westward route. Magellan was convinced that a strait must exist between the Atlantic and the Western Ocean, and having studied the voyages of Vespucci he concluded that it lay far to the south, below the latitude of 50 degrees south reached by the Italian. In the spring of 1518 this plan received the approval of the Spanish King, and after lengthy preparations, Magellan and his fleet of five ships left Sanlucar de Barrameda on September 20, 1519 on what was to prove the longest and most hazardous voyage in history. We are fortunate that among those who sailed in the fleet was an Italian, Antonio Pigafetta, who kept and published a journal which provided an eyewitness account of this epochmaking journey.

Reaching the Brazilian coast, they moved steadily south probing the bays and estuaries for a possible strait, especially the Rio de la Plata. By April 1520 they halted at 49 degrees south at San Julian,

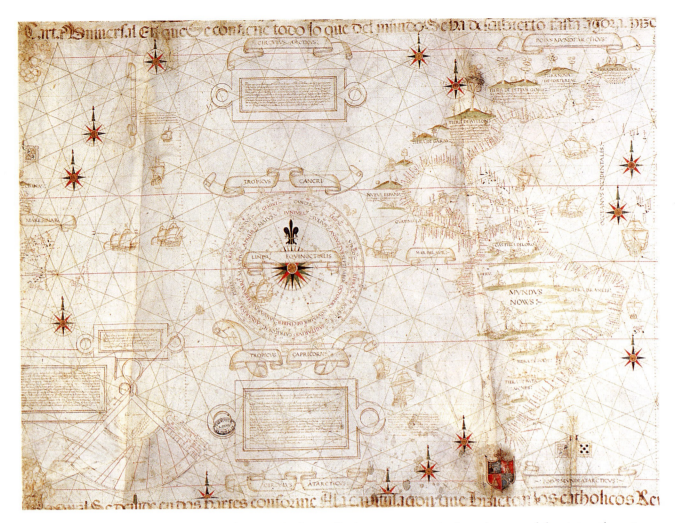

Part of Ribero's World Chart, 1529. This record of Magellan's great voyage is the only map of the sixteenth century to give a true idea of the vastness of the Pacific – and its emptiness: there is nothing between the Magellan Strait and the Marianas.

Vatican Library

where Magellan quelled a mutiny among his men before settling for four winter months. During this period they saw some Patagonians whose giant stature amazed them and whose pictures were to adorn the maps of this region for centuries. In late August they put to sea and resumed their south-ward course, until on October 21 Magellan's ships rounded Cabo Virgenes and 'We found by a miracle a strait which is a hundred and ten leagues long . . . and it issues in another sea which is called the Peaceful Sea'. Menaced by icebergs, fogs and reefs, the passage of the strait was long and dangerous, so that even the iron-willed commander wept with joy when they passed Cape Pilar into a calm, open sea. Little guessing the challenge that now awaited them, the fleet, reduced through loss and desertion to three vessels, set a course at first due north to escape the intense cold, then north-west into the ocean whose tranquility prompted Magellan to name it the Pacific. They made good speed running before favourable easterly winds, but if storms were not a threat the unimagined vast-ness of the Pacific was: for one hundred days they sailed steadily west, sighting only one island which provided neither food nor water. Tortured by starvation and disease, they were compelled to sail onwards, for to turn back in the face of the easterly wind only to reach the desolation of Patagonia was impossible. Above all perhaps was the fear of the unknown: geographical logic told them that the Indies lay ahead, but each new day revealed only the empty ocean, and they were disorientated, alone in a world without maps. Magellan never weakened, but his chosen course was an unlucky one, missing the chains of islands in the southern and central Pacific, and carrying him so far north that he at last found land and fresh supplies on Guam in the Mariana Islands, by which time more than twenty crewmen had died, including the only English sailor in the fleet, Master Andrew of Bristol. Magellan's choice of this course is mysterious, for while the longitude of the Spice Islands was uncertain, their latitude must have been known to him, and latitude sailing was then the dominant and universal technique of navigation. Magellan's subsequent actions are also puzzling, for rather than heading directly south for the Moluccas, he continued west to the islands later named the Philippines. It is reported that, while in India many years before, Magellan had employed as his servant a Filipino named Enrique, who had travelled with him constantly, and that on arriving in the Philippines, Enrique thus became the first man in history to circumnavigate the world. During the next few weeks Magellan attempted to evangelize the islands' inhabitants, became involved in a needless conflict and was killed on the small island of Mactan in April 1521, mourned by his men for his 'constancy in the most adverse fortune; in the midst of the sea he was able to endure hunger better than we; most versed in nautical charts, he knew better than anyone the true art of navigation, of which it is certain proof that he knew by his genius and his intrepidity . . . how to attempt the circuit of the globe.'

Sebastian del Cano assumed command of the fleet, and they arrived at last in the Moluccas where they found the long sought-for spices growing in profusion, as well as other delights such as 'parrots of many kinds, white ones and red ones which are the most sought after, not so much for the beauty of the plumage but because they talk most clearly'. Further trials and a voyage of almost a year lay before del Cano and his men as they turned for home. Only one ship, the *Vittoria* was fit to sail, and hoping to avoid the hostile Portuguese they shaped a course by Timor and crossed the Indian Ocean far to the south of the Portuguese routes. After circumnavigating the whole of Africa, they fell foul of the Portuguese at Cape Verde, and on 22 September 1522 the *Vittoria* dropped anchor outside Seville, with fewer than twenty survivors of this extraordinary voyage.

Magellan's energy and vision equalled that of Columbus, and he shared with his great predecessor the tenacity of a man driven by something deeper than common ambition. What Magellan's personal drive was we can only guess at, since no personal statement of his aims and beliefs survives, but a desire for revenge against the country that had spurned him must have played its part in forging his implacable determination to destroy the Portuguese monopoly in the spice trade. Ultimately other historical forces accomplished this aim, for the immensity of the Pacific meant that there were few immediate results for Spain from Magellan's achievement. But he dispelled two beliefs that had been widely held in Europe during the immediate post-Columbus era: that there was an easy way to penetrate the barrier of the Americas, and that, once a way had been found, the Indies and Cathay were within easy reach. The subsequent quests for the North-East and North-West Passages would demonstrate that European geographers failed to absorb the lesson of the Magellan's Pacific voyage and what it showed about the size of the earth.

In the wake of Magellan, at least four Spanish expeditions crossed the Pacific seeking to establish a Spanish route to and presence in the Spice Islands, and most important of all, a return route to Central America, which would enable Spain to conduct its own eastern trade. Del Cano himself sailed from Spain in 1525 with Garcia de Loyasa and a considerable fleet of seven ships on a disastrous voyage in which only two vessels survived the crossing to the Moluccas, both Del Cano and Loyasa dying at sea. On a second ill-fated enterprise, Hernan Cortes dispatched three ships from Mexico in 1527 commanded by Alvaro de Saavedra. Despite having halved the sailing distance and having found a favourable route at around latitude ten degrees north, only one ship made port in the Moluccas, where Saavedra joined forces with the survivors of Loyasa's fleet, and attempted the first

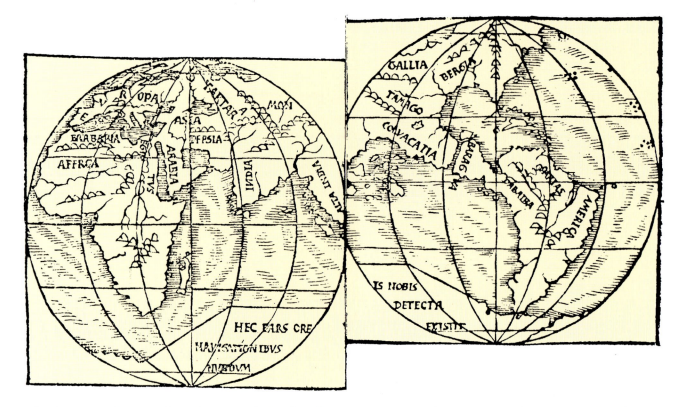

The first printed map to show the Strait of Magellan, by Franciscus Monachus, 1527. North America is thought to be joined to Asia. The huge southern continent bears the enigmatic words 'This part of the world not yet discovered by our navigators'.

west-east crossing of the Pacific, back to America. The prevailing easterly winds in the central Pacific completely defeated the Spanish and forced them back to the Moluccas, though not before they had touched the northern coast of New Guinea, which was to become a major, if enigmatic, feature on the Pacific map.

News of these failed expeditions – failed in that they were unable to return – did eventually reach Spain, and the Spanish crown determined in 1529 to acquiesce in the Portuguese monopoly, in return for a large payment from Portugal. The theoretical question of the position of the Moluccas was never agreed in strictly geographical terms, despite a lengthy conference at Badajoz in 1524 which replayed the Tordesillas arguments, but this time on the other side of the globe. This failure was inevitable due to the inability to determine longitude. The Portuguese cosmographers considered that the Spice Islands were situated 43 degrees west of the anti-meridian of the Tordesillas line, well within their sphere of control, while the Spanish argued that they lay 3 degrees east of it, and were therefore rightfully Spanish. The failure of the Loyasa and Saavedra fleets no doubt contributed to Spain's recognition that she was on weak ground, and the Tordesillas anti-meridian was finally placed by mutual consent at 17 degrees east of the Moluccas, leaving the islands clearly Portuguese. The calculation was in fact an impossible one in its own time, since by modern reckoning the Tordesillas line was 55 degrees west of the Greenwich meridian, placing the Moluccas exactly on the dividing line, 180 degrees distant.

However, decisions taken in Europe could not apparently deter the viceroys of New Spain from seeking possible new lands in the Pacific and from attacking the Portuguese Empire from the rear.

The Americas, by Sebastian Münster, 1544. Münster was a highly influential geographer, yet the proximity of America to Japan and China is quite inaccurate, and could easily have been challenged at this date.

The British Library Maps C.8.a.14.

Another expedition which left Mexico in 1537 under Hernando de Grijalva was rent by mutiny, although the mutineers did continue to the Moluccas. The final Spanish-Mexican attempt on the Moluccas was in 1542 when five ships under Ruy Lopez de Villalobos departed from Navidad. They touched the Marshall Islands, and named the island of Leyte 'Filippina', which was later extended to that entire group, but they were repulsed from the Moluccas themselves by the Portuguese, and again the Spanish were unable to retrace their route across the Pacific. The survivors of these many expeditions were dependent on the doubtful mercies of the Portuguese for their eventual repatriation via the Indian Ocean route. By 1550 the Spanish had decided to renounce their ambitions in the Moluccas, and turned their attention instead to the Philippines, claimed by no other European power, although it was not until 1565 that a colonizing expedition was sent, under Miguel Lopez de Legaspi. Spanish settlements were founded at Cebu and Manila, and this expedition had enormous additional significance, for its pilot, Andres de Urdaneta succeeded in finding a viable return route by sailing northeast from the Philippines to a latitude of almost 40 degrees north, where he encountered favourable westerly winds which carried him to the coast of California. Although this route was long and

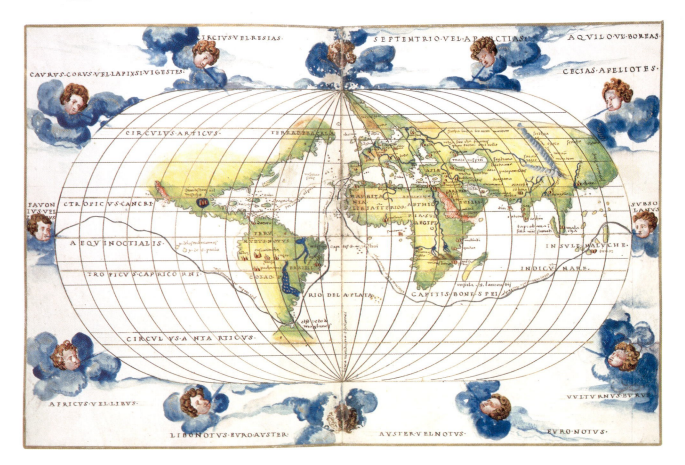

World Map by Battista Agnese, c.1540. The distinguishing feature of this map is the silver lines encircling the world, representing the tracks of Magellan's fleet. Agnese was the first mapmaker to employ this device.

The British Library Egerton MS 2854, ff. 13v–14.

circuitous, it was reliable, and it transformed the prospects for further exploration in the Pacific. Sailing directions founded on Urdaneta's original navigation became standard for all Spanish vessels for the next two centuries, as their galleons plied between the Americas and the Philippines.

THE FIRST MAPS OF THE PACIFIC

What was the impact on the world map of Magellan's historic voyage, and those of his successors in the Pacific? The Strait of Magellan, the vital gateway linking the Atlantic and the Pacific, was shown among the many expressive illustrations to Pigafetta's texts, which appeared in manuscript from 1525 onwards, although these illustrations cannot perhaps be regarded as serious maps. The Vespucci chart of 1526 however is a copy of the Spanish master-chart from the *Casa da Contratacion* in Seville, and is one of the earliest surviving maps to mark unmistakably the all-important strait. The strait's first representation in print was in a small world map illustrating a geographical work by Franciscus Monachus, published in Antwerp between 1527 and 1529. This map is rough and schematic, but it is remarkable for its assumption that the land south of the Magellan Strait was itself a huge continent, across which the mapmaker has written, enigmatically, 'This part of the world not yet discovered by our navigators'. None of these maps attempted to do justice to the immensity of the

Pacific, and are understandably inaccurate about the northern Pacific, perpetuating the belief that that America and Asia are one continent. The map which first showed the true scale of the Pacific is the world chart of 1529 by Diego Ribero, in which the distance west from Magellan's Strait to the Moluccas is shown, correctly, to be equivalent to that eastward from the same point to southern India – some 10,000 miles. Ribero was, like Magellan, a Portuguese who had transferred allegiance to Spain, and had actually represented the Spanish case at the Badajoz conference and become Pilot Major in the *Casa da Contrtacion*. It is ironic that this ground-breaking map was drawn by a Portuguese to embody the discoveries of a Portuguese, both working in the service of Spain. Ribero was naturally able to show very few features in the Pacific; westwards from Peru he marks only the 'Island of Tribulation' where Magellan found neither food nor water, then the Ladrones, or Mariana Islands. To the north, Ribero is equally original, placing ships in the ocean where other mapmakers showed a northern link between America and Asia. In its realistic depiction of the newly-discovered expanse of the Pacific, Ribero's chart remained unique in the sixteenth century, for all other maps sought to compress this ocean whose emptiness and mystery seemed so intimidating. The influential printed maps of Sebastian Münster and the manuscripts of Joan Martines continued to suggest that that the American coast was but a brief voyage from Japan and the coasts of Cathay.

Faced with the overwhelming problem of the Pacific, European mapmakers sought refuge in what was to become the most enduring geographical myth in European thought: the great southern continent. Classical thinkers, Ptolemy among them, had suggested that continental land-masses would be found symmetrically disposed on the earth's surface, east and west, north and south, in order somehow to balance the globe. This idea was taken seriously by Renaissance geographers, and Mercator spoke of a continent 'under the Antarctic Pole so great that, with the southern parts of Asia and the new India and America, it should be a weight equal to the other lands'. Interest in the Pacific as merely a trade route to the Indies was replaced by the search for the new territories it might contain, and the emptiness of the map provided geographers with an irresistible temptation to locate imagined lands there. The sighting of each new island was greeted as the long-sought coast, and dreams of new empires comparable to the Americas grew among the Spanish, the English, the French and the Dutch. Before Magellan the most telling clues to the southern land had been found in Marco Polo, with his reports of lands and kingdoms far to the south of Cathay named 'Beach', 'Lucach' or 'Maletur', and of a second, greater Java. The land south of Magellan's Strait was widely believed to be the coast of a southern continent, and appears as such on maps from 1540 onwards, often assuming gigantic proportions on printed maps of the Venetian school by Gastaldi and Forlani, and on the maps of Ortelius. One of the first islands to be identified as part of the continent was New Guinea, understandably, since its northern coast extends for 1,000 miles. Perhaps sighted by Portuguese mariners as early as 1526, and by Saavedra in 1528, it made a belated appearance on maps from the 1560s, sometimes drawn as a large island, sometimes as part of a continent which would typically be named *Terra Australis sive Magellenica Nondum Detecta* – 'Southern Land or Magellana, not yet discovered'. French manuscript sea-charts of the sixteenth century – those drawn in Dieppe between c.1540 and 1580 – also show a great southern continent, but often with the significant addition of certain place-names in Portuguese. The French themselves had no direct knowledge of this region, and it has been argued that these names must represent an authentic record of Portuguese landfalls in Australia. The evidence is inconclusive, but if the Portuguese did land in Australia in the 1520s or 1530s, they evidently did not consider it worth exploring.

THE SPANISH IN THE PACIFIC

The first recorded expedition into the Pacific to have new discoveries as its avowed motive rather than route-finding to the Moluccas, sailed from Peru in November 1567. Inspired by the scholar, historian and mathematician, Pedro Sarmiento de Gamboa (who would later make the first detailed survey of the Magellan Strait), its brief was 'for the discovery of certain islands and a continent, because many men versed in mathematics had deduced that they existed for certain'. Commanded by Alvaro de Mendaña, this expedition, like that of Magellan, took an unlucky route which missed all the significant island groups, until after eighty days at sea, land was reached in February 1568 in the Solomon Islands. This fanciful name, bestowed by the eager Spaniards, in anticipation of its riches, was most ill-chosen, for, as the official record says, 'the islands they discovered were of little importance, although they say they heard of better lands, yet they found no specimens of gold and silver, nor of merchandise nor any other source of profit, and all the people were naked savages'. After several months' fruitless reconnaissance among the islands, Mendaña and Sarmiento had little choice but to turn for home, taking the newly-pioneered northern route of Urdaneta. The harrowing four-month voyage and the failure to find any significant territory meant that once again the Pacific had preserved its secrets and defeated the Spanish. No new expedition followed for twenty-five years, and the Solomons themselves remained unvisited for a further two centuries.

Yet Mendaña tenaciously clung to the idea that the Pacific held secrets worth revealing. In 1595 he departed on his second and final crossing of the ocean with the avowed aim of colonizing the Solomon Islands. He had four ships and nearly 400 men under his command, but the adventure proved a catalogue of error, conflict and misfortune, for the Spanish and for the islanders they encountered. Mendaña proclaimed confidently, but quite wrongly, that the Solomons were 1450 leagues (around 5,000 miles) west of Peru, yet when he encountered a substantial group of islands on the latitude of the Solomons barely 3,500 miles out, he announced that their goal was reached. After a quarter of a century he may be forgiven for not recognizing the terrain, but nothing could illustrate more tellingly than this the challenge of the Pacific and the problem of longitude in particular. The islands were the Marquesas, but the amiability of their people did not protect them from Europeans' weapons, and some 200 islanders were killed in the few weeks during which the ships were resupplied. Realizing his mistake, Mendaña resumed his westward course for a further 3,000 miles, anchoring off a volcanic island which was indeed close to the Solomons, which he named Santa Cruz (now Ndeni), and here worse awaited: massacres of the islanders, fighting between the Spanish mariners and soldiers, and death from malaria, including that of Mendaña himself, who for twenty-five years had dreamed in vain of a glorious return to the Pacific. Command was assumed by the navigator, a Portuguese named Pedro Fernandez de Quiros, who set sail at once for the haven of the Philippines. Two ships were lost en route, but Quiros succeeded in bringing the flagship *San Jeronimo* into Manila, and finally in December 1596 to Mexico.

Despite this blood-drenched failure, Spanish hopes of territorial conquest in the Pacific were still not extinguished, for Quiros took up the mantle of the fallen Mendaña, and conceived grandiose, almost Messianic plans to evangelize the mythical Southern Continent for Spain. He secured Papal approval, and with three ships, he sailed from Peru in December 1605, accompanied by soldiers and Franciscan friars, as if embarking on a crusade. After touching various small islands in the Tuamotu Archipeligo and westward, on May 1, 1606 Quiros's fleet entered a wide bay on a forested coast with a mountainous hinterland, which Quiros was convinced was continental. It was in fact Espiritu Santo in modern Vanuatu. In a re-enactment of Columbus's first landing, Quiros ceremoniously took possession for Spain of 'Australia del Espiritu Santo', and celebrated the first mass. He enrolled his men as members of a spiritual order of his own devising, the Knights of the Holy Ghost, who were to rule in the New Jerusalem. What happened subsequently is difficult to understand, for only three weeks

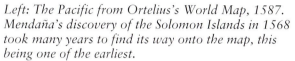

Left: The Pacific from Ortelius's World Map, 1587. Mendaña's discovery of the Solomon Islands in 1568 took many years to find its way onto the map, this being one of the earliest.

The British Library Maps C.2.d.4.

Below: The vital Strait of Magellan, by Joan Martines.

The British Library Harley MS 3450, f.12.

later the three ships departed from the island never to return. Quiros was physically ill, and possibly mentally ill too, the islanders were implacably hostile, and reconnaissance had suggested that this was after all an island. Like Mendaña's before him, Quiros's visions of paradise could not withstand the cold touch of reality. In a few days the weather worsened and the ships became separated; Quiros began the weary, dispiriting homeward voyage by the northern galleon route. In Mexico and in Spain Quiros faced hostility and derision, and when he died in 1614, Spanish dreams of Empire in the Pacific finally died with him. Yet there was one important footnote to this bizarre expedition. When the ships of Quiros's fleet became separated, the navigator on board one of the other vessels, Luis Vaez de Torres, made away to the north-west for New Guinea and Manila. Reaching the extreme eastern capes of New Guinea, Torres recorded that 'I could not weather the east point, so I coasted along to the westward on the south side', from where he sailed on through the Moluccas. Torres had in fact made a remarkable passage of the strait which now bears his name, littered with dangerous reefs and with the continent of Australia on his port bow. The inhabitants of eastern New Guinea were savage and hostile, but further west they appeared more friendly, and Torres could not fail to perceive that some were Moslems, noticing evidence among them of trade with China. The existence of the Torres Strait did not become generally known, and the name was bestowed much later, in the eighteenth century.

The Spanish experience in the Pacific had been a grim one for them and for the Islanders they encountered. They had secured a stronghold in the Philippines. But a succession of exploratory ventures had all ended miserably. They were defeated by the vast scale of the Pacific and they had failed completely to discover any imperial prizes remotely comparable to the Americas. As the seventeenth century opened political forces in a weakened Spain now brought an end to any new imperial ambitions. Little of any significance had been added to the map, and the positioning of discoveries such as the Solomons or the Marquesas remained inaccurate. One further ill-documented voyage deserving mention was that of Juan de la Fuca in 1592 who touched the coast of North America around latitude 47 degrees north and reported finding a strait into the interior of the continent. This strait was much discussed and sought for at the possible exit from the North-West Passage. Of course it was not, but de la Fuca's name was bestowed on the strait which now marks the western border between Canada and the United States.

For fifty years after Magellan, Spanish hegemony over the Pacific was total, and their intention to maintain it was vividly demonstrated when Thomas Cavendish penetrated the Magellan Strait in 1587, and found there 'King Philip's City which the Spaniards had built . . . They had contrived their city very well and seated it in the best place of the Straits for food and water; they had builded up their churches by themselves; they had laws very severe among themselves, for they had erected a gibet whereon they had done execution upon some of their company . . . These Spaniards which were there were only come to fortify the Straits, to the end that no other nation should have passage through into the South Sea saving only their own; but as it appeared, it was not God's will so to have it. For during the time that they were there, which was two years at the least, they could never have anything to grow or in any wise prosper. And on the other side the Indians oftentimes preyed upon them, until their victuals grew so short that they died like dogs in their houses. To conclude they were determined to have travailed towards the river of Plate, only being left alive twenty-three persons, whereof two were women, which were the remainder of four hundred.'

DRAKE'S CHALLENGE TO THE SPANISH MONOPOLY

The Pacific Ocean itself was a geographical barrier more daunting than any such garrison, quite aside from the accepted doctrine of sovereignty and monopoly among the European powers. Yet political events in Europe, especially conflicts between Catholic and Protestant nations, provided the pretext for rejecting that doctrine. The first English voyage into the Pacific was a more or less blatant attack on Spanish interests, and the narrative of Sir Francis Drake's voyage of 1577–80 is of interest equally for its geography and its psychology. Drake's instructions did not mention the word circumnavigation, but were couched entirely in the language of contemporary geographical myth. He was to enter the Pacific by Magellan's Strait, and discover *Terra Australis* otherwise known as 'Beach', as plainly mapped by Ortelius in his great atlas of 1570, where he was to make treaties with the local rulers for the trade in English cloth in return for the anticipated gold and spices. He was to return if possible by the 'Strait of Anian' which was believed to lead from the northern Pacific into the north Atlantic. Privately Drake was instructed by Queen Elizabeth that she 'would gladly be revenged on the King of Spain for divers injuries that I have received', thus licensing him to cause the maximum damage to Spanish ships and bases. Sailing from Plymouth in December 1577 officially for Alexandria, some of his crew were astounded and dismayed when their true destination was announced at sea. At Port San Julian on the Patagonian coast, Drake experienced a mutiny just as Magellan had, and the bones of the English rebels joined those of the Spanish, which were still to be found by the shore. The Patagonians Drake found to be 'five cubits viz. seven foot and and a half in full height, if not somewhat more', and their savagery he explained thus, 'This is certain, that the Spanish cruelties have made them more monstrous in mind and manners than they are in body . . . for the loss of their friends, the remembrance whereof is assigned and conveyed over from one generation to another, breedeth an old grudge.'

After three months at San Julian, Drake entered Magellan's Strait, which he confirmed was narrow and dangerous, and only to be passed with constant soundings from pilot boats preceding the ships. Drake cleared the strait in seventeen days, but unlike Magellan emerged into a furious westerly storm which scattered his small fleet and drove Drake's ship south and east to latitude 57 degrees south, 'towards the Pole Antarctic as a pelican alone in wilderness . . . with the most mad seas, the lee shores, the dangerous rocks, the contrary and most intolerable winds, the most impossible passage out'. Drake felt sure he had reached 'the uttermost cape or headland of all these islands. It stands near in 56 degrees, without which there is no main nor island to be seen to the Southwards, but that the Atlantic Ocean and the South Sea meet in a most large and free scope.' Drake had accidently touched on what was to become the Cape Horn passage, and had incidentally undermined part of the myth of the great southern land. The storms at last abated, permitting Drake, now alone in the *Golden Hind*, to turn north along the Chilean coast, where he raided Spanish territory and shipping unhindered, even looting Callao, the port of the the Peruvian capital Lima, for the Spanish had never seen a foreign warship in the Pacific before. Laden with plundered treasures, the *Golden Hind* wallowed deep in the water. Continuing north, Drake probed the coast as far as latitude 48 degrees, seeking, without perhaps any great conviction, for the 'Strait of Anian'. He landed for supplies in July 1579 in a bay somewhere on the Californian coast around latitude 38 degrees (at a site whose identification has long been disputed, perhaps near present-day San Francisco) naming the region New Albion.

Overleaf: Drake's circumnavigation map. The map as news report: colourful but inaccurate, despite its claims to have been 'seen and corrected' by Drake himself. Two English coats of arms appear, one near Cape Horn, while the Magellan Strait is not shown; the other in California – Drake's 'New Albion' – although the text describing New Albion is placed in Greenland, whose discovery is credited to Drake!

The British Library Maps C.2.a. 7.(1).

LA HERDIKE ENTERPRINSE FAICT PAR LE

La vraÿe description du voiage du s.ͬ fransoÿs draeck
Cheualier Lesquel estant acompaigne de cinq nauires deux
desquel il brula ung aultre sen retourna et la quatre
fuit peris il partit dang.ͬ Le 13 desembre 1577 passa
oultre et fit Le sirquit de toute La terre et retourna audict
royaume Le 26.ͤ septembre 1580

TERRA   ART N

GROEN LA

premierem.ͭ descouuert par Le signeur
sainct Iulian 1579 fut Le sig.ͤ couronne
par les habitans dudict païs duex diu

catala.

QVISAI

Tournede
la a caue
de laglasse

NOVA ALBIO

NOVA
HIS
PANIE

cuola

Ygapan

Moluccai

faru

NOVA france

circuli

MARE   DEL

CVS

NOORT

Roelt de Retour

190 200 210 220 230 240 250 260 270 280 290 300 310 320 330 340

AEQVINOCTIALIS

Tumbis BANA

petuma

Arica

Tibi
chicali

TERRAGINANTIN

BRESI
LI
A IVVA

ACVTIA
REGIO

Route dels plat

NOVA GVINA

MARE DEL

SVR

MARE
OCEANO

S. elisabei

combien que Lon pense que La partie meridio
nale du destroit soit terre ferme chÿ et ce quell et tre
ietant que ne soutquies desquieies la prossam de terre
a este nomme elisabet par le dict sig.ͤ dack
qui pmier La descouerite

la magnifiq; reception du roÿ des moluques
faicte au sig.ͤ dracke le faisant tire au port
par quater de ses galeres et Luÿ mesme costoia
des vassiau dudict drack et prenoit graad
plaisir a ouir la musique

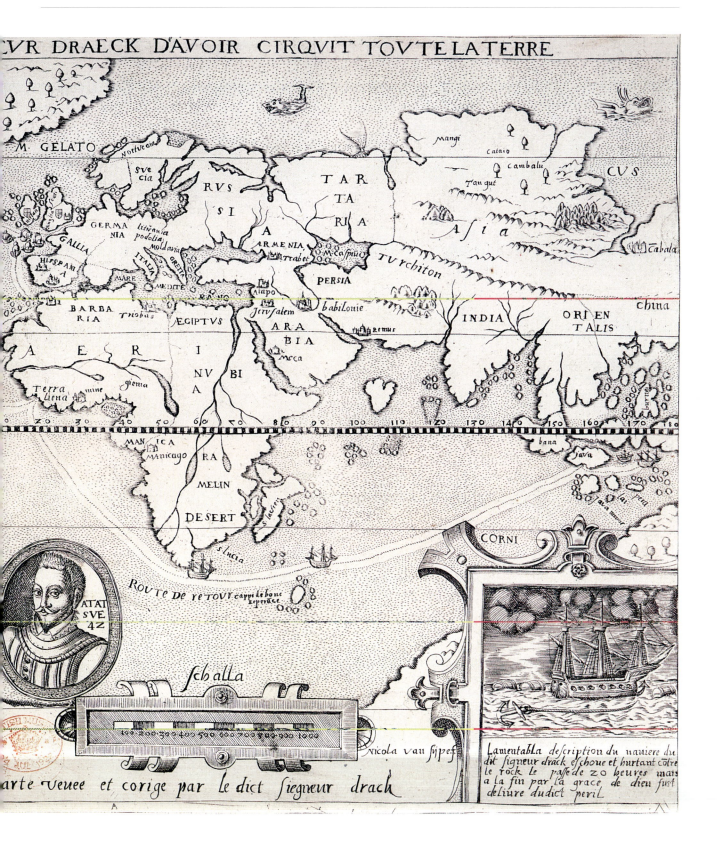

Daunted by the coast of Vancouver, he turned south-west into the ocean, and committed himself to circumnavigation. He reached the Moluccas in three months, and was royally received by the ruler of Ternate, who had quarelled with the Portuguese, and took on still more merchandise in the form of spices. However several tons of the the precious cargo had to be sacrificed as ballast to free the *Golden Hind* from a reef off Celebes. Sailing south of Java, Drake headed out into the Indian Ocean south of the Portuguese routes, just as Del Cano had done half a century before. Passing the Cape of Good Hope in June, Drake brought his ship into Plymouth harbour on September 26 1580, the first captain to navigate his ship around the world. It is idle to debate whether Drake was a consummate seaman, or, as the Spanish saw him, 'the master-thief of the unknown world', for he was clearly both.

The original idea of locating *Terra Australis* had apparently been forgotten, but his feat aroused enormous interest and found its cartographic expression in several commemorative maps engraved in the 1580's. These celebrated maps trace Drake's tracks across the three oceans and are enlivened with pictures of the *Golden Hind* in California and the Moluccas. Yet as maps of the Pacific they have probably less value than Ribero's chart of 1529. Once again longitude is the problem; the distance from Peru to the Spice Islands is understated by some 2,000 miles, while the trend of the American coast from Mexico towards Alaska is grossly exaggerated, occupying some ninety degrees of longitude. A vast continent fills the entire southern portion of the globe, although no European eye had ever seen it, and no identifiable island group is placed between New Guinea and South America. Such was the cartographic result of this famous voyage. Yet even the great Ortelius was similarly at a loss, for his world maps of this period achieve little more, although they place the Solomons correctly in relation to New Guinea. With that exception the mapmaker could only make informed guesses about

Right: Japan from Millo's World Map of 1582. This is an unusually accurate rendering of the Japanese islands, suggesting that the mapmaker had access to some special source material, now lost.

The British Library Add. MS 27470.

Left: Japan by Luiz Teixeira, published by Ortelius in 1595. This depiction of Japan, wrongly aligned and with only two principal islands, became standard in Europe.

The British Library Maps C.2.d.7.

the location of islands briefly touched on, then lost and possibly refound and re-named by other Spanish ships – islands with names such as San Pedro, Nombre de Jesus, or Santa Anna, depending on which feast-day they were sighted. The triple problems of the phantom Southern Land, the absence of any really significant island groups to act as landmarks in the immensity of the Pacific, and the measurement of longitude would persist for decades. Drake's voyage was emulated in 1586–88 by Thomas Cavendish, most of whose narrative is occupied with tales of rapacious and bloodthirsty raids upon Spanish America. Two further English ventures into the Pacific in the 1590s achieved little, but the fragility of Spanish maritime power had been exposed, and new men with new motives would claim the freedom of the seas in the seventeenth century.

THE DUTCH DISCOVERY OF AUSTRALIA

The same religious and political animosity which threw England into conflict with Spain, created a second enemy to assail the Spanish and Portuguese maritime trade, and it was the Dutch who, initially by accident, solved some of the mysteries of the Southern Ocean. The rise of Dutch sea power was an aspect of the Dutch revolt against their Spanish rulers. The Dutch fishing fleet formed the basis of a formidable navy which by the 1570s was able to challenge and defeat the Spanish. After the establishment of the Dutch Republic in 1579 the maritime economy continued to grow, while religious animosity gave the Dutch a further motive to attack Spanish interests overseas. The union of the Spanish and Portuguese crowns in 1580 made Portugal's seaborne empire equally a target. One consequence of the Dutch-Spanish hostility was the closure of all Iberian ports to Dutch merchant shipping. Lisbon was the arrival port for all East Indian goods, thus the Dutch were provided with a pragmatic, commercial motive to seek their own routes to the east. In 1595 the first Dutch fleet to sail beyond Europe rounded the Cape of Good Hope, in open defiance of the Portuguese monopoly, and opened trade with the ports of Java and Bali. Other fleets followed, and in 1598 the first Dutch attempt was made on the westerly passage to the Moluccas via Magellan's

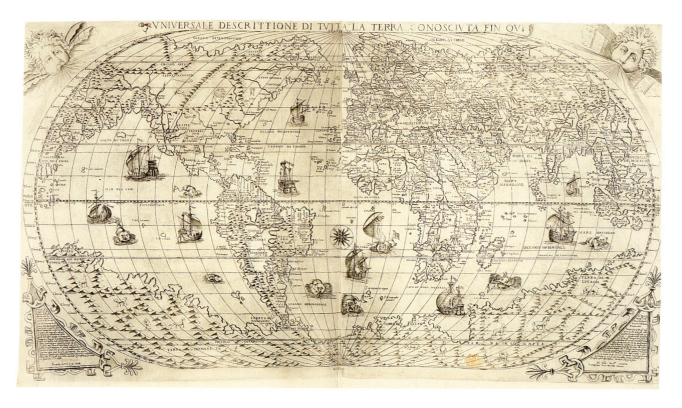

The imagined southern continent extending across the entire globe, seen in a world map by Paolo Forlani of 1571.
The British Library Maps K.Top.IV.5.

Strait. This fleet was dispersed by storms in the south Atlantic, but there was a strange sequel, for one vessel succeeded in passing the strait and sailing to Japan. There the English pilot, William Adams, so impressed the rulers with his knowledge of ships and shipbuilding that he was detained permanently, and officiated between the shogunate and the European traders who began to visit Japan. He never returned to England again, but became a semi-legendary figure in the orient. In the same year as the Adams expedition, a second fleet left Amsterdam under Olivier van Noort, which crossed the Pacific westward from Magellan's Strait and returned via the Indian Ocean route, to complete the first Dutch circumnavigation. During these voyages any Spanish or Portuguese ships and ports were treated as legitimate targets for attack. Van Noort returned to Holland in 1601, and in the following year the Dutch East India Company was formed, which arrogated to itself its own monopoly, for no captain who was not a member of the Company was permitted to sail east via the Cape or west via Magellan's Strait. The English East India Company was formed in 1600 like the Dutch to exploit Spanish-Portuguese weakness. Conflict with the Dutch in the East Indies however, and the securing of trading concessions from the Mughal Empire, dissuaded the British from further adventures in the Indies and the Pacific, and they concentrated instead on India.

It was the Dutch navigators who discovered that, when sailing east from the Cape of Good Hope, at around latitude forty degrees south, they encountered strong, favourable west winds (later known as the 'Roaring Forties') which carried them some 3,000 miles east, at which point they changed course northwards for Java. It was in the course of these voyages that Dutch mariners, running slightly too far to the east, came upon an extensive, uncharted coast. In 1616 the ship *Eendracht* commanded by Dirk Hartog made a landfall at around latitude 26 degrees south, on an island facing a large bay with the mainland coast trending away north to south. Following this coast for several

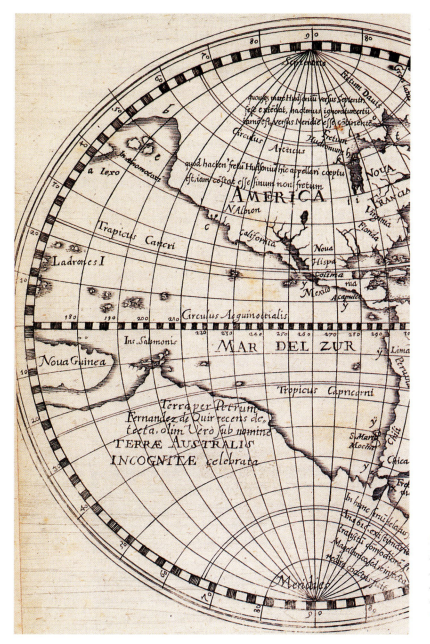

The Pacific from a world map published by Eliud Nicolai, 1619. The Torres Strait separating New Guinea from Australia, seen clearly here, was first sailed by Luis de Torres in 1606, but its existence was doubted until the age of Cook.

The British Library 790.c.27.

hundred miles, Hartog unofficially named it 'Eendrachtsland', before sailing north to Java. During the following twenty years further sections of coast were touched in this way and were roughly charted. In 1619 Frederik Houtman marked the prominent rocks at 28 degrees south, known ever since as 'Houtman's Abrolhos' or Houtman's Look-Out. In 1622 the ship *Leeuwin* rounded the cape of that name, and found that the land ran now east, a coastline followed for an immense distance in 1627 by Francois Thijszoon and Pieter Nuyts when their ship, the *Gulden Zeepaerdt*, became separated from their fleet. When they finally turned to retrace their course, they had added almost 1,000 miles of coastline to the chart. None of these ships, after Hartog's, seems to have landed and explored the new territory, a fact which can only be explained by the desolate aspect of this coast, and its appearance of being uninhabited. In 1629 a landing was forced when Francois Pelsaert's vessel, the

Batavia, was wrecked on Houtman's Abrolhos. In open boats some thirty survivors reached the mainland, which they found to be desolate, and inhabited by people with whom they were unable to make any contact. Pelsaert and his crew succeeded in escaping to Java, but he marooned two mutineers on the coast, who thus became, reluctantly, the first white settlers in Australia; they were never heard of again.

Geographers were faced with the question of what this land might be: was it the unknown southern continent, or the 'Beach' of Marco Polo? Even before Hartog's discovery, another Dutch skipper, Willem Janszoon, sailing east in 1605–6 from Java and Timor in the *Duyfken* on a reconnaissance expedition, had entered the Gulf of Carpentaria and taken its eastern coast for New Guinea. Was this new land then the southern extension of New Guinea? Further exploration of the north coast in the 1620s and 1630s suggested that it was, for they failed, strangely perhaps, to find the Torres Strait. During these voyages, by Jan Carstenszoon in 1623 and Pieter Pieterszoon in 1636, the inhabitants were found to be primitive and without seafaring or technical skills, and the land apparently unpromising in natural resources. In other words, it was similar in character to 'Eendrachtsland' to the west, but whether it was connected to it was impossible to say.

Meanwhile an important Dutch expedition independent of the Dutch East India Company set out to explore the Pacific. Jacob le Maire and Willem Schouten had studied all available charts of South America, including those resulting from Drake's voyage, and they convinced themselves that open sea existed to the south of the known land. In June 1615 their two ships left the Texel, and in January 1616 were off Tierra del Fuego, well past the entrance to Magellan's Strait. 'Early on the morning of the 24th we sighted land to starboard, lying not more than a good mile away . . . The land ran east by south with very high mountains which were all white with snow. We continued to sail along the land, and about noon we came to the end of it and saw more land east of the last, also very high and dangerous looking. These countries lay in our opinion about eight miles from each other and there appeared to be a good channel between them both . . . On the morning of the 25th we were close to the more easterly land . . . We gave this the name of Staten-Landt but the land to the west of us we called Mauritius de Nassauw . . . We had a northerly wind to carry us into the channel, sailing sou'sou'-west with good progress . . . and we then ran southward that night with a very heavy roll from the south-west and very blue water, from which we opined and were certain that it was the Great South Sea, whereat we were very glad, holding that a way had been discovered by us which had until then been unknown to man, as we afterwards found to be the truth . . . (On the 29th) we again saw land to the north-west . . . it consisted entirely of high mountains covered with snow, and ends in a sharp corner, which we called the Cape of Hoorn. . .' Schouten and Le Maire had revealed one of the great maritime passages of the world, linking the Atlantic and Pacific Oceans, avoiding the long, dangerous Strait of Magellan. They made good their crossing of the Pacific, only to be arrested in Java for breaching the East India Company's privilege, for no one would believe that they had entered the Pacific by a new route. For many decades after this voyage, the 'Staten-Landt' to the east of Le Maire's Strait was taken to be part of the great southern continent, just as Tierra del Fuego had been before: the land was shifted when necessary, but faith in it persisted as strongly as ever. In spite of this, all ships entering the Pacific from the east shaped a course north-west in search of warmer latitudes, thus forgoing the possibility of finding it.

The Dutch seem to have displayed a distinct lack of urgency in the steps they took to explore the new south land. After Hartog's accidental landfall in 1616, the years passed by and no deliberate attempt was made to follow this coastline north or south, or to investigate the interior. Two reasons suggest themselves for this. Firstly there was the arid, forbidding nature of the coast itself, lacking in bays, rivers-mouths or natural harbours, while the few glimpses obtained of the inhabitants offered no promise of a civilization worth contacting. After all the speculation concerning an unknown southern land, there was a certain reluctance to accept that this could be it. Secondly was the fact that

The Dutch attacking Portuguese-held Tidor, one of the richest of the Spice Islands, from De Bry.
The British Library 568.i.1. (8–13).

the Dutch were heavily involved in the East Indies trade, which was already providing all the merchandise their fleet could handle. This apparent lack of interest in the new land demonstrates very clearly the pragmatic motives of explorers and seafarers: the disinterested search for knowledge took second place to the commercial value of any discoveries. What was the mapmakers' interpretation of these events? The Dutch East Company of course recorded on its archive charts the latest findings of its navigators, and its hydrographer of the time, Hessel Gerritsz published a map locating the early landfalls of Hartog and his successors, both on the west coast and in the Gulf of Carpentaria. Yet mapmakers were unable to forget the fabled kingdom of 'Beach', and from the 1620s to the 1640s limited traces of the new discoveries were shown alongside Beach and the protean land-mass of *Terra Australis Incognita.*

Nevertheless by the year 1640 the Company felt that the time had come to investigate the extent and potential of this half-discovered land. Sponsored by the Governor-General of the Dutch East Indies, Anthony van Diemen, an expedition was prepared under the command of Abel Tasman, a captain already experienced in exploring the northern Pacific, with an expert pilot in Jacobszoon Visscher. Tasman's two ships sailed from Mauritius, now established as a Dutch base, in October 1642, with his first objective to discover whether the new land was part of a great continent stretching south to the pole. Since the coast of Hartog's 'Eendrachtsland' was known to extend from around latitude 22 to latitude 34 south, it seems surprising that Tasman took a westerly course along the 50th parallel, intending to reach the longitude of New Guinea before turning north. This course ensured that he completely missed the coast of Australia, indeed it was only bad weather which forced him north far enough to touch the southern tip of 'van Diemen's land' (later named Tasmania), the 'first land we had met with in the South Sea.' Although they landed, exploration of the island was cut short by the apparent discovery that it was inhabited by giants: notches were found cut into trees, obviously to facilitate climbing, but the notches were five feet apart! In spite of the giants, Tasman took possession of it in the name of the Dutch States-General although he did not discern that it was an island. Tasman continued east until he came upon the west coast of New Zealand, naming it 'Staten Landt' considering that it was probably the same land discovered south-east of Cape Horn by Le Maire and Schouten. That Tasman and Visscher could link these two discoveries, which were separated by 5,000 miles of ocean, is testimony to the tenacious hold which the the legendary southern continent had on the European imagination. During his reconnaissance of 'Staten Landt', four of Tasman's men were killed by Maoris in what he named 'Murderers' Bay': the hostility

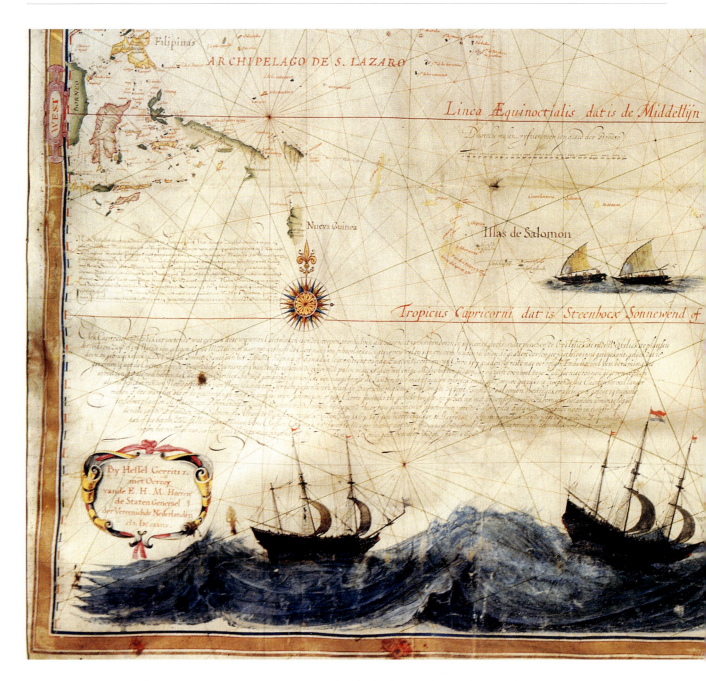

The Southern Pacific by Hessel Gerritsz, 1622. The map by the hydrographer to the Dutch East India Company commemorates the first passage of the Cape Horn route by Schouten and LeMaire in 1616.

Bibliothèque Nationale, Paris

of the Maoris was one of the reasons for Tasman's early departure, before he could discover the strait separating the North and South Islands or indeed that they were islands. Sailing north-east, the Tonga and Fiji Islands were reached before the ships turned west and followed the north coast of New Guinea. Like so many other navigators, Tasman missed the Torres Strait, and so failed to establish the insularity of New Guinea.

Tasman and Visscher were critically received on their return, and it is hard to see their 5,000 mile voyage as anything other than a splendid failure. They had circumnavigated Australia without ever seeing it; their interpretation of the New Zealand coast was perversely inaccurate; and they had failed to find New Guinea's southern coast. What they had achieved was to set definite limits to the

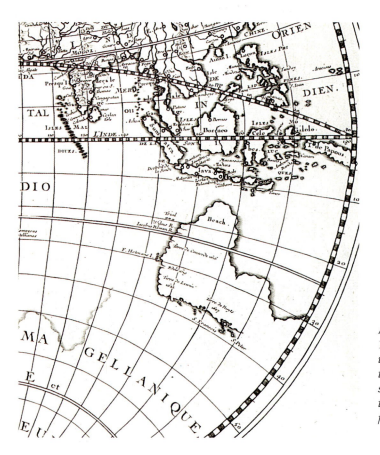

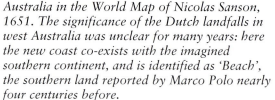

Australia in the World Map of Nicolas Sanson, 1651. The significance of the Dutch landfalls in west Australia was unclear for many years: here the new coast co-exists with the imagined southern continent, and is identified as 'Beach', the southern land reported by Marco Polo nearly four centuries before.

The British Library Maps K.Top.IV.8.

southern land newly discovered, and to separate it from the supposed *Terra Australis* which must now be shifted to the east and south, into a region of the southern Pacific where no European had ever sailed.

In search of the hard facts which this voyage had not provided, Tasman was dispatched upon a second in 1644, this time with the specific aim of exploring the coasts of the new land, first in the north, to seek an exit into the Pacific, or failing that he was to turn west and trace the coast as far as Cape Leeuwin. Tasman duly explored the Gulf of Carpentaria, but once again failed to find the Torres Strait. Turning west, he demonstrated that the coast was continuous with 'Eendrachtsland' and beyond to the south coast seen by Nuyts and Thijszoon in 1627, a total of some 3,000 miles. Yet Tasman could not pretend to have seen anything very memorable or alluring on his voyage, and the Company showed its disappointment, first in its judgement that in future such important exploration should be entrusted to 'more vigilant and courageous persons', and second in its conduct, for no further interest was taken in this 'New Holland': the poverty and savagery of both its coasts and its naked inhabitants had quenched any desire to investigate further, and for a further century few people would disagree with them. Ironically, it was after this demonstration of its barrenness that the new south land became known as 'New Holland'. Following this second voyage, the coasts of Australia were shown complete on three sides, excepting the east, with the incomplete outlines of Tasmania and New Zealand. New Guinea was represented as a great northern peninsula of Australia, although some mapmakers continued to hint at a strait between them – some vague tradition concerning the Torres Strait had evidently taken deep root among geographers, and if a vast continent could be conjured into existence, why not a tiny strait?

THE PROBLEM OF THE NORTHERN PACIFIC

But if one southern continent had been found and dismissed as worthless, the Dutch did not yet abandon the aim of expanding their activities in the Pacific. As early as 1609 they had established a trading base in Japan, and the seas north and east of Japan were rumoured to hold further islands, promontories of Cathay or Tartary, as well as the long-cherished dream of a strait to the Atlantic. Tasman himself had made one attempt to chart these waters in 1639, without any clear result, and in 1643 the Dutch authorities in Java dispatched a second expedition under Maarten Vries whose results were to confuse the geography of the northern Pacific for the next hundred years. Vries sailed along the eastern coast of Yezo (the modern Hokkaido, the north island of Japan), and then between the largest of the Kuril Islands, Iturup and Urup, before turning west to Sakhalin Island. Vries portrayed Yezo as a promontory of mainland Asia, failed to discern that Sakhalin was an island, and formed a highly exaggerated impression of the size of the Kurils, which he named 'Staten Land' and 'Compagnie Land'. These two lands and the distorted form of Yezo, together with yet another mysterious coast thought to have been sighted by a Spaniard named Joan de Gama, haunted all maps of the region, sometimes extending to the coast of North America, a vast phantom Dutch empire. These incomplete coastal surveys produced totally misleading results, and the haste to establish a claim to sovereignty seems to have overridden all else. It is a striking fact that no Europeans with knowledge of Japan, traders or Jesuits, were able to confirm from Japanese sources the true geography of its northern regions, and that it was always represented on maps as two islands rather than three.

It was the Russians who dispelled these fantasies, in the course of their eastward expansion inaugurated by Peter the Great. By 1710 they had occupied the whole of the Kamchatka Peninsula and began the process of establishing the true geography of the northern Pacific, in which a major part was played by Vitus Bering, a Dane in the service of the Russian navy. The Russians were deeply interested in the possible existence of a northern sea route to the Pacific and the countries of the east, and also in the relationship between Russia's eastern territories and the Americas. In July 1728 Bering sailed from southern Kamchatka, with instructions to follow 'the shore which bears northerly and

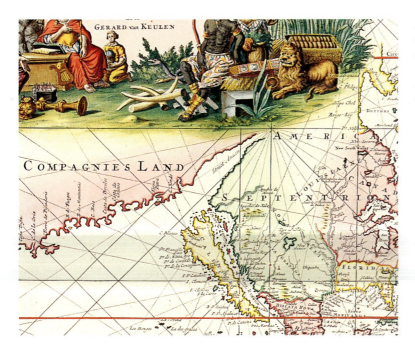

Left: The Northern Pacific by Van Keulen, c.1720. Dutch exploration in this region created two phantom lands – 'Iesso' and 'Compagnie Land', which sometimes assumed the monstrous proportions seen here.

Private Collection

which, since its limits are unknown, seems to be part of America' and to determine where it joined America. In August Bering passed the East Cape of Asia, and beyond to latitude 67 degrees north and saw the coast now trending away north-west. Bad weather prevented his sighting the opposite coast of Alaska, but he had passed through the strait which now bears his name, located where the long-fabled Strait of Anian had been placed by mapmakers in the sixteenth century. In June 1741 Bering sailed again from Kamchatka to explore the eastern or American side of the strait. He rounded the Alaskan Peninsula, passed Kodiak Island and sighted Mount St. Elias, before turning back, but the return voyage was a nightmare of cold, hunger and disease which Bering failed to survive. But he and the Russians who had explored south from Kamchatka had shown Vries's lands to be illusory, and had opened the Russians' way to Alaska,

The last Dutch voyage of exploration in the Pacific came in 1721–22 when Jacob Roggeveen, sailing between Cape Horn and the Tuamotu Archipeligo, became the first European to land on Easter Island, whose people and monuments have provided one of the Pacific's most enduring mysteries. Roggeveen remained only one day and missed an invaluable opportunity to understand the celebrated statues, although the Dutch observed the inhabitants lighting fires before them and apparently worshipping them. A subsequent brief visit by a Spanish ship in 1770 noticed that the islanders possessed the remnants of a unique form of written script. When Captain Cook arrived in 1774 he found the island apparently ravaged by civil war and the statues overthrown. The moment had apparently passed when the traditions of the Easter Islanders could have been recorded and understood.

PACIFIC EXPLORATION IN THE AGE OF REASON

La Perouse with Louis XV: Pacific exploration being planned in the salons of Europe.

Giraudon

By the mid eighteenth century the limits of the Pacific had been defined on three sides, the Asian, the American and the northern. But, over two centuries after Magellan first ventured on its waters, the map of the ocean itself was still desperately incomplete and its multitudinous peoples unknown. It was during the eighteenth century that a new spirit of exploration emerged among the European nations, a spirit which found its clearest expression in the Pacific. For it was beginning to emerge that the great secret of the Pacific was that it held no great secret: no hidden continent, no new civilization, no fountain of wealth. What it held was a myriad of islands, whose variety of peoples, flora and fauna challenged the European mind to observe, analyse and understand this richness. It stimulated both their intellect and their imagination, and the Pacific became both a place where real

The Pacific by Zürner, c.1720. Two centuries after Magellan, very few Pacific island groups had been firmly located. Here the Solomons have drifted some ninety degrees east and have been confused with the Marquesas.

The British Library K.Top.IV.15.

ships sailed, and a philosophical playground where questions about man and nature were explored. In this sense the Pacific became a more rational version of the medieval twilight realm beyond Europe, filled not with demons and monsters, but with exotic, natural, verifiable phenomena. Rousseau was to complain that during the three centuries in which Europeans had been exploring and colonizing the world, they had accumulated pathetically little scientific knowledge of it, ascribing this failure to the fact that voyages of exploration were undertaken not by scientists and philosophers, but by sailors, soldiers, merchants or missionaries. By the mid-eighteenth century this situation was changing: 'Any blockhead can go to Italy', said Joseph Banks, while his idea of a grand tour was to accompany Captain Cook into the Pacific. The advance of scientific methods in the eighteenth century demanded enquiry, measurement and comparison in fields such as zoology, earth science and

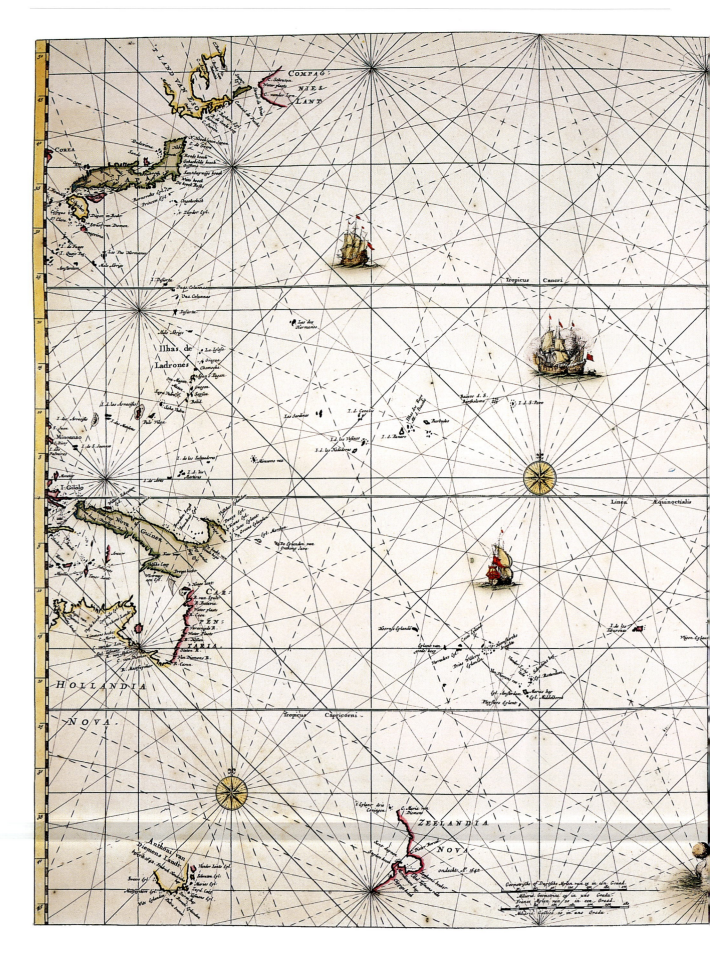

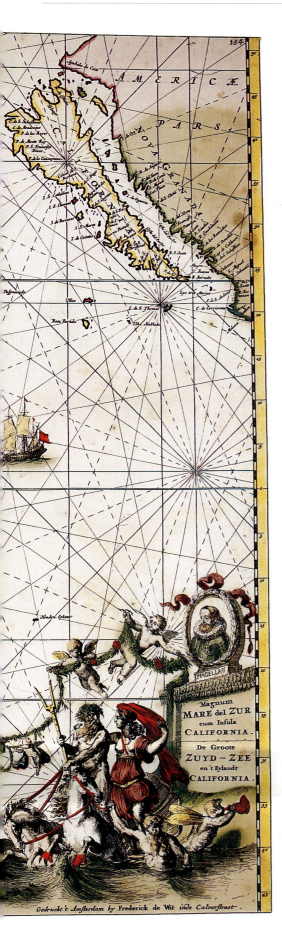

astronomy. Above all perhaps was the desire to articulate an understanding of Nature in which the concept of design would sustain both a rational and religious perception of the world. Seen in this perspective, the rich variety of islands and peoples in the Pacific might be seen as alternative and miniature worlds in which Nature could be seen experimenting with her powers. The image which the Pacific islands overwhelmingly evoked was that of Paradise, with their lush environment, their beneficent climate and their people innocent of tyranny, hunger and poverty. European travellers had for centuries set out with their minds filled with images of old or fabled worlds which they sought to rediscover – Arcadia, Eden, Atlantis, Hesperides, Jerusalem or Cathay. The character of the Oceanic peoples provoked questions about man's nature which chimed precisely with those which the philosophers of the age were asking about government, liberty, and happiness in human society. For two centuries the European nations had sent adventurers into the unknown in a ruthless search for wealth and domination, during which they had struggled against the forces of nature and the savagery of pagan man. In the eighteenth century there were signs that this phase was being overtaken by a genuine desire to observe and understand what had been discovered. Travel narratives sought to enlarge their reader's knowledge of the natural and human world by precise, authentic description, not to amaze them with tales of danger and conquest. The very language of eighteenth century travel writing reflects this new spirit: discerning, humane, and self-effacing, yet precise – these were the qualities to which English and French explorers aspired during the century in which the map of the Pacific was brought to completion. All thoughtful visitors to the Pacific were struck by the cultural similarities shared by the innumerable islands, and the question of how and why these people had migrated across thousands of miles of ocean became central to all study of the region. Both the islanders and the inhabitants of Australia provoked doubts about European culture in the minds of the eighteenth century explorers. Captain Cook denied that these people were savage or wretched: 'In reality they are far happier than we Europeans, being wholly unacquainted not only with the superfluous but with the necessary conveniences so much sought after by Europeans; they

The Pacific after Tasman, by De Wit, 1668. Tasman circumnavigated Australia without seeing it, and touched the west coast of New Zealand and the Islands of Vanuatu. He had limited the possible extent of Australia, but the blanks on the Pacific map remained huge.
The British Library Maps C.45.f.2.

are happy in not knowing the use of them. They live in a tranquility which is not disturbed by the inequality of condition. The earth and sea of their own accord furnish them with all things necessary for life.'

One of the first representatives of the new approach was the contradictory figure William Dampier, whose achievements as an explorer were secondary to his role in stimulating interest in travel narratives and in the Pacific. A buccaneer by trade, but certainly not the illiterate, bloodthirsty bully that most of them were, he was judged by one who knew him as 'the mildest-mannered man that ever scuttled ship or cut a throat'. After some years raiding on the American coast, he crossed the Pacific in 1688 and explored the northern coast of Australia, whose inhabitants he considered to be 'the most miserable in the world'. In 1697 his book A *New Voyage Round the World* became something of a bestseller, for he was a keen observer and a lively stylist. On the strength of this work he was commissioned by the Admiralty to command a new expedition in 1699 to explore and chart New Guinea. Dampier succeeded in finding a strait between New Guinea and New Britain, but this experience somehow led him to the extraordinary conclusion that 'other parts of this great Tract of Terra Australis were certainly islands', and this became the source of a century-long search for an imagined strait that was supposed to bisect Australia entirely. Dampier returned to the Pacific in 1703, and in the course of that voyage Alexander Selkirk, the model for Robinson Crusoe, was marooned on Juan Fernandez Island off the coast of Chile, and it was Dampier who returned to rescue him in 1708.

In the last decade of the seventeenth century, a new factor entered Pacific exploration with the arrival of French ships and scientists. Dutch maritime activity was now in decline, and the growing rivalry between the French and the British was carried into the Pacific, both nations anxious to claim new possessions and new scientific achievements. The French had formed a 'Compagnie des Indes Orientales' and a 'Compagnie Royale de la Mer Pacifique', and their early voyages deep into the southern hemisphere have perpetuated on certain islands explorers' names such as those of Bouvet, Crozet and Kerguelen. The importance initially assigned to these discoveries proved to be wildly exaggerated: suggestions that Bouvet's Island, discovered in 1739, was the promontory of a 'Southern India' provoked many searches for it, but it was not relocated until 1898, because Bouvet made an enormous error in calculating its position.

In the early eighteenth century, before French and British explorer-scientists turned their eyes on the Pacific, how many islands had been securely placed on the map? The answer is remarkably few, and there is the additional problem of identifying reported island landfalls where the geographical position could not be given with any precision. A feature such as the Cape of Good Hope, once found and described, was unlikely to be mistaken by later mariners, but this is plainly not true of a small island separated by weeks or months of open-sea sailing from any known point. The problem of naming and re-naming adds to the uncertainty. The Marianas were discovered by Magellan and were long known as the Ladrones – Islands of Thieves – and their position relatively close to the Philippines became secure, as did some of the Caroline Islands to the south. The reverse is true of the Solomon group which Mendaña discovered in 1567, but failed to re-find. It is considered that the English circumnavigator Philip Carteret sailed through them in 1767, but that the identification with Mendaña's islands was made only in the following year by Bougainville. In the intervening two centuries they had been placed at widely differing longitudes, migrating to positions as far as 120 degrees east on some eighteenth century maps, and becoming conflated with the Marquesas of Mendaña's second voyage in 1595. Quiros's island of Espiritu Santo was likewise re-located many times in the regions east of Australia and New Guinea, sometimes even being placed on the mainland of Australia itself. Tasman explored the Tonga and Fiji groups, which appeared with Dutch names such as Amsterdam Island, Rotterdam Island etc., on maps after 1650. Roggeveen, after leaving Easter Island, touched some of the Society Islands and what was probably Samoa. With these

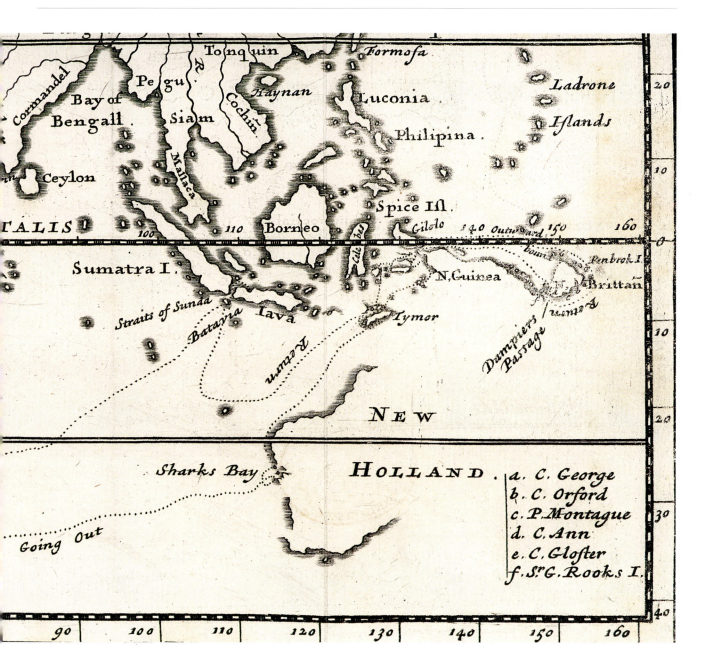

Dampier's tracks around Australia, published 1703. Despite months of exploration, Dampier was unable to clarify the geography of Northern Australia, or its relation to New Guinea. He stated his belief that the north and east of 'New Holland' consisted of islands and were not continental at all.

The British Library 303.h.24(2).

exceptions, a map of the Pacific from the 1720s or 1730s would either be empty, or it would include a number of islands whose identification is quite uncertain, having names such as 'Isla Solitaria', 'Isla Desolata' or 'Isla Traditores' – 'Traitors' Island'. These islands were drawn from contemporary narratives, or were copied from one map to another, so that their geographical reality is almost as problematic as the Atlantic islands of the fourteenth century. Some showed extraordinary vitality,

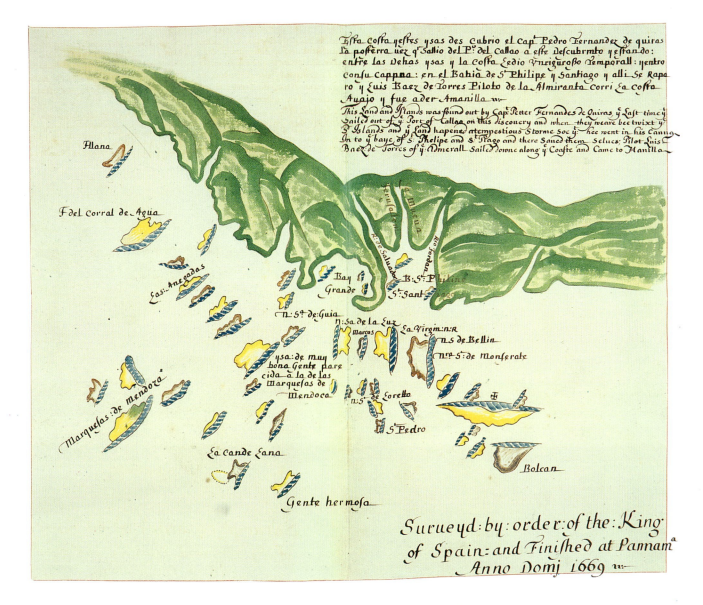

Within the image, the following text appears:

Effa cofta yeffes ysas des cubrio el cap.t Pedro Fernandes de quiras
la pofferra uez q.e Sallio del P.o del Callao a effe Defcubrmto y effan do:
entre las Dehas ysas y la Cofta Eedio Ynriguroso Temporall: yentro
confu cappna: en el Bahia de S.t Philipe y Santiago y alli Se Rapa
ro y Luis Baez de Torres Piloto de la Almiranta corri Ea cofta
Auajo y fue ader Amanilla m

This Land and Islands was found out by Cap.t Petter Fernandes de Quiras y Laft time y
Sailed out of y Port of Callao on this difcouery and when they weare bee twixt y
S.d Islands and y Land hapened atempestious Storme soe y hee went in his Canno.
In to y baye of S.t Phelipe and S.t Jago and there Saued them Selues; Pilot Luis
Baez de Torres of y Admerall Sailed downe along y Coafte and Came to Manilla

Flana

F del Corral de Agua

Las: Anegadas

N: S.a de: Guia

ysa: de muy
bona Gente pare
cida a la de las
Marquefas de
Mendoca

Marquefas: de mendora

Ea cande Eana

Gente hermofa

Bay
Grande

Marcos

B: S.t Philine
S.t Sant

n: Sa de la Luz
Ea Virgin: n: R
n.s de Bellin
n.ra S: de Monferate

n: S.a de Loretto

S.t Pedro

Bolcan

Surueyd: by: order: of the: King
of Spain: and Finifhed at Pannam.a
Anno Domj 1669 m

Espiritu Santu discovered by Quiros in 1606, copied from Spanish charts by William Hack in 1698.

The British Library Harley MS 4034.

such as 'Davis Land' reported in 1687 by the English buccaneer Edward Davis west of Juan Fernandez, which was specifically mentioned as a target for discovery in the sailing orders of Roggeveen, and later of John Byron in 1764. Any island which held no fresh water, or where a landing, proved impossible because of reefs, was likely to be called 'Disappointment Island', which was the name given by Byron to one of the Tuamotu group. Whether such islands found their way onto maps lay in the hands of European map publishers who had to decide how important such a 'discovery' was. The history of Pacific exploration between 1520 and 1720 had been unable to advance beyond this kaleidoscopic game of chance, which was so unsatisfactory in an age of science.

No figure more clearly exemplifies the new breed of eighteenth century explorer than Louis-Antoine de Bougainville, who was a soldier, diplomat and mathematician before he was a seafarer. Bougainville's voyage of 1766–69, the first French circumnavigation of the globe, was commissioned by the French government as a deliberate world reconnaissance, manned by naturalists, scientists and artists. Bougainville's own account is full of reflection on what he saw, both in the natural and the human world. Passing Magellan's Strait, he sailed northwest to the Tuamotu Archipeligo where 'The verdure charmed our eyes and the cocoa-trees everywhere exposed their fruits to our sight, and over-shadowed a grass plot adorned with flowers; thousands of birds were hovering about the shore, and seemed to announce a coast abounding with fish, and we all longed to descend . . . Some of our people cried out that they saw three men running to the seashore . . . these men seemed very tall and of a bronze colour. Who can give an account of the manner in which they were conveyed hither, what communication they have with other beings, and what becomes of them when they multiply on an isle which is no more than a league in diameter. Such descriptions made explicit the comparison of the Pacific Islands with paradise, an impression made even more strongly in Tahiti, which the French called 'Nouvelle Cythère' after the classical island of Venus. Where had these people come from, and how had they evolved a state of society so different from the European? Observations such as Bougainville's were influential in building the concept of the 'noble savage', and the radical philos-ophers were bleakly prophetic about the impact which Europeans would have on such cultures. The most celebrated statement of this pessimism was that of Diderot, who penned what has become a classic tirade against European exploration: 'Ah, Monsieur de Bougainville, steer your vessel far, far away from the shores of these innocent and fortunate Tahitians. They are happy and you can only bring harm to their happiness. . . You took possession of their country as if it did not belong to them . . . No sooner had you appeared among them than they became thieves; no sooner had you set foot on their land than it became stained with blood . . . At length you sailed away from Tahiti. These good and simple islanders bade you farewell. Oh that you and your compatriots and all the other inhabitants of Europe might be engulfed in the depths of the ocean rather than see them again . . . One day they will come with the crucifix in one hand and the dagger in the other to cut your throats or to force youto accept their customs and opinions: one day, under their rule, you will be almost as unhappy as they are.'

In fact Bougainville had been forestalled in his discovery of Tahiti by an English ship, the *Dolphin*, under Captain Samuel Wallis, which had landed in June 1767 in the course of one of three English circumnavigations of this period. The others were John Byron's voyage, also in the *Dolphin*, and Philip Carteret's in the *Swallow*. All were fully documented and added further islands to the map, for example on 2 July 1767, one of the *Dolphin's* company, 'the son of Major Pitcairn of the marines', sighted the tiny island which was named for him, and which became so famous as the refuge of the *Bounty* mutineers. Yet all these voyages followed so nearly the same course north-west from Cape Horn that nothing major was gained in terms of the overall geography of the Pacific. That was only to be achieved through the deliberate, measured and systematic reconnaissance of Captain James Cook, who brought the modern map of the Pacific near to completion.

COOK IN THE PACIFIC

Cook undertook three voyages between 1768 and 1779, each outstanding in its results. His instruc-tions from the Admiralty called for a final answer to the problem of the existence of a southern continent, which still had its advocates in England and in France. His first voyage demonstrated the insularity of New Zealand and revealed the potential of Australia's eastern seaboard, which was green and fertile in contrast to the barren coasts previously observed in the west and north. Avoiding and partly charting the Great Barrier Reef, he succeeded in passing through Torres Strait, thus 'being able to proove that New Holland and New Guinea are two separate lands or islands, which until this day hath been a doubtful point with geographers.' It was Cook's second voyage of 1772 – 1775

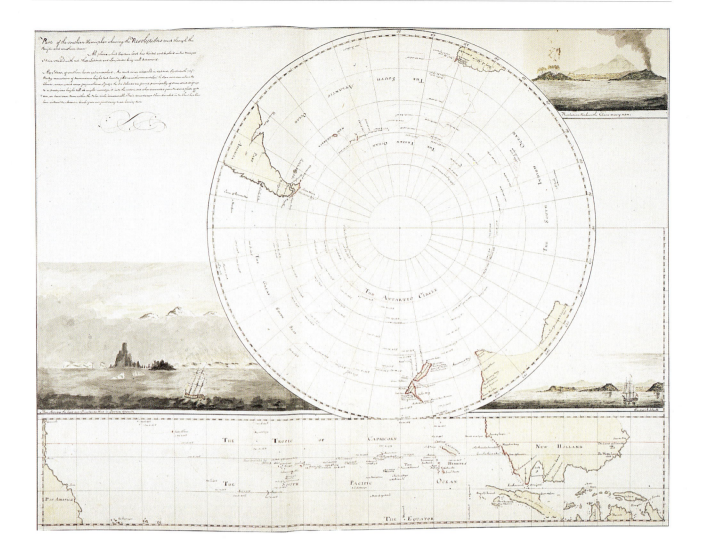

The tracks of Cook's southern voyages, c.1775. Cook's primary achievement was to remove finally the belief in the long-imagined southern continent; of course he narrowly missed sighting Antarctica.

The British Library Add. MS 15,500.1.

which finally dispelled the possibility of a great southern continent existing in any habitable latitudes. This time the route lay via the Cape of Good Hope, then south-east to unprecedented latitudes, making the first recorded crossing of the Antarctic circle and encountering walls of ice. At one point, approximately 106 degrees west, 2,000 miles due south of Easter Island, he was only a few miles off the Antarctic coast, which he never sighted. Cook cautiously observed: 'It was my opinion that this ice extended quite to the pole . . . As we drew near this ice, some penguins were heard but none seen; and but few other birds or any other thing that could induce us to think that land was near. And yet I think there must be some to the south behind this ice; but if there is, it can afford no better retreat for birds or any other animals, than the ice itself with which it must be wholly covered.' Thus Cook plainly demonstrated that though land might still exist beyond the limits he reached, it must be 'near the pole and out of the reach of navigation.' This was, he added, 'the final end put to the searching after a southern continent, which has at times engrossed the attention of some of the maritime powers for near two centuries past, and been a favourite theory among the geographers of all ages.'

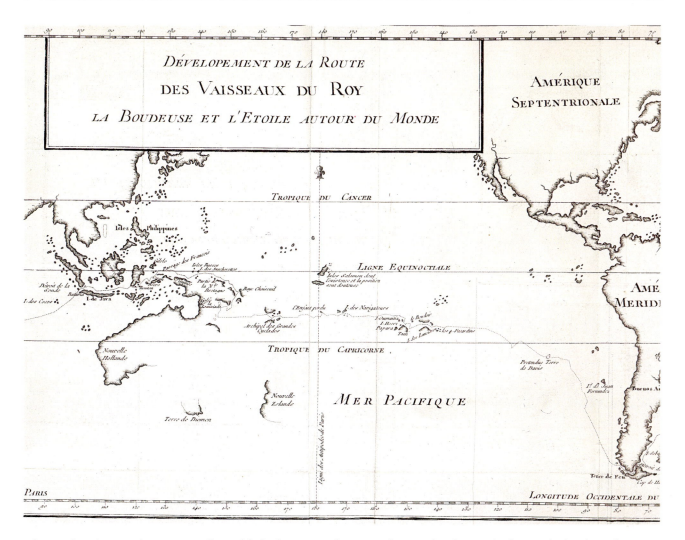

The tracks of Louis de Bougainville, published 1771. Sailing west from Tahiti he touched several islands such as New Hebrides, which he calls 'Grandes Cyclades'. The Solomons are marked, but their very existence is said to be doubtful.

On this voyage Cook had for the first time the benefit of using Harrison's new chronometer which at last made possible the accurate calculation of longitude, and the charts made on this occasion set new standards of precision. In some ways, Cook's methods were as significant for the future as his achievements: painstaking, practical and humane, he took as much pride in the fact that his discoveries were accomplished without loss of life among his crew as in the discoveries themselves. At this time it was common for disease and malnutrition to claim half a ship's crew during any extended voyage. The merchant ships he specified for his voyages made inshore navigation in uncharted waters safer, for their draft was shallow and their flat bottoms enabled them to be 'laid on shore' as naval ships could not. Emerging from the Antarctic ice, Cook made northwards, charting the Marquesas, the Society Islands, the Friendly Islands, Vanuatu and other groups.

The mysteries of Pacific geography were being resolved one by one, and Cook's third and final voyage had an additional objective. Developing trade in North America, particularly the fur trade centred on Hudson Bay, had raised again the old question of a passage from Canada to the western

Left: The Marquesas, a chart with inset view drawn on Cook's ship Resolution *in 1774. East is at the top, and 'La Dominica' is Hiva Oa.*
The British Library Add. MS 15,500.8.

Right: The Australian coasts by Matthew Flinders, 1814. Two centuries after the first Dutch sightings, the southern continent was at last circumnavigated and charted after two years' painstaking work.
The British Library Maps Tab.437.a.

sea. The British Government regarded this route as potentially so valuable that it offered a reward of £20,000 for any British ship that should discover a passage from Hudson Bay to the Pacific. Cook's record of exploration in the Pacific made it natural that he should he be sent to search for it from the western end. Sailing in 1776, Cook traversed the Pacific yet again, this time due north from Tahiti, to discover the Hawaiian Islands (named initially the 'Sandwich Islands' after the First Lord of the Admiralty) which Cook guessed to be the northernmost extension of the Polynesian world, for he recognized the linguistic and cultural similarities between the Hawaiians, the Tahitians, the Marquesans and others. 'How' he mused 'shall we account for this nation's spreading itself so far over this vast ocean?' Sailing east to California, Cook followed the coasts northwards, probing in vain for any strait. Rounding the Alaskan Peninsula he entered the Bering Strait and reached his most northerly point at latitude 70 degrees, before being turned back by ice. Withdrawing south to Hawaii to winter and refit, Cook met his tragic and needless death at the hands of the islanders in February 1779, an uncanny re-enactment of the death of Magellan so many years before. His crew were stunned, feeling that with him went 'the spirit of discovery, the decision, the indomitable courage.' Dutifully they attempted the Bering Strait again, but again failed to penetrate it, and returned by Japan, the China Sea and Indian Ocean.

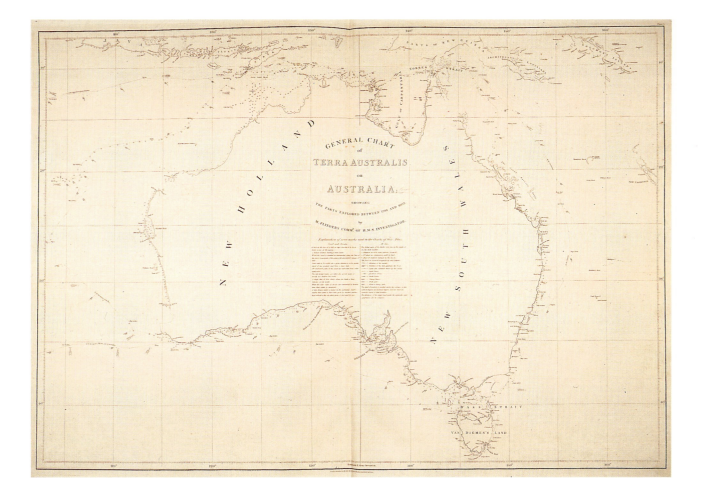

Cook's achievements marked both the close of an era in Pacific navigation – the end of the quest for a great secret which had never existed – and the beginning of a new phase of scientific reconnaissance. Doubtful sightings and partial surveys would no longer transform islands into imaginary continents. After 1780 virtually all maps of the Pacific, and many world maps, paid tribute to Cook by showing his tracks and often his portrait. It has been said that Cook explored more of the earth's surface than any other single man in history, and it was recognized by his contemporaries that he had completed the re-drawing of the map of the world's oceans begun three centuries before by Columbus. Of course there were still uncharted regions, and new islands to be discovered, and in the thirty years following Cook's death, La Pérouse clarified the geography of north-east Asia, Vancouver made an exemplary survey of the intricate coast of western Canada, D'Entrecasteaux made improved charts of Australian and Melanesian waters, and Flinders finally circumnavigated Australia in 1803, charting its entire coastline for the first time. Slightly later, in the 1820s, Dumont D'Urville combined research and analysis of the human and natural worlds with his exploration, and it was he who proposed the threefold division of the region into Polynesia, Micronesia and Melanesia which still stands. These were prolonged technical assignments: undertaken in a scientific spirit very different from the conquistador culture which drove the first Europeans through the dangerous Strait of Magellan into the great Southern Sea.

The exploration of the Pacific had occupied almost three centuries, for its scale, its intricate geography, and its remoteness from Europe made it a far greater challenge than the Atlantic or Indian

Oceans. During that time the motives and the conduct of the European explorers evolved to reflect different phases of European civilization itself: gold-seeking Spaniards, Calvinist Dutch traders, French scientists and English surveyors. Yet before 1800 none of these were more than passing visitors, and their effect on the region was shortlived. The islands were preserved in their isolation because they were so small and so scattered, and lacked tangible sources of wealth. After c.1800 new factors led to permanent or semi-permanent settlement of the islands by Europeans. Among these factors were the colonization of Australia and New Zealand, which created a European centre to the region; the coming of the whaling industry with its need for bases; the growing trade in pearls, tortoise-shell, sandalwood and cocoanut-products; later came the cultivation of crops such as sugar-cane, with its associated plantation economy. The impact on island culture was often catastrophic: disease, near-slave labour, dispossession of land, and the collapse of traditional culture. Diderot's savage prophecy had been fulfilled. It is easy to say that it was inevitable, that a dynamic, technical and commercial culture will always destroy a static, traditional one. It was not the end that the explorers had sought, especially the humane ones such as Bougainville and Cook, and once again we are faced with the paradox of the history of exploration that something conceived as courageous and idealistic becomes coarse and material. Only for the discoverer was the act of discovery the end of the story, unfortunately.

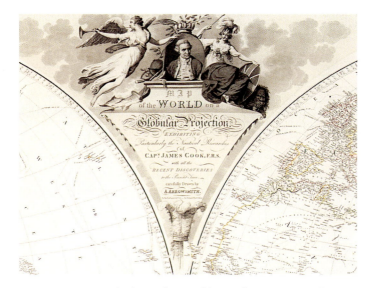

Captain James Cook, from the world map by Arrowsmith, 1794.
The British Library Maps

CHAPTER 5

THE CONTINENTS
AND THE POLES

Dumont D'Urville's ship in ice-floes in 1840.

ASIA

THE STORY OF EUROPEAN KNOWLEDGE of Asia contrasts sharply with the historical discovery and exploration of America and the Pacific. Contacts between the two continents had existed since ancient times, and an imprecise, semi-legendary knowledge of Asia remained part of inherited European tradition throughout classical and medieval times: Asia formed one of the great divisions of the tripartite world – Europe, Africa and Asia – accepted by Greek, Roman and Christian geographers. The barriers to precise geographical knowledge of Asia were partly physical – steppe, desert and mountain – and partly political – the hostility of its many peoples to Europeans, especially of course the fact that, from the eighth century AD, Islamic states controlled the direct routes into Asia. These barriers explain the paradox that a landmass continuous with Europe should become accessible only by sea. The opening of the seaway to Asia around the year 1500 was decisive, for it cannot be said that regular overland communication was ever established between Europe and India or China, even in modern times. However, before and after 1500 many individuals succeeded in penetrating Asia's defences and exploring the interior, travelling as traders, missionaries, spies, scientists or merely as curious observers. In many cases these travellers were not the first to explore their chosen region of Asia, but simply the first to write down what they saw. These journeys rarely had any lasting results in terms of establishing permanent contacts between Europeans and Asians; they were isolated experiences, significant only because they were given literary form, and so inspired other travellers. Nor did they often result in the diffusion of precise geographical knowledge or improved maps, since the travellers were rarely trained geographers. From the European perspective, the outstanding fact about the peoples of Asia was that they possessed technical or military skills which meant that they were not to be subdued by Europeans, as those of America, the Pacific or Africa could be, and their lands were not to be occupied by a handful of armed invaders. This situation began to change in northern Asia in the seventeenth century, with the eastward advance of Russia across Siberia, and in the eighteenth century with the British expansion into India from their foothold in Bengal. During the three centuries from 1400 to 1700 there was no systematic process of exploration in Asia, only a series of isolated incursions from the west, the south or the east.

Asia, and above all its Moslem states, were always regarded as inaccessible, dangerous, even forbidden regions, and perhaps for that very reason attracted adventurous spirits who were determined to probe their secrets. One of the earliest post-medieval travellers was the Italian Ludovico di Varthema, who left Europe in 1502 on a journey which took him to Arabia, Persia and India, during which he became the first known European to visit the Moslem holy cities of Mecca and Medina, which he achieved by disguising himself among a large group of pilgrims. Varthema's account of his travels, published in Rome in 1510, is lively and picturesque, but it contributed little to geography in the precise sense, and in this it set the pattern for many Asian travel narratives. The typical map of Arabia in the sixteenth and seventeenth centuries was understandably sparse in detail, and merely highlighted Mecca and Medina, although their true location was unknown. Not until the nineteenth century did European adventurers succeed in crossing the desert and in making accurate surveys of their routes.

Central Asia in the European imagination: desert and mountain, oases and ancient cities. From Desceliers' World Map, 1550.

The British Library Add. MS 24065.

The Asian interior was of course accessible to the north of the Moslem lands, where the State of Muscovy had emerged from the shadow of its Tartar overlords. Yet around the year 1500 Muscovy lay in a condition of such extraordinary isolation from the outside world that its very existence was barely known in western Europe, and its only contact with the west was via a few diplomatic envoys from Rome or Vienna. The first description of Muscovy published in

Arabia, from Waldseemüller's World Map, 1516. Geographical knowledge was almost non-existent: only the domes of Mecca and Medina are noteworthy.

Schloss Wolfegg

Europe was that of Sigismund von Herberstein in 1549, based on his earlier visit to Moscow as an envoy of the Holy Roman Emperor. It seems unlikely that this was known to the English merchant-adventurers Willoughby and Chancellor in 1553 when they set out on their pioneering voyage around the North Cape, for no mention of Muscovy was made in their commission, and Chancellor discovered the White Sea and the port of Archangel quite by accident (see chapter 2). His overland journey from Archangel to the court of Ivan the Terrible in Moscow opened diplomatic and trading relations between England and Russia. This opportunity was welcomed enthusiastically in London, despite Chancellor's unflattering account of Russian life: aside from the imperial palace, Moscow was little more than a jumble of wooden huts, where the inhabitants relieved their miserable existence with endless drinking, and where the dead lay in the frozen streets to be eaten by dogs. Chancellor died in the course of a second voyage in 1556, but he was succeeded as representative of the newly-formed Muscovy Company by Anthony Jenkinson who travelled by sea and land to Moscow in 1557. In the following spring he received the Czar's permission to explore to the south and east, and he journeyed down the Volga to Astrakhan, where the effects of Ivan's conquest were pitifully evident: the once-feared Mongols were suffering from famine, plague and deportation into slavery, and Jenkinson reported that children were being sold for bread. Hoping to reach Cathay, he crossed the Caspian Sea and proceeded to Bukhara where fighting between rival tribes made further progress very unsafe, and he returned to Moscow and England, having negotiated trading privileges, mainly for furs, but also for hemp, tallow and cordage. In 1561 Jenkinson made a second journey to the Caspian, this time reaching Kazvin, the capital of Persia. The commercial results of his exploratory ventures were short-lived, but he published a map in 1562 of 'Russia, Moscovy and Tartary' which was incorporated in Ortelius's great atlas of 1570 and became the standard map of the region for a century or more. It is one of the few Asian maps before the eighteenth century to embody new and authentic geographical data, extending from the White Sea to Tashkent and Bukhara, although its scope is undeniably limited: Jenkinson marks the course of the River Ob and, very inaccurately, the Syr Darya, but he clearly knew of the Ural Mountains and the Aral Sea only through distant reports.

Jenkinson had entered Persia from the north and had returned with enticing merchandise – gems and silks – and the promise of more. During the next half-century a number of Europeans turned their eyes on Persia as the imagined 'Gateway to the East', and succeeded in entering the country

Left: Russia by Anthony Jenkinson, 1570. Jenkinson travelled to Moscow in 1557, and followed the Volga down to the Caspian Sea.
The British Library Maps C.2.c.3.

Right: Persia from Blaeu's Atlas, 1668. Persia was the most accessible Moslem country, receiving European ambassadors, and many European travellers contributed to the high level of geographical data seen here.
The British Library Maps C.5.b.1.

overland or via Ormuz. European interest in Persia was increased when it became known that the Persians were long-standing enemies of the Ottoman Turks, who threatened Christian Europe for centuries. The adventures of Sir Robert Sherley and his brother Anthony from 1599 to 1628 are well-documented, and give a vivid picture of the splendour, the culture and cruelty of the court of Shah Abbas at his new capital in Isfahan. Sir Robert married a Persian princess – they were both painted in Persian costume by van Dyck – and spent many years as an ambassador of the Shah, attempting to form alliances between Persia and European countries against their common enemy Turkey. Persia acquired the reputation of being the most civilized and accessible of the Moslem countries, and attracted many more gentlemen-adventurers, and their narratives provided the high degree of detail found on maps of Persia in the seventeenth century, showing a greater density of place-names than the maps of any other Asian country. European activity in Persia diminished in the eighteenth century due to foreign invasions and civil wars, and the English, the French and the Dutch developed other trading bases further east. It was during the early nineteenth century that European politics caused a re-awakened interest in Persia as the 'Gateway to the East'.

To the Europeans the most enticing and celebrated country in Asia was the Cathay of Marco Polo. But even in the mid-sixteenth century, when contact with Asia had been revolutionized by the opening of the sea-routes, the question remained: Where was Cathay? As early as 1513, the Portuguese, although concentrating their attention on the spice-producing islands, had first visited the estuary of the Pearl River and made contact with the mainland kingdom which came to be called China (the origin of the name is unknown, it is not native Chinese). By 1557 the Portuguese trading settlement at Macao was established, and first Dominican then Jesuit missionaries arrived in the country. The Europeans were struck by the advanced culture of China, presented in Gonzalez de Mendoza's influential book *The History of the Great Kingdom of China*, 1585, and suspected that China was indeed the Cathay described by Marco Polo. The Jesuits, particularly after the founding by Matteo Ricci of their mission in Peking in 1601, gathered a great deal of information about their host country. Ricci and his colleagues are remembered for introducing western geography into China

through their maps and globes, but they were also the chief source of western knowledge of China. A number of maps copied from Chinese originals found their way to Europe in the early years of the seventeenth century, so that the principal rivers, the Chinese provincial names, and of course the position of the Great Wall, became fairly well known. The Dutch and then the British, at Formosa and Amoy respectively, supplanted the Portuguese as traders, but the Jesuits remained more important as mapmakers, culminating in the comprehensive atlas of China compiled by Martino Martini and published by Blaeu in 1655.

Dutch and English attention was directed to India as part of their policy of attacking Spanish-Portuguese monopolies, and the first English ship to pass the Cape of Good Hope and reach the Malay Peninsula – the *Edward Bonaventure* commanded by Captain James Lancaster – did so in 1591, several years before the first Dutch fleet, and it brought back from Java the first cargo of spices shipped direct to England. Several English travellers Thomas Stevens, John Newberry and Ralph Fitch – visited India in the 1580s and 1590s, and their accounts of the country and the spice trade, published by Richard Hakluyt, were influential in the founding of the East India Company in 1600. Fitch saw the capital of the Mogul Emperor at Agra, and subsequently moved on to Bengal. In 1615 the East India Company sent an important mission under Sir Thomas Roe to the Mogul Emperor which secured the position of the Company in India, at the same time as the Dutch determinedly

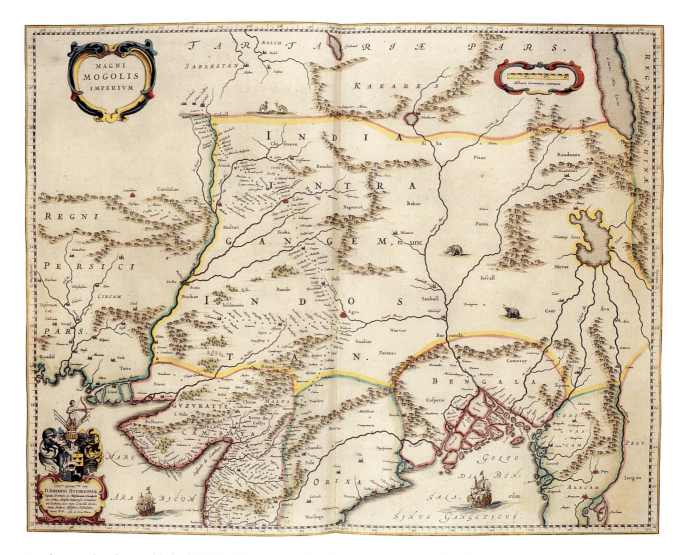

Northern India, first published 1619. This map resulted from the embassy of Sir Thomas Roe to the court of the Great Mogul. It was drawn by William Baffin, the arctic explorer.

The British Library Maps C.5.b.1.

drove the British out of the East Indian islands. These two developments ensured that India and not the Far East became the chief theatre of English activity in Asia. The Portuguese wife of Charles II brought Bombay as part of her dowry, and by the later seventeenth century Calcutta, Madras and Bombay constituted the three bases on which British India was founded. Roe furnished the information for an important early map of central and northern India which was drawn by the Arctic explorer William Baffin, who happened to be on board the ship which carried Roe back to England. The French with their 'Compagnie des Indes' made their slightly later bid for trade and influence in India, and eighteenth-century French cartographers such as D'Anville published increasingly detailed maps of the subcontinent. Throughout most of India, densely settled with towns and villages, exploration was not a physical or logistical problem, although it might often be politically difficult or dangerous, with the multiplicity of local rulers. The great geographical problems lay in the north, in the mountains which connected the subcontinent with Persia, with 'Tartary' and with China.

These same problems had already attracted the first group of western visitors to the Himalayas,

China, 1609. An anonymous manuscript which must have used authentic sources, possibly Jesuit. It shows the fifteen provinces of the Ming Empire, with their principal cities, and the Great Wall.

The British Library Cotton MS Aug.1.ii.45.

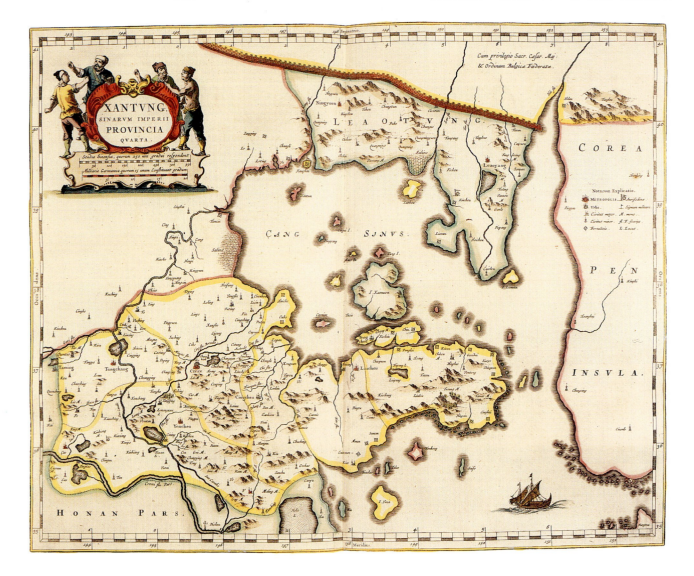

the Jesuit missionaries based in India. Their motive was initially religious, for rumours had reached them of a trans-Himlayan kingdom whose deeply religious culture, with its rituals conducted by unmarried priests, revived medieval ideas of a lost Christian community somewhere in Asia. The first of these remarkable Jesuit explorers was the Portuguese Bento de Goes, who had acted as an ambassador between Goa and the court of the Mogul Emperor, Akbar the Great. Leaving Delhi in 1602, de Goes joined a caravan for Peshawar and Kabul via the Khyber Pass. Crossing the Pamirs to Yarkand he navigated the Taklamakan desert and reached Suchow (in modern Sichuan) where he died after his five-year journey. He was the first European in modern times to enter China from the west, and he had succeeded in communicating by letter with Ricci in Peking with the result that both men were satisfied of the identity of China and Cathay, based on the geography of de Goes's route compared with that of Marco Polo. De Goes failed however to find the lost Christians, and Antonio de Andrade left on a second expedition in 1624 direct to Tibet via the pilgrim route through the Garhwal Mountains to Badrinath. In the small Tibetan town of Tsaparang, Andrade established a mission where other priests later served for many years. Andrade was thus the first European to cross any part of the Himalaya, to see the sacred source of the Ganges, and to encounter Tibetan Buddhism, for this he learned was the country's religion, and not a lost form of Christianity. Between 1626 and

Left: Shantung, published by Blaeu, 1655. One of a series of detailed provincial maps of China compiled by the Jesuit Martino Martini.
The British Library Maps C.5.b.1.

Right: Part of Tibet, by D'Anville, 1737, from Nouvel Atlas de la Chine, showing the Tsangpo River and the region west of Lhasa, based largely on the work of Jesuit missionaries.
The British Library Maps C.1.0c.21.

1630 two more Jesuits, Stephen Cacella and John Cabral, entered Bhutan and Nepal, Cabral becoming the first European to visit Kathmandu. Still more significant was the Himalayan passage from north to south by John Grueber and Albert D'Orville, who travelled from Peking in 1661 to Koko Nor lake, and toiled across the bleak Tibetan plateau, becoming the first Europeans since Friar Odoric in 1330 to enter Lhasa. The great Potala palace had recently been completed, and like all later travellers, the two priests were astonished by its majesty, and equally appalled by the squalor which surrounded them in the streets of Lhasa. D'Orville died in Agra, worn out by his mountain journey. Among subsequent explorations that of Emmanuel Freyre and Ippolito Desideri in 1714 – 1721 was perhaps the most important. They travelled from Srinagar to Leh, traced the headwaters of the Indus near Lake Manasarawar and the sacred mountain Kailas, then followed the Tsangpo-Brahmaputra to Lhasa. The achievements of these Jesuits in the beautiful but daunting terrain of the Himalayas, wild, untravelled and unmapped, commands our amazed admiration. Their avowed missionary intentions may have had short-lived results, but they had recovered the threads of classical geography; they linked India and China by traversing the heartland of Asia; they identified medieval Cathay; and they penetrated the most formidable mountain range in the world. They were not equipped to map the region, but their narratives were studied especially by French cartographers and helped to improve

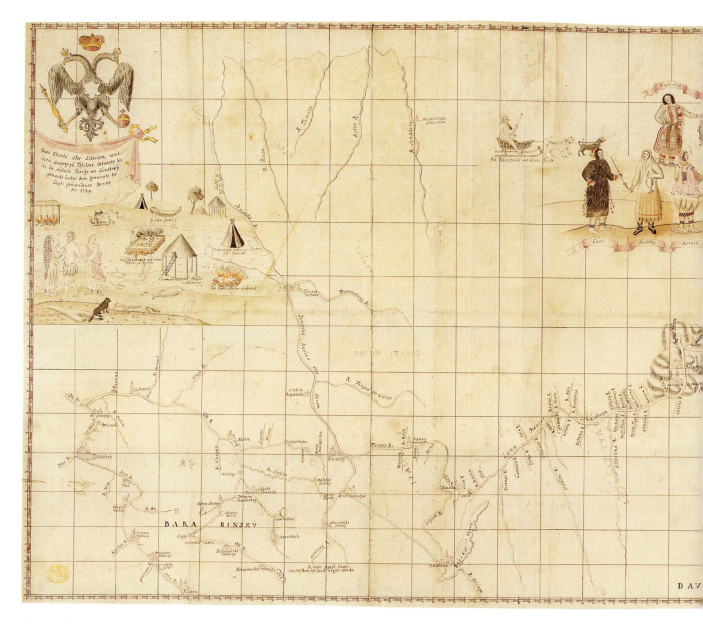

Siberia, drawn to record Vitus Bering's expedition of 1725–29. Bering followed the rivers Yenisei and Lena, crossed the Sea of Okhotsk and Kamchatka Peninsula, here mapped for the first time.

The British Library K.Top.114.43.1.

the map of central Asia. The mature mapping of India and its northern neighbours belonged to the new era of scientific surveying that came with the British imperial age.

In the later eighteenth century the British, entrenched in India, sought to discover more about their Himalayan neighbours. Emissaries such as George Bogle, Thomas Manning and Samuel Turner (a cousin of Warren Hastings) entered Tibet, Bhutan and Nepal, while slightly later William Moorcroft and John Wood explored Ladakh, the Hindu Kush and the Pamirs. These men brought back colourful accounts of their adventures, and it was in this period that the glamour, the fascination, almost the myth of Tibet and Central Asia took its hold on the European imagination, enticing scores of travellers with varying motives to undertake their 'golden journey to Samarkand', to Lhasa

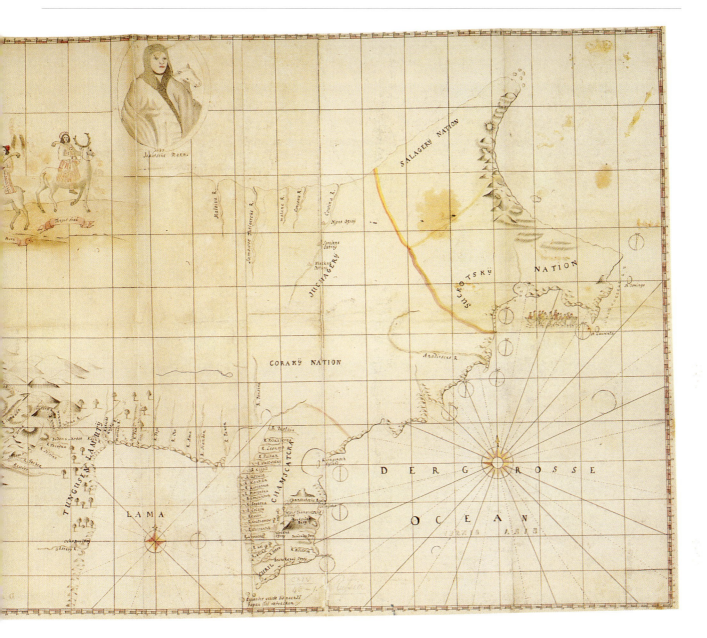

or elsewhere. The mountains and the desert appealed to something in the romantic imagination of the nineteenth century, as the imagined Eden of the Pacific had appealed to the rationalism of the eighteenth. Central Asia was of course the reverse of paradise: bleak, uninhabited, barely endurable, it offered an existential solitude for restless Europeans. Amongst others the Swedish explorer, Sven Hedin, promoted in his books this mystical sense of central Asian travel. This glamour was only heightened by the political dangers, for not merely individual travellers were likely to meet a violent death, but even European armies found themselves vulnerable, as in the case of the defeat and massacre of the British army in Afghanistan in 1842. Moreover by 1820 the Tibetan authorities had become alarmed at the interest the European powers were showing in their country, and sealed their borders to foreigners, a policy which merely intensified Tibet's mystique as a forbidden land. After repelling such determined individuals as Przhevalski and Hedin, this isolation was decisively broken by the British military mission in 1903–4, commanded by Younghusband, an invasion in all but

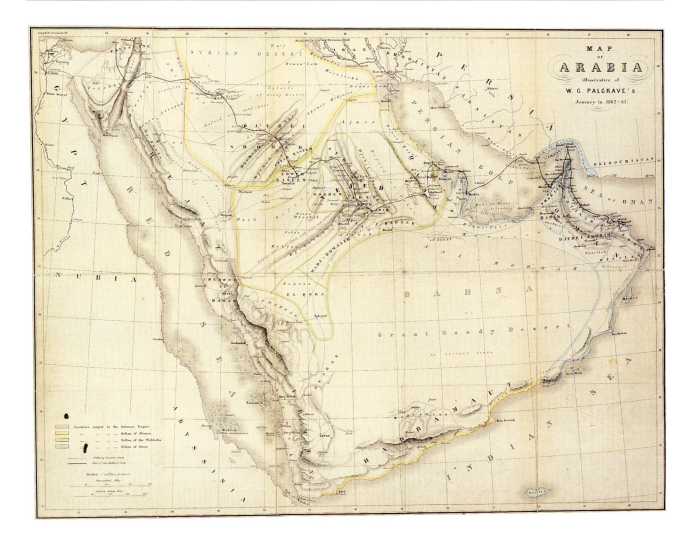

Arabia, by William Palgrave, the result of his journey in 1862–63, the first documented west-east crossing of the Arabian Peninsula.

The British Library 10077.dd.21.

name, bringing Tibet into the realm of international politics, with ultimately tragic consequences for her people.

The most consistent force in Asian exploration however had come from Russia, and it occured in several phases. In the sixteenth century, pioneering fur traders began to venture beyond the Ural Mountains into the unknown wasteland of Siberia. The most important single event was the invasion in 1579 by a party of Cossacks of the Mongol-held territory east of the Urals. Led by Yermak Timofeiev, they fought as mercenaries for Russian merchants, but victories over the Mongols and the native Samoyed inhabitants were given the blessing of the Czar, and Siberia was annexed to Russia. Travelling mainly via the great rivers – the Ob, the Yenisei, and the Lena – fur traders moved steadily east, and by 1638 Russians were on the shores of the Sea of Okhotsk facing the Pacific Ocean. Vasili Poyarkov explored the Amur River marking the border between Russia and China, while another Cossack, Semeon Dezhnev is thought to have descended the Kolyma River in 1648 and rounded the East Cape, the extreme easterly point of Asia, eighty years before Bering's expedition. These adventures are ill-documented, but the few records suggest that these pioneers were rapacious and bloodthirsty, their approach to the native peoples being similar to that of the Spanish conquistadors, and just as American gold enriched Spain, so Siberian furs poured into Moscow. The first systematic map-surveys of Siberia were conducted by Semyon Remezov early in the eighteenth century, and the French cartographers Joseph and Louis Delisle were later invited to expand and improve the work.

It was Czar Peter the Great who desired a more exact knowledge of his eastern territories, and in 1734 he initiated the Great Northern Expedition in which parties of Russian officers explored, surveyed and mapped the plateaux, river system and coasts of Siberia. Russian expansion into Asia continued during the eighteenth and still more the nineteenth century, as territories were acquired by conquest or diplomacy from Turkey and Persia in the Black Sea and Caucasus region, and independent tribal lands in Kirghizia and Turkestan were annexed. It was in this phase that Russian imperialism came into conflict with British, and the so-called 'Great Game' developed as soldiers, envoys, scientists and spies criss-crossed Persia, Afghanistan, the Himalayas, the Tibetan plateau, the Tien Shan mountains and the Taklamakan desert. It was Lord Curzon who remarked that 'Frontiers are the razor's edge on which hang suspended the issue of war or peace and the life of nations', and the location of frontiers was a vital problem in this forbidding terrain. The exploration and mapping of this huge expanse of hostile terrain suffers from problem of definition: significant places may have been 'discovered' and marked on a seventeenth century map – as Tashkent, Lop Nor, or Lhasa were – but the scale, positioning and topography of such maps were all totally inadequate for the purposes of the nineteenth century soldier or scientist, so a new generation of maps was called into being, drawn from a very different standard of reconnaissance. Russian scientists such as Peter Semyonov, through his carefully-planned journey of 1856–57, effectively added the Tien Shan to the map of Russia, while the Survey of India began in the 1850s the process of surveying the Himalayas which revealed their stature as the greatest mountains in the world, but which was still far from complete when the first serious climbers arrived in the mountains in the 1920s. Far smaller than the Russian or British presences in Asia, the French colony in Cochin China made a significant attempt to explore the interior through the Mekong Expedition of 1866–68. Hopes that the river would provide a practical means of access to China and Central Asia were dashed, but Doudart de Lagrée and Francis Garnier worked upstream from the plains of Cambodia for almost 2,000 miles into the mountains of Yunnan, en route revealing to Europeans the great temple complex of Angkor.

Like Central Asia, Arabia was a place where politics and romanticism met and drew European visitors in search of the exotic, the dangerous, the un-European. Certain journeys and narratives stand out as landmarks because they were unique in their time, but they were isolated, unrepeated adventures, and their significance often lay in the field of literature, or cultural and anthropological studies, rather than in strict geography. They opened up no lines of communication, indeed they led, not infrequently, to the death of the explorer. One of the earliest in modern times was a Danish expedition to the Yemen in 1764–64, whose sole survivor and narrator was Carsten Niebuhr. His observant, scholarly report initiated the modern tradition of descriptive writing about Arabia. Egypt and Palestine of course attracted a growing number of historians and archaeologists, but the main part of the Arabian Peninsula remained unvisited and unmapped. Scholars such as the German Ulrich Seetzen in 1809–11 and the Swiss J. L. Burkhardt in 1815–13 explored the *Hejaz* – the western coastal plain of Arabia – and visited Mecca. It was Burkhardt who was the first European to see the great ruins of Petra in Jordan. The first documented crossing of the desert was made by an English Jesuit, William Palgrave in 1862–3, who travelled from Jordan over the An Nafud desert to the Persian Gulf, and published a significant new map of the region. The celebrated Arabian travels of Sir Richard Burton were surprisingly limited in scope, concentrated entirely in Mecca and Medina. Far more extensive were the journeys of the other English author indelibly associated with Arabia, C. M. Doughty, who spent the two years 1876–78 exploring the great central desert, the *Najd*. The context of travel in Arabia was transformed by a series of political events: the British occupation of

Aden from 1839, the engineering of the Suez Canal in the 1860s, the steady decay of Ottoman power, and the events which followed from World War One. Yet the parched expanse of the *Rub'al Khali*, the infamous Empty Quarter, remained unexplored by Europeans until the 1930s.

Europe's relationship with Asia was older and more complex than with any other continent. Although geographically continuous with Europe, its vast extent and the diversity of its peoples permitted only a slow, intermittent process of exploration spread over centuries. This process was on the whole less mercenary than exploration in other regions: Europeans were fascinated by the 'otherness' of the Asian landscape and its civilizations, and over five centuries or more a literary tradition developed which drew fresh travellers into the encounter with Asia, although permanent European settlement was long-delayed. No single river crosses more than a quarter of the continent, one entire coast is virtually walled by ice, and its heartland contains the most inhospitable desert-mountain complex in the world. In these circumstances the mapping of Asia awaited the nineteenth-century demands of science and imperialism before attaining any degree of completeness.

NORTH AMERICA

'America is a vast conspiracy to make you happy' may be a twentieth-century joke, yet it has strikingly deep historical roots, for it might have been written to evoke the early European vision of North America: a new-found land, immense, fertile, apparently risen from the sea, and undefended. This last point was crucial: its people were 'naked' – meaning uncivilized; they were not numerous (there were perhaps one million people in the whole continent in the year 1600); those first encountered on the eastern seaboard had no cities and no science; they did not farm or mine their land in any systematic way; and they lived in fragmented tribes without unity or statehood. For Europeans to explore, settle and master this land seemed to them so natural that the morality of the process was never questioned. North American exploration, in contrast to that of Asia, was inspired from the outset by this innate sense of territorial freedom. But at the same time it was shaped by a number of specific motives. The earliest was that enduring quest, an access to the western sea which must lead to China, for, as Richard Hakluyt wrote, 'The Northwest passage to Cathay and China may . . . be searched out as well by river and overland as by sea.' The English American colonies were conceived partly as bases from which the western coast of the continent and hence this western sea might be reached, but the land soon revealed attractions of its own. In 1602 Bartholomew Gosnold made the first direct voyage from England to Massachusetts Bay, discovered the rich fishing grounds there, traded with the Indians, and first noted the hook-shaped peninsula of Cape Cod, which was to become such a landmark on maps of the east coast. After the failure of the earliest colonies (see chapter three), Virginia was successfully settled in 1607, Massachusetts in 1620, New Hampshire and part of Maine in 1622, Maryland in 1632, Connecticut in 1635, Rhode Island in 1636. In 1622 the Dutch founded New Amsterdam – later New York – and two years later New Netherland on the Hudson River, and in 1638 a group of Swedish emigrants settled on the Delaware. The English colonies were authorized by royal charters, which also encouraged them expand 'Into the land throughout from sea to sea west and north-west'. As the colonists probed inland they heard many Indian reports of a 'great water beyond the mountains', but the Appalachians, rugged, complex, and densely-wooded, presented for many years an impenetrable barrier to expansion. The rivers and bays of New England were explored and charted, and in time the majority of colonists forgot the dreams of Cathay, and discovered that the edge of America had become the centre of their world and they desired to go no further.

A clearer path to the interior of the continent lay to the north via the St. Lawrence River, explored so much earlier by Cartier. After Cartier's voyages, French political interest in North America had waned, but her fishermen regularly visited the waters of Newfoundland, and from this

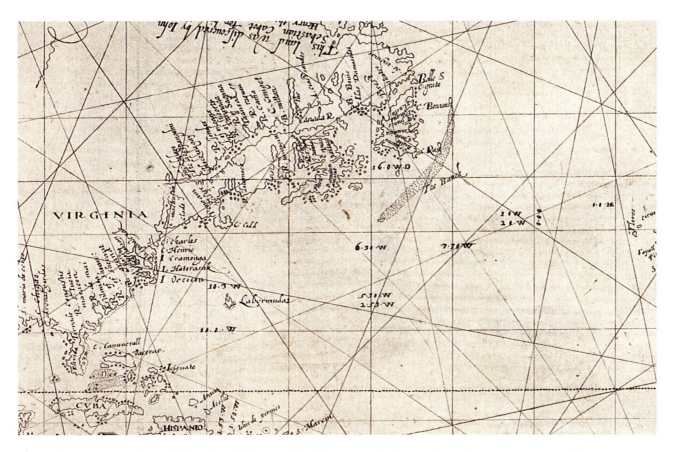

Cape Cod, from the Wright-Kipp World Map, 1610. The distinctive hook of the Cape was first noted by Bartholomew Gosnold during his voyage of 1602 exploring the fishing-banks.

Bodleian Library

trade grew another potentially richer still – that in furs. By the 1590s French traders were bartering with the Huron and the Iroquois for pelts to ship back to Paris, and the French crown conceived the policy of granting monopolies in the St. Lawrence region to entrepreneurs who would settle colonies in New France. It was on such an expedition that the outstanding figure of Samuel Champlain first arrived in Canada in 1603. Already an accomplished mapmaker, Champlain made a number of pioneering journeys up the St. Lawrence, the Ottawa and the Richelieu Rivers; he reached Lake Huron and Lake Ontario and, of course Lake Champlain; he founded Quebec in 1608, and the settlement of Place Royale on the site named by Cartier Mont-Royal, the future Montreal. Wounded in 1615, Champlain himself ceased active exploration, but instead commissioned others to continue his work. One of them, Etienne Brulé explored southward from Lake Ontario in 1616, descending the Susquenhanna River to Chesapeake Bay, and some years later in 1622 he reached Lake Superior. Another, Jean Nicolet, crossed Lake Huron and Lake Wisconsin in 1634. The hope that the rivers of New France would finally lead to the western sea and to China was entertained by Champlain and his disciples, and it is a familiar story that Nicolet donned Chinese robes when he landed on the western shore of Lake Michigan, in anticipation of meeting the people of Asia; however he could scarcely have believed that the freshwater lake, large as it was, was the Pacific Ocean. He was unable to report his findings to Champlain when he returned to Quebec, for the latter had died in 1635, but not before he had embodied his discoveries in a series of important maps between 1612 and 1632, in which the Great Lakes took shape for the first time.

Above: Canada by Samuel Champlain, 1632. Champlain explored the St. Lawrence and reached Lakes Ontario and Huron, but what he heard of the other lakes was plainly confused. South of the St. Lawrence he penetrated to Lake Champlain and the Hudson valley.

The British Library 981.d.21.

Right: The Mississippi, 1697, from Louis Hennepin's narrative. There is some uncertainty about the routes of La Salle, Joliet and Hennepin in this region. By 1684 however, these explorers had claimed a vast new empire for France.

The British Library Maps 69917(2).

These journeys and these discoveries would have been impossible without the cooperation of Indian guides. The relationship of the Europeans with the Indians remained highly ambivalent, both in New France and in the English colonies. The Europeans brought certain goods and skills which the Indians envied, and for which they were prepared to assist the newcomers. They brought other gifts from Europe – diseases, alcohol, firearms – which would weaken and destroy the Indian culture. The Indians in turn possessed knowledge and skills without which the colonists and traders could scarcely hope to expand and prosper: an uneasy alliance was thus formed, which might at any time break down into conflict.

In 1659 two French hunter-guides named Groseillers and Radisson reported descending a river west of Lake Michigan – the Wisconsin River – until it reached a junction with a 'Great River' flowing south: it is difficult to be certain, but they may have been the first Europeans since de Soto to see the Mississippi. As so often, courageous Jesuits followed the explorers, and the missions established in the 1660s in the area between Lake Superior and Lake Michigan were to be important bases for further advances. In a crucial journey in 1673 the Jesuit Father Marquette, accompanied by Louis Joliet, re-discovered the Wisconsin-Mississippi link and followed the great river for a thousand miles,

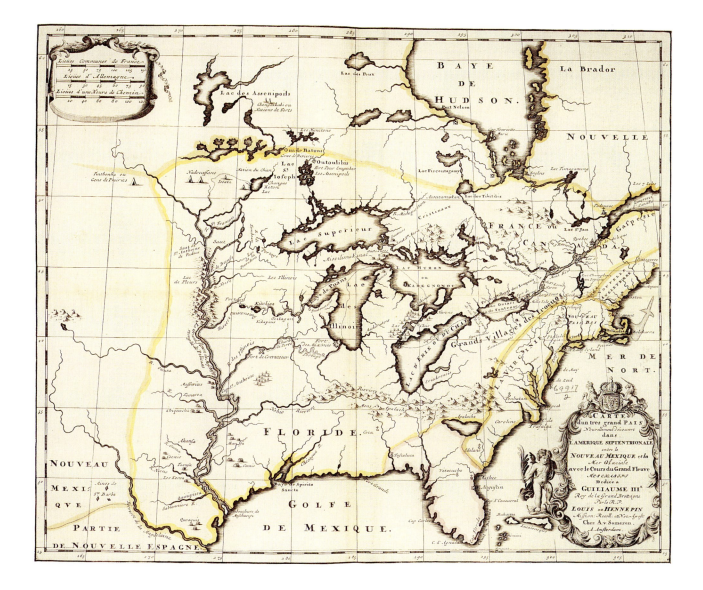

down to its junction with the Arkansas River, returning via the Illinois River to Lake Michigan. In 1681–2 Robert de La Salle retraced this route from north to south, this time following the 'Great River' to its delta on the Gulf of Mexico. Near the river mouth La Salle formally took possession of the vast tract of territory between the Great Lakes and the Gulf of Mexico, naming it Louisiana, for the French king.

La Salle had earlier discovered the Ohio River during an expedition in 1669 with Iroquois guides, although it is uncertain whether he followed it to the confluence with the Mississippi. It was La Salle's party who had been the first Europeans to sight Niagara Falls in 1678, an event fully described in the narrative of the Jesuit Louis Hennepin, published in Europe in 1697. La Salle had conceived a grandiose plan to link the St. Lawrence artery with the interior via a sailing fleet on the Great Lakes, recognizing that portage around the Niagara Falls would be necessary. With enormous effort he had a sixty-ton ship built on Lake Erie above the Falls, which became the first sailing ship to cruise the Great Lakes, crossing Lakes Erie, Huron and Michigan, piling up a rich cargo of traded pelts. La Salle ordered the ship back to the falls, while he prepared for his Mississippi Journey, but the ship vanished somewhere on its return voyage, and no trace of it was ever found. The final chapter in

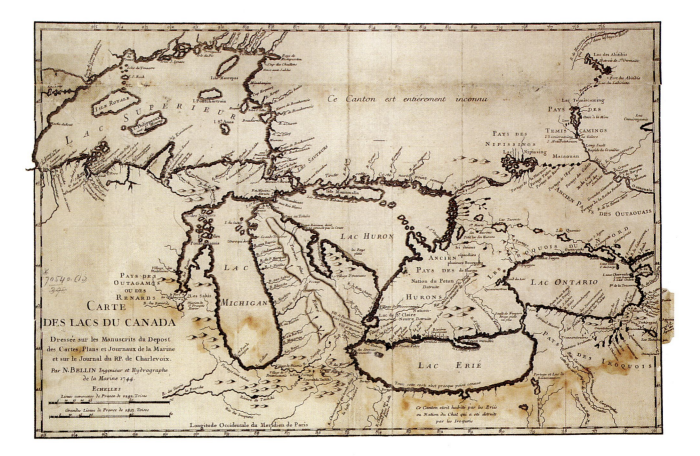

The Great Lakes, 1744, by Jacques Bellin. Prepared with the aid of the Jesuit explorer Pierre de Charlevoix, this map at last established the true configuration of the Great Lakes.

The British Library Maps 70540(1).

La Salle's career came in 1684–87, when he sailed from France for the Gulf of Mexico intending to found a French colony at the mouth of the Mississippi. Not surprisingly, the coast looked totally unfamiliar from seaward, and he failed to find the delta. The party landed and made repeated fruitless attempts to locate the Great River overland, until the despairing crew mutinied, and La Salle, whose courage and achievements deserved a better fate, was murdered in a marshy wilderness near the Brazos River in Texas.

The French explorers between 1603 and 1682 had opened a vast tract of country, and had demonstrated that an even vaster one still lay hidden, for it was plain that the major rivers Arkansas, Missouri and Mississippi must drain a huge, probably mountainous region to the west. All hopes that the Pacific was just over the horizon were fading, and the true extent of North America was beginning to be understood. The French hold on this great region existed in name only, and European rivalries would inevitably threaten it. The French had made two principal errors which would cost them dearly in North America. The first was to incur the hostility of the powerful Iroquois, which Champlain had done as early as 1609 in a battle in which he had sided with the Huron; this event was to reverberate down the years, causing the Iroquois to ally themselves with the British in the struggle which ultimately lost Canada for the French. The second was to neglect the northern regions around Hudson Bay, permitting the British Hudson's Bay Company to thrive, ironically guided in the first instance by French trappers. In the Anglo-French hostilities of the eighteenth

New England, manuscript chart c.1680. The mapping of coasts is strikingly accurate, but inland the rivers and lakes are more difficult to identify.

The British Library Add. MS 5414, f.21.

century, it was inevitable that the French stronghold of the St. Lawrence – Great Lakes region would be caught in a pincer between the British in the north and those in the south.

Meanwhile on the eastern coast the British settlers had not ceased their steady, persistent probing of the Appalachians. Although lacking landmark discoveries comparable with those of Champlain or La Salle, explorers ascended a dozen major rivers from Georgia to Maine, seeking the watershed which would lead them to the western coast. In 1699 John Lederer reached the summit of the Blue Ridge Mountain, and thought he saw the Atlantic Ocean from the top. One of the most significant achievements was that of Gabriel Arthur, who in 1674 passed the Cumberland Gap and descended to the Ohio Valley – the route that later became legendary among westward migrants – and some years later followed the Alabama River to the Gulf of Mexico. South Carolina traders now ventured across the mountains to the territories of the Creek and the Cherokee, and in 1698 Thomas Welch of Charleston became the first known Englishman to cross the Mississippi. In 1664 the British had seized New Amsterdam from the Dutch, thus inheriting the Hudson River trade centred in Albany, and widening their power-base. For the next hundred years a complex three-way conflict was maintained in eastern North America between the British, the French and the Indians, in which exploration was a function of the search for commercial and political advantage, a search which culminated in the Seven Years War of 1756–73, known to American history more precisely as the French and Indian War. Before that crisis, the French did attempt to outflank the Hudson's Bay traders by pushing north-west from the Great Lakes. Between 1731 and 1749 Sieur de La Vérendrye and his three sons reached Lake Winnipeg, the Saskatchewan River and the upper waters of the Missouri, yet despite persistent rumours of western seas and westward-flowing rivers, the completion of the map to the Pacific coast seemed to remain perpetually out of reach.

The British fur trading companies responded by sending out agents in a determined attempt to unravel the mysteries of the north-west. In 1770 Samuel Hearne of the Hudson's Bay Company left Churchill and crossed one thousand miles of unexplored territory before striking the Coppermine River, which he followed to its mouth, thus becoming the first European to reach the Arctic Ocean overland. En route Hearne discovered a major lake, which he called 'Athapuscow' but which was almost certainly the Great Slave Lake. Others returned to this region, the most celebrated being Alexander

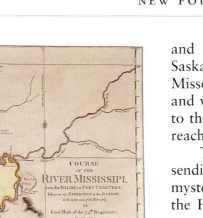

Left: The Mississippi 1775, by John Ross. The last and most detailed British survey of the river, made after the region was taken from the French and shortly before the War of Independence commenced.

The British Library Maps 1.Tab.44.

Right: Spanish North America, a manuscript map by Mascaro, 1782. The Spanish sought to forestall British expansion in the continent by planting settlements beyond Mexico, as far as Northern California, and exploring inland to the Great Salt Lake.

The British Library Add. MS 17652.a.

Below: The mouth of the James River, by Robert Tindall 1608. The colonists dispatched by the Virginia Company of London established their settlement, Jamestown, about 60 miles up river.

The British Library Cotton MS Aug.1.ii.46.

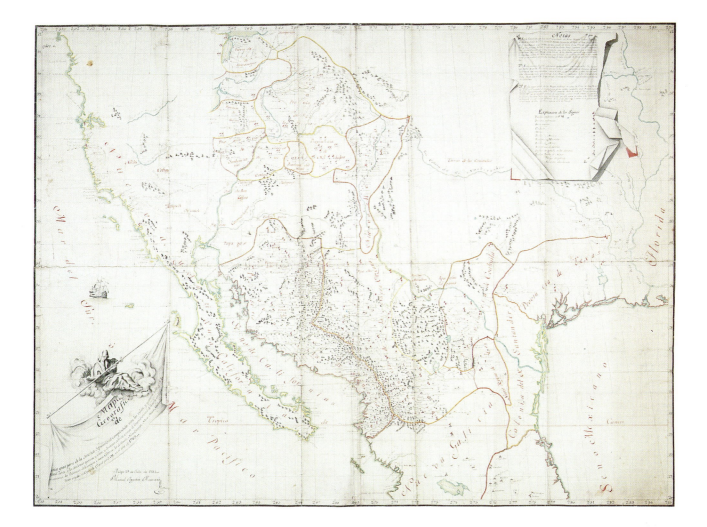

Mackenzie who was employed by the rival North West Company. In 1789 Mackenzie made his historic river journey of 2,000 miles from the Great Slave Lake down the river which bears his name to the Beaufort Sea, having a rugged mountain range always to his west. Ironically he referred to this waterway as the 'River of Disappointment' because it had failed to lead him to the Pacific. In 1792 he made his second historic river-journey from Lake Athabasca via the Peace River, crossing the Rockies near the modern Prince George, and reaching the Pacific coast at Dean Channel. Mackenzie was the first European to cross the Rockies and to cross America north of Mexico. Hearne and Mackenzie had demonstrated that a strait or river linking the Hudson Bay region with the Pacific was geographically impossible. The maritime surveys of Captain Vancouver during 1792–95 of the complex coastline between latitudes 45 and 60 degrees north confirmed the absence of any seaway to the American interior: a three hundred year old mirage was finally dispelled. Curiously, MacKenzie arrived at Dean Channel just six weeks after Vancouver had coasted by the same spot, and inscribed on a rock the words 'Alexander Mackenzie from Canada by land, the twenty-second of July 1793.'

Britain and France were not the only European nations involved in exploring the continent. Spain, the oldest colonial power, sought to consolidate her position in Mexico by expanding into Texas, Arizona and California. Spain was always interested not merely in trade but in the occupation and Christianization of her subject territories. This task was always partly military and partly missionary, and it fell to Jesuits, Franciscans and Dominicans to extend Spanish power in North

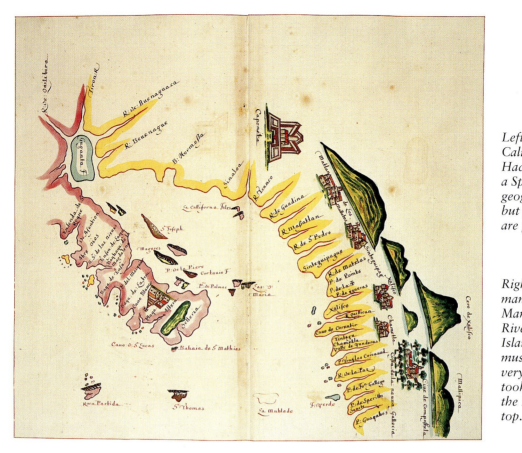

Left: The Gulf of California by William Hack, 1682, copied from a Spanish chart. The geography is unmistakable, but few of the place-names are familiar.
The British Library Harley 4034 Map p.3.

Right: An anonymous manuscript chart of Manhattan, the Hudson River and part of Long Island, c.1665. This map must have been drawn very soon after the English took the settlement from the Dutch. East is at the top.
The British Library Add. MS 16371.K.

America. The most significant individual was the Jesuit Father Eusebio Kino, who between 1687 and 1711 founded missions in Sonora, explored the Gila and Colorado Rivers, initiated the settlement of Baja California, and finally established that California was a peninsula, demolishing the one hundred year old myth of its insularity. The Spanish were alarmed by the British settlement of Georgia in 1733, which they considered part of Spanish Florida, and in response a major expedition was sent across the Rio Grande to found towns and missions in southern Texas. After the conclusion of the French and Indian War, the British Empire in North America had doubled, while France ceded to Spain control of all territory west of Mississippi. In the 1760s and 1770s Spain maintained her policy of defensive expansion, sending missionaries and settlers north into California to found Los Angeles, Santa Barbara, Monterey and San Francisco, and to penetrate inland as far as the Great Salt Lake. At the same time seaborne expeditions explored the coast much further north than their compatriots of the sixteenth century had done. In 1775 Juan de Ayala first entered the Golden Gate, and Bruno de Hezeta reached the mouth of the Columbia River, and passed on to Vancouver Island. However the links between the Spanish settlements and Mexico were tenuous, and they were left to develop alone; ultimately they were unable to resist encroachments from the east.

The fourth colonial power, and one which provoked an alarmed reaction from the others was, perhaps surprisingly, Russia. Following the voyages of Bering and Chirikov around the Alaskan coast in 1741, a Russian-American Fur Company was established to import pelts from the unclaimed territory of America's far north-west. The first base was on Kodiak Island from 1783, and in 1799 New Archangel (the modern Sitka) was founded by Alexander Baranov, the first governor of Alaska. Destroyed by Tlingit Indians three years later, it was rebuilt and became 'The St. Petersburg of the

Pacific', with shipyards, workshops, churches and an observatory. From here Russian trappers and traders ventured as far south as California, and by the 1820s Russia was claiming as her own the territory down to the northern point of Vancouver Island.

The last quarter of the eighteenth century saw political upheavals in America which completely transformed the context of exploration. American independence freed the former colonists of all the restrictions on movement and trade imposed from Britain, and settlers streamed in their thousands through the Appalachians into Tennessee, Kentucky and Ohio. Freedom to use the Mississippi and its tributaries were crucial to these new communities, and the United States government was deeply alarmed when, in 1800, Napoleon induced King Charles IV of Spain to return all Louisiana including the strategic port of New Orleans to France. Napoleonic plans for dominance were as unwelcome to Americans as they were to Europeans, and several years of diplomacy followed, as well as several serious reversals for Napoleon, before the celebrated Louisiana Purchase of 1803 was accomplished. It was the largest land-purchase in history, and by its terms a vast territory west of the Mississippi was acquired by the United States; but precisely what had been acquired remained unknown. On the political level, boundaries must be agreed with Spain to the south-west, and with Britain to the north; on the geographical level almost a million square miles of land were waiting in which no American or European had ever travelled. It was the single most important geographical challenge in American history, the challenge to which the achievements of Cartier, Champlain, La Salle and Mackenzie had unconsciously been leading.

President Thomas Jefferson immediately initiated an expedition to ascend the Missouri River to its mountain headwaters, and to attempt the crossing of the watershed to the Pacific coast. It was led by Meriwether Lewis and William Clark, both soldiers with a good scientific background and proven survival skills. In May 1804 they left St. Louis with a large keelboat, and in a matter of weeks they had passed the final European settlements and entered the unknown territory of the Great Plains.

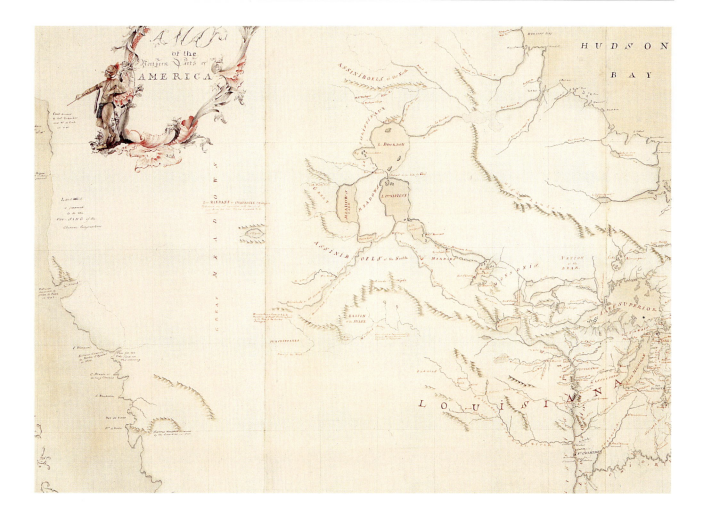

After several tense but bloodless encounters with Sioux Indians, they made winter camp at Mandan, in modern North Dakota, where they were joined by a French fur-trader and his wife, a Shoshone Indian named Sacagawea, whose presence was to prove vital to the success of the expedition. Years earlier she had been captured by an enemy tribe, and her reunion with her people in the Bitterroot Mountains ensured the friendship of the Shoshone towards the explorers. In spring 1805 the expedition resumed its journey, taking to canoes near the junction with the Yellowstone River, and making an arduous portage around the Great Falls of the Missouri. They now entered the high mountains of present-day Montana and Idaho, the first white men to do so, and the month of September was spent threading, with Indian help, the passes which would lead west to the coast. Via the Snake River they entered the Columbia River, which they descended to its mouth, arriving on November 19 at the Pacific coast. Here they wintered before commencing the six-month return journey to St. Louis. They had travelled 7,600 miles, most of it across unexplored country, bringing back maps, journals, specimens and data from this huge new territory, and their encounters with Indians had been amicable. The outstanding geographical feature of North America – the Rocky Mountains – had been revealed in detail for the first time, three centuries after Europeans first landed in the continent. They had not found an easy route to the Pacific coast, for none existed, and they had not completed the map of North America; but they had taken the vital step which would lead to its completion, and the Great Plains, the Rocky Mountains and the Pacific coast now beckoned a stream of explorers and settlers.

The subsequent opening of the American west belongs to the social and economic history of the

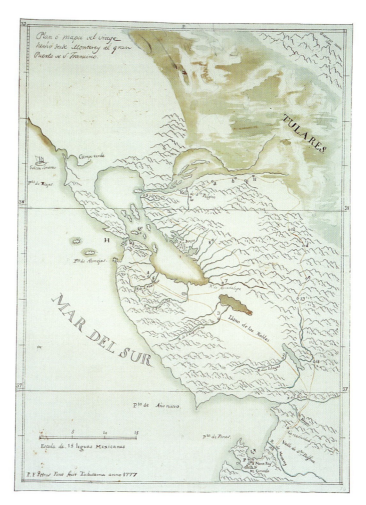

Left: Northern North America, c.1759. This fine manuscript map displays the vast empty space that awaited exploration west of the Mississippi.

The British Library K.Top.CXIX.7–2.

Right: San Francisco Bay, 1777, by Pedro Font. A chart recording Juan de Ayala's reconnaissance of the Golden Gate during his voyage from Monterey in 1775.

The British Library Add. MS 17651, f.9.

United States rather than to the history of exploration. As Europeans arrived on the east coast in their thousands, landhunger drove thousands more to the west, and the identity of the United States was transformed. The great losers were the Indians, the dispossessed victims of a historical process beyond anyone's control. There was now no longer any ambivalence in their relations with the white men, but by the time the Indians understood that they were enemies, they were already defeated.

From the first European landings in North America outside New Spain – those of Cartier in the 1530s – the great motive had been to penetrate from the eastern seaboard to western coasts. As always, the problem of longitude was all-important, for the true extent of the continent lay hidden for two centuries. But while explorers were vainly seeking routes to the west, a new nation was taking shape in the east, and it was political and demographic pressures in the nineteenth century which would reveal the true geography of North America. The exploration of the continent was not a search for scientific knowledge, or for the experience of the exotic: it was a function of the migration of Europeans across the continent, in the course of which a new nation was formed, and an ancient culture died.

Western North America by William Clark, 1810, recording Lewis and Clark's historic crossing of the continent from Missouri through the Rockies to the mouth of the Columbia River.

Beinecke Rare Book and Manuscript Library, Yale University

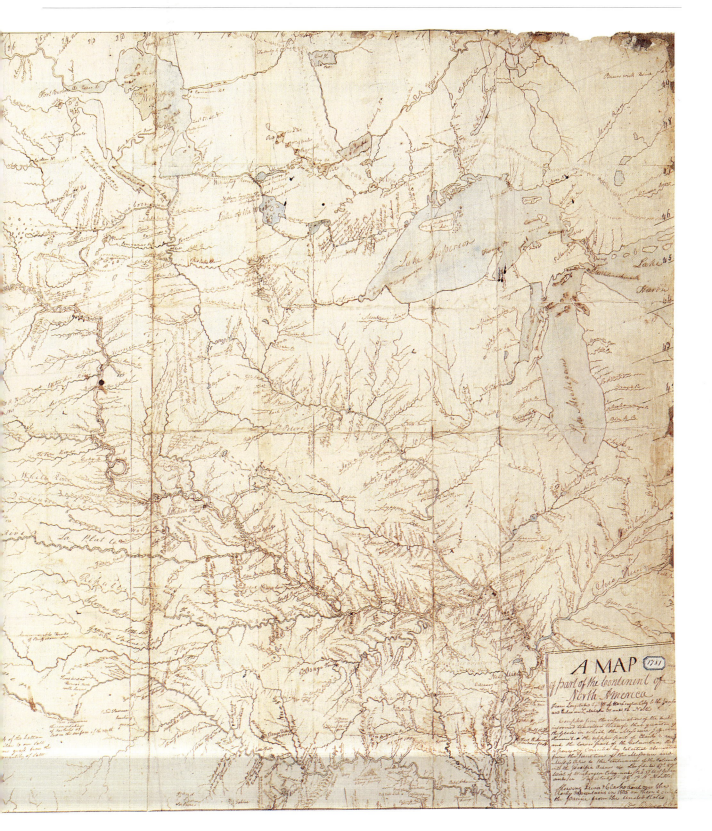

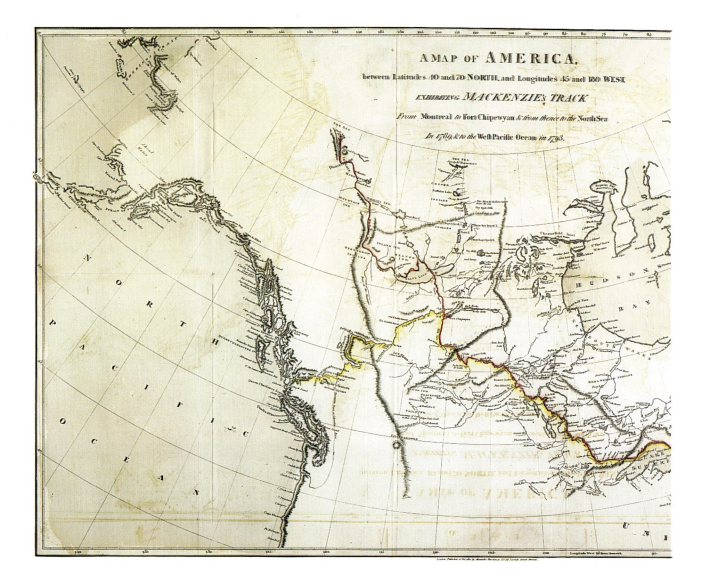

SOUTH AMERICA

If the exploration of North America was the product of gradual colonization, that of South America was accomplished by conquest, swift, ruthless and complete. Both the terrain and the climate were more hostile to Europeans than those of North America, but this apparently did not deter the Spanish conquistadors. To their military, crusading minds topography, natural science, ancient civilizations held no interest unless they could be subdued and exploited, as they sought other Mexicos in which they could cut their way to gold and glory. The indigenous peoples were merely part of the local flora and fauna; in Vespucci's words 'They have no law and no creed, they live in accordance with nature'.

The continent's eastern coast was touched by Columbus, Cabral, Vespucci and Magellan prior to 1520, but the modern history of South America began in 1531 when Francisco Pizarro landed in Peru with the avowed aim of conquering 'New Castile', which he accomplished in three short years. From Peru, the Spanish fanned swiftly outwards, notwithstanding the difficult terrain. As early as 1533 a force under Sebastian de Benalcazar moved north to seize present-day Ecuador, pressing on into western Colombia, reaching the valley of the River Magdalena in 1536 where he heard the

Right: Oregon and Upper California, 1845, by John Frémont. Frémont was an army engineer who surveyed these mountainous regions with the help of Indians and trappers. His map became vital for settlement and railroad-building in the west.

The British Library Maps 72321(3).

Left: North-Western Canada by Alexander McKenzie, 1801. McKenzie's two historic river journeys in 1789 and 1793, were the first recorded crossings of Canada, first to the Beaufort Sea and then to the Pacific.

Hydrographic Office, Taunton

earliest rumours of El Dorado. On the northern coast of Colombia colonies had been established at Santa Marta in 1525 and Cartagena in 1532, the latter becoming one of the great maritime centres of Spanish America. In 1537–8 Gonzalo de Quesada ascended the Magdalena valley from the north, subdued the Chibcha Indians with vicious efficiency, and founded Santa Fé de Bogota as the head-quarters of the province of 'New Grenada'.

South of Peru, Chile was invaded, first by Pizarro's lieutenant Diego de Almagro in 1535, who made a harrowing first crossing of the Andes into Bolivia, which cost the lives of hundreds of Spaniards – with little result, for Almagro hastened back to help crush the revolt in Peru. More decisively Pedro de Valdivia led a new force into Chile in 1540. Valparaiso and Santiago were founded, but fierce resistance by the Araucanian Indians limited Spanish progress for many years to the Biobio River, near the modern Concepcion. Valdivia conceived a grandiose plan to push the Spanish dominion south to the Straits of Magellan, but he was killed before it could be fulfilled. In 1545 the celebrated silver mines at Potosi in the Bolivian Andes were discovered and acted as a magnet for the Spanish, so that Potosi became the greatest single source of wealth in South America. The speed of the Spanish advance was astonishing: in little more than a decade they had swept through the western half of the continent in a series of military campaigns, in which geography was disregarded, and native cultures all but extinguished. It was an assault on the environment which

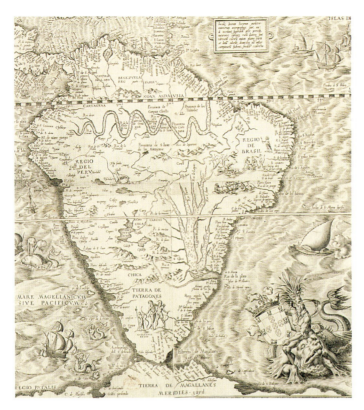

South America, 1562, by Diego Gutierrez. The coasts are complete, with the Amazon and Rio Plata strongly but inaccurately marked; the Orinoco is unexplored, but after only four decades of European settlement, the map is remarkably finished.

The British Library Maps 68910.

belongs only incidentally within the history of exploration. In 1560 when the governor of Peru, Don Hurtado de Mendoza sponsored a new expedition into the Amazon, he frankly recorded that his reason was 'to relieve the Provinces of Peru of much corrupt blood, by sending forth many idle men who might otherwise cause fresh insurrection.'

Geographically, the most important of these early expeditions from Peru was that of Francisco de Orellana in 1541–2. In human terms, Orellana's is probably the most compelling narrative from the entire conquistador period, for the simple reason that this time it was the Europeans who suffered so desperately, and who needed all their powers of endurance as they battled with a savage environment. The avowed motive for the expedition was to search for forests of cinnamon trees reported to lie east of the Ecuadorian Andes, and it was Pizarro's own brother Gonzalo who led the force of some 220 Spaniards, and a large number of Indian slaves. Orellana was second-in-command, but it was he who was to achieve the greatest fame. Leaving Quito in February 1541, the force made a punishing winter crossing of the snow-covered Andes close to the great volcano of Cotopaxi. Passing the watershed of the mountains, they reached one of the many eastward-flowing rivers, the Napo, though they had no concept of the vast tract of country which lay before them. After spending two months building a substantial boat from materials taken from the surrounding jungle, some fifty men commanded by Orellana set out to reconnoitre downstream, among them the Dominican Gaspar de Carvajal, who made the vivid, historic record of their journey. Gonzalo Pizarro waited for their return, but he waited in vain, for whether by design or whether they found themselves powerless in the river's current, Orellana's boat swept steadily on towards the confluence with the Amazon. When he received the news, Pizarro had no choice but to turn and re-cross the mountains; his men dragged themselves, half-naked and starving, back into Quito in June 1542.

For weeks, Orellana and his men drifted down-river with 'no food but toads and serpents', until they encountered a group of friendly Indians, who fed them and watched them as they built a second, larger boat, a sailing brigantine, in which they embarked on the Amazon itself. In three months they sailed 2,000 miles through unknown territory, suffering starvation, sickness, and attacks by hostile Indians, in one of which Orellana was blinded in one eye. The Spaniards saw, or imagined that they saw, that the Indian women were taller and fiercer than the men, and that they were foremost in the fighting; for this reason they named the river the Amazon, recalling the warrior-women of classical legend. In July they noticed that the river had become tidal, and soon it was so wide that the land was often invisible. Putting ashore, they refitted their boats, using vines as cordage and blankets as sails,

The Amazon. This anonymous manuscript of c.1549 is one of the earliest known representations of the Amazon, following Orellana's epic journey of 1541–42. The 'City of the Kings' is Lima, Pizarro's capital founded in 1535.

Bibliothèque Nationale, Paris

and after fighting the tide for days, they passed the mouth of the Amazon and turned north into the Atlantic. Sailing for more than a thousand miles off the coast of Guiana, the third stage of their epic journey ended when they landed in September 1542 at the Spanish settlement on Cubagua Island, eighteen months after leaving Quito. They were the first men to navigate the Amazon, indeed the first to cross South America. Orellana, accompanied by Carvajal, hastened back to Spain and secured the king's commission to explore the land he had discovered, but he died on the voyage returning to South America. He had however placed on the map the world's largest river, and after 1542 the snake-like course of the Amazon dominated the map of South America, which had formerly been almost featureless. Orellana's journey had not been in any sense a precise survey, and the absence of printed maps in Spain meant that no accurate chart of its course was available. In many maps of the sixteenth century, the Amazon is shown flowing wildly north-south across the whole continent. In this and in their other ventures into the jungles east of the Andes, the Spanish found little to attract them, and the huge territory traversed by Orellana was left to the Portuguese to explore.

The exploration of the Orinoco River was far less clear-cut, occupying sixty years and being

largely inspired by the search for the legendary El Dorado. This tradition was first encountered by the Spaniards in the 1530s and told of a king – the 'Golden One' – of a fabulous realm who visited each day a miraculous lake where he was anointed with gold dust. The effect of such a story on the Spanish can easily be imagined. Its location was vaguely supposed to be somewhere among the head-waters of the Orinoco, but whether in the west or the south of that great arc was unknown. Various tributaries were explored, many of them by agents of the German finance house of Welser of Augsburg, which had purchased exploration rights from the Spanish crown, and which maintained a base at Coro from 1528 until 1546. The notorious adventurer, Lope de Aguirre, was reported to have discovered in 1560 the Amazon-Orinoco link which exists via the Casiquiare River, a link much doubted by geographers, but which was confirmed by von Humboldt more than two centuries later.

The Orinoco itself was largely explored by Antonio de Berrio in 1582–84 who followed the Casanare and Meta Rivers from the Colombian Mountains. Just a few years later Juan Martin de Albujar, the sole survivor of an Orinoco expedition, struggled out of the jungle after spending ten years with the Indians, as he claimed, in a fabulous city which he called Manao. His story was widely reported and the interest it revived in El Dorado spread far beyond Spanish America, most famously to Sir Walter Raleigh in England, who sought to restore his flagging position at court by winning 'a better Indies for her Majestie than the King of Spain hath any'. Raleigh sailed from Plymouth in

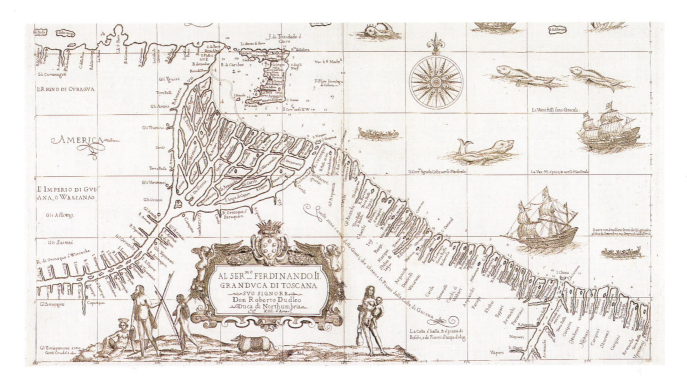

Above: *Guyana, by Sir Robert Dudley,
1646. The region between the Orinoco
and the Amazon was the only part of
South America where nations other than
the Spanish and Portuguese found a
foothold: British, French and Dutch
trading settlements were founded in the
supposed 'Gold-bearing kingdom of
Guiana'.*

The British Library Maps C.8.d.10.

Left: *North-East Brazil, 1647. These
maps showing the Portuguese
settlements were drawn up by the Dutch
scholar Caspar van Baerle, working from
Dutch Guiana; no maps of this large
scale were published for any other part
of South America.*

The British Library Maps C.5.b.1.

Right: *Paraguay: a map of the Jesuit
missions drawn by Father Joseph
Quiroga, 1749. Paraguay became almost
a kingdom within a kingdom until the
Jesuits were expelled in 1767.*

The British Library Add. MS 17665B.

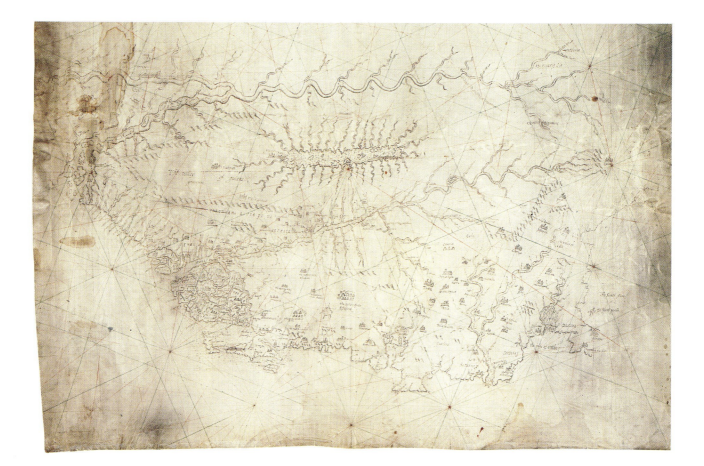

February 1595 for Trinidad, where he met Antonio de Berrio, whose warnings about the country ahead Raleigh ignored, For three months he and his men struggled against the waters of the Orinoco before abandoning the attempt and returning to England empty-handed. Raleigh sought to rescue his reputation by publishing his *Discoverie of the Large, Rich and Beautiful Empire of Guiana*, and by claiming that native chiefs had willingly ceded this territory to English rule, so that English colonies could legitimately be founded there. It was largely as a result of Raleigh and his quest for El Dorado that Guiana acquired its distinct identity on European maps. Raleigh worked on a large unfinished chart of the Orinoco, whose true geography however remained so unknown that nineteenth-century writers could still site lost worlds in its southern mountains. Although first investigated in the 1530s, the Orinoco made no distinct appearance on maps before the 1590s. The inhospitable region between the Amazon and Orinoco deltas was long known as the 'Wild Coast', and it was the only region in South America where Europeans other than Spanish and Portuguese were permitted to find a foothold, with Dutch, French and British trading colonies established there in the seventeenth century.

To the south lay the most massive region of the continent, Brazil, claimed by the Portuguese as early as 1500, but over which they exercised only a shadowy power, for there was no obvious source of wealth to be found there, and the Portuguese were fully occupied in the Indian Ocean. This situation changed with the accession of John III who determined to establish efficient colonies in Brazil. By 1550 Bahia (Salvador) and Pernambuco (Recife) were founded, and Rio de Janeiro followed in 1567. In the absence of precious metals, the colonies were agricultural, and sugar, rice, tobacco, indigo and cacao were grown successfully, while exotic hardwoods and animal skins were also exported. Of

Left: The Region of El Dorado by Sir Walter Raleigh, 1596. South is at the top, and between the Amazon and the Orinoco lay the 'Lake of Manoa', where the imagined gold-kingdom was believed to lie.

The British Library Add. MS 17940

Right: Guayaquil and Puna, 1682. One of a series of Spanish charts covering the entire western coast of South America, taken by a British ship and copied in London by William Hack.

The British Library Harley MS 4034, ff. 142v–143.

Below: The Amazon, 1707, by the German Jesuit missionary Samuel Fritz. Fritz enlarged his mission from Quito to the Rio Negro. He strongly opposed Portuguese slaving activities and hoped to extend Spanish authority eastward into Brazil.

The British Library Maps 83040(4).

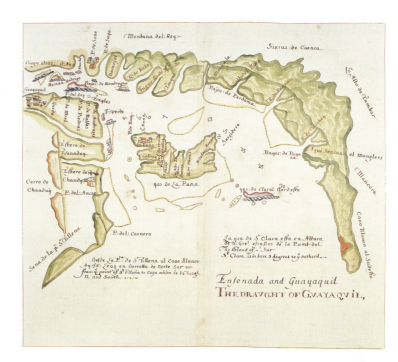

course the boundaries of Brazil were at first quite indeterminate, and in the seventeenth century the colonists pushed west far beyond the Tordesillas line to the slopes of the Andes. In this movement they were matched by the Jesuits who established missions along the Amazon to protect and Christianize the Indians. Conflict between the Jesuits and the rapacious colonists who sought to enslave the Indians became endemic, and ironically helped to stimulate the import of slaves from Africa, a traffic which eventually brought more than three million Africans to Brazil over the next three centuries. One of the outstanding Jesuits was the German-born Samuel Fritz who served in missions in the western Amazon for forty years. His map of the region in 1707 was the most accurate published to that date, and he believed firmly that the western half of the river belonged rightly within Spain's jurisdiction, for Spain, officially at least, did not make slaves of the Indians. Brazil's borders were defined effectively when bands of exploring or raiding colonists – *the bandeiras* – met Spanish resistance in the north, west or south.

The huge territory of Brazil broke into the Spanish dominions, but to the south was a further natural point of entry into the continent, the Rio de la Plata, whose importance had been recognized in the 1520s. There are ill-documented reports of several expeditions in the region before that of Sebastian Cabot, who was then in the service of Spain, in 1527–28. Cabot was en route for Asia via the Straits of Magellan when he turned aside to explore the estuary, ascending the Parana River to beyond its junction with the Paraguay. Cabot's voyage produced little direct result, but the Spanish were anxious to define the southern limits of Portuguese power, and sent further ships to the Rio de la Plata. Buenos Aires was founded in 1536 when Pedro de Mendoza arrived with a massive Spanish force, which however was decimated by starvation and Indian hostility. Some survivors led by Juan de Ayolas settled on the site of Asuncion, and may have followed the Paraguay River almost to the borders of Peru. After Mendoza's failures, Cabeza de Vaca, survivor of an earlier epic adventure in North America, was sent in 1541 to re-establish the Spanish position. Buenos Aires was rebuilt, Asuncion was strengthened, and the rivers explored, including the discovery of the great falls at Iguacu. In 1548 a group of explorers under Martinez de Irala made the first crossing from Paraguay into Peru via the headwaters of the Paraguay River. The link between the eastern and western regions of Spanish America was shortened by the founding of Santiago del Estero and Mendoza in the 1550s, providing bases in the trans-Andean route. Maps of the sixteenth century invariably exaggerated the size and importance of the Rio de la Plata, sometimes showing an imagined link between the Paraguay River and the Amazon, a link which indeed, via the Amazon's tributary the Juruena, misses completion by a mere twenty miles in the watershed of the Parecis Mountains.

In Paraguay itself the Spanish merged relatively peacefully with the Guarani, and from the early seventeenth century the Jesuits built a network of missions which served as centres of culture as well as trade. So successful were they that they were perceived as a state within a state, and excited the envy of the Spanish and the Portuguese to the north. In a complex political intrigue, the Jesuits were expelled from Paraguay in 1767 and the missions were cruelly suppressed, ending a brief golden age in Spanish American history. This was a campaign out of its true time, the final phase of the Hispanic conquest, cynical and bloodthirsty, delayed by historical accident for two centuries.

By the early seventeenth century, geographical knowledge of South America had reached a plateau which continued unchanged for a century. The Hispanic control of the continent was total, and all exploration was carried out by Hispanic traders or missionaries. Maps were dominated by the three great water systems, and with certain features such as the silver town of Potosi or the legendary El Dorado given prominence. It is certain that the colonists themselves possessed more detailed manuscript maps, as did the governments in Spain and Portugal, but mapping and geography in those countries were always subject to a culture of secrecy, and little of this material was ever published. Had other colonial powers ruled in South America, the situation would have been different, as is shown by the series of detailed maps of north-eastern Brazil published by the Dutch scholar Caspar van Baerle in 1647, under the auspices of the governor of Dutch Guiana. Van Baerle's maps showed the estates and divisions of the Portuguese prefectures at scales larger than any other maps of South America published at this time. The eagerness with which the British navy received in 1682 a collection of captured Spanish charts of the western coast, is evidence again of the closed nature of Hispanic South America. These charts were widely copied and became the standard guides to these waters during the eighteenth century. As with North America, the longitudinal extent of the continent was invariably exaggerated, to almost 60 degrees instead of the true 47 degrees.

It was in the mid-eighteenth century that the geographical study of South America began to change and a new, more scientific spirit of exploration emerged, as it did also in the Pacific region and elsewhere. The first event was, in a way, accidental, springing from a French scientific project for determining the figure of the earth by measuring an arc of longitude in the Arctic and at the equator. In 1735 Charles-Marie de la Condamine travelled to Ecuador with the geophysicist Pierre Bouguer to carry out the necessary measurements. During this work, which occupied eight years, La Condamine had become fascinated by the South American environment, and when his task was finally complete, he embarked on a journey from the Andes to the mouth of the Amazon, observing in detail the ethnography, flora and fauna of the region, and later publishing the first scientific study of South American geography. La Condamine was the first to introduce the rubber plant and its product to Europeans. In the years which followed, long-delayed topographic surveys were at last initiated, such as that of Felix de Azara who in the 1780s mapped much of what is now Paraguay. Spain also recognized the need for new hydrographic surveys, and entrusted the task to an Italian, Alessandro Malaspina, who charted almost the entire South American coast in the 1790s. From 1799 to 1804 Alexander von Humboldt and Aimé Bonpland travelled first in the Orinoco region, then through the Andes from northern Colombia to Lima. Darwin described von Humboldt as 'the greatest scientific traveller who ever lived', and his observations during this journey are often considered to mark the foundation of modern scientific geography. He spent the next thirty years analysing and publishing his studies of geology, climate, botany, zoology, and as a result South America became a magnet for scientists of all disciplines, but especially for naturalists. It was in South America in the three years from 1832 to 1835 that the most important naturalist of all time, Charles Darwin, found the immense wealth of material which led him to understand one of nature's deepest processes.

The exploration of South America was inextricably linked to its position as a Hispanic colonial empire. Its geography was established quickly but imprecisely, and it was virtually closed to outsiders for almost three centuries. In all this it differed fundamentally from North America or Asia, and it illustrates sharply the impossibility of divorcing the progress of exploration from European political and commercial ambitions. Nowhere was the cost of exploration in human terms more terrifying than in South America, with its native peoples murdered or enslaved, their lands seized, their cultures destroyed and their names forgotten, while those of their conquerors became honoured as historic figures. The haunting questions about European exploration are nowhere more sharply focussed than in the history of South America.

AFRICA

While Africa had formed part of the world map from classical and medieval times, only the regions north of the Sahara were known, indeed the existence of this burning desert was the basis of the classical doctrine that the world was divided into climatic zones, and that the torrid zone between the tropics and equator was uninhabitable. Throughout the classical era, North Africa was considered as part of the Mediterranean world; only with the Islamic conquest of the seventh century AD, did it become closed to the west and linked to the culture of the Middle East. Contacts had existed between

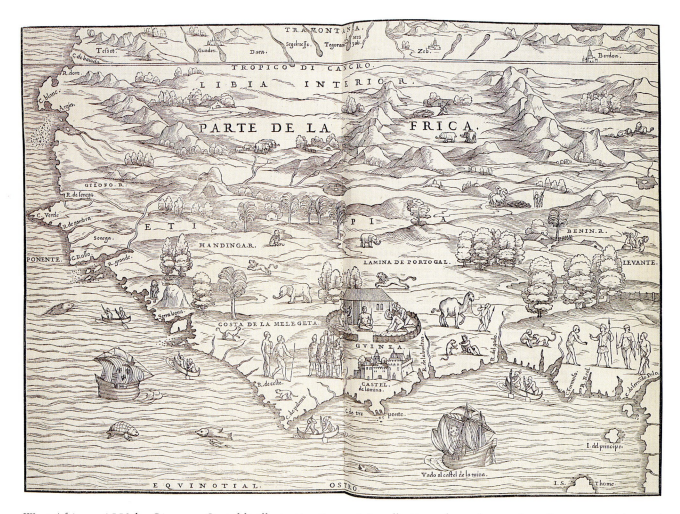

West Africa, c.1550 by Giacomo Gastaldi, illustrating Ramusio's collection of travel narratives. Portuguese ships and the fort of El Mina are prominent, but the unknown interior is a fantasy of forest and mountain.

The British Library 566.K.3.

sub-Saharan Africa and the Mediterranean for many centuries, contacts with both Egypt and Carthage for example, and the desert trade routes were inherited and developed by the Arabs. By AD 1000, settled pastoral and agricultural communities with metalworking skills existed throughout Africa, especially in a wide belt from the Guinea coast to the Nile, and centralized states and kingdoms were beginning to emerge. Medieval European maps often showed a large westward-flowing river in Africa, but whether this represented some tenuous knowledge of the Niger is impossible to say. Thanks to the Portuguese navigators, the continent's outline was charted with great accuracy by 1502, with the exception that the Gulf of Guinea was always drawn too deeply, by ten longitude degrees or more.

It is often claimed that European knowledge of the interior of this vast territory was non-existent before the early nineteenth century; this is certainly untrue, although it is true that that knowledge was very fragmentary. The reasons for this are clear: the almost total absence of harbours and navigable rivers throughout the entire western coast, from Morocco to the Cape; the difficult terrain, consisting of either desert or jungle, which fronted the ocean; the diseases such as malaria which

Abyssinia, the 'Empire of Prester John', 1573, by Ortelius. Based partly on the reports of Portuguese embassies to the court, a number of modern names are recognisable – Goiame and Tigrai; yet the extent of Abyssinia is greatly exaggerated.

The British Library Maps C.23.e.12.

claimed the lives of Europeans as soon as they landed; and the Islamic presence in the ports of the more hospitable east coast. Islamic power was widespread in northern and coastal east Africa when the Portuguese arrived. The great traveller Ibn Battuta and other Arab geographers are vital sources for our historical knowledge of Africa, although they were not always reliable. The Arab scholar known to the west as Leo Africanus travelled widely throughout Africa north of the equator between 1510 and 1520, and his *Descrittione dell'Africa*, published in Venice in 1550, remained the authoritative guide to the continent for two centuries or more. It was his error of observation that gave rise to

The Kingdom of Monomotapa, by João Albernas, 1677. The gold-bearing kingdom on the Zambezi opened up by the Portuguese as early as 1512.

Bibliothèque Nationale, Paris

the belief that the River Niger flowed west, so that mapmakers invented huge lakes in West Africa as its source, and portrayed the Rivers Gambia and Senegal as forming its Atlantic delta.

The Portuguese called the entire Guinea coast *El Mina* – the Mine, for they recognized that the peoples of this coast had access to huge amounts of gold, indeed during the sixteenth century the largest source of gold available to Europe was the 'Gold Coast', and it came through Portuguese hands. A still richer and more widespread trade was slaving, which developed with the colonization of the Americas, and from 1500 to 1800 European interest in Africa was confined to the slave trade from the west coast, in which the British, Dutch, French and Portuguese were the leaders. In contrast to the swift European seizure of the Americas, little attempt was made to explore or settle in Africa. Nevertheless, before Africa attracted serious European attention in the early nineteenth century, there were several pioneering phases of exploration, which did establish some important features and regional names upon the map of the continent.

Within a few years of arriving on the East African coast, the Portuguese heard reports of gold-rich kingdoms in the interior, and they set out to investigate inland from the port of Sofala and along the Zambezi. It was in 1512 that the adventurer Antonio Fernandes first encountered the kingdom of Mutapa (where Zimbabwe now lies); trading bases were quickly located at Sena and Tete on the Zambezi, and in 1542 ambassadors were exchanged. In 1560 the Jesuit Gonçalo de Silveira converted the king to Christianity, although this proved temporary and Silveira was later martyred. A military expedition in 1573 under Francisco Barreto re-established Portuguese power, and their presence in the lower Zambezi was to last until Mozambique was formally elevated into a Portuguese

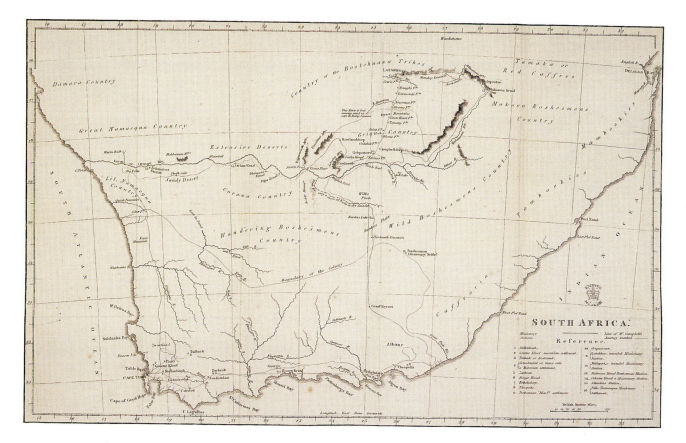

South Africa, by John Campbell, 1815. Campbell was a missionary who succeeded in tracing the entire course of the Orange River.

The British Library 981.d.20.

colony in 1891. In 1616 Gaspar Bocarro made a significant journey from the middle Zambezi to the coast at Kilwa, passing the southern end of Lake Nyasa, raising the possibility of inland exploration by boat. The bases and the rivers of 'Motapa', or 'Monomotapa' as it was also known, were mapped by the Portuguese, although the area was shown inaccurately in printed maps of the seventeenth century.

On Africa's west coast, the River Congo was explored within a few years of its discovery by Diego Cão in 1482; the kingdom of the Kongo was discovered, its court converted to Christianity, and the possibility of ascending the river to Abyssinia was considered, without result however. Another permanent Portuguese settlement grew up to the south of the Kongo, having Luanda as its headquarters. In 1575 Dias de Novais was appointed governor, and reports of silver mines led to some penetration inland along the Cuanza River; however native resistance, disease and the absolute failure to find any silver cut short this initiative. The Portuguese remained in the future Angola, which had the slave trade at the the heart of its existence, and at least one unsuccessful attempt was made in 1606 to push east and link with the Portuguese settlements on the Zambezi. Maps of southern Africa in the sixteenth and seventeenth centuries were accustomed to combine these slight elements of real geography with the long-held belief that the source of the Nile must lie in mountains or lakes south of the equator, where other rivers, such as the Congo and the Zambezi might also rise. Further north, the most significant penetration of the interior occurred in the River Gambia, where a British expedition ascended more than 300 miles in 1618–20. Not until a century later did the French

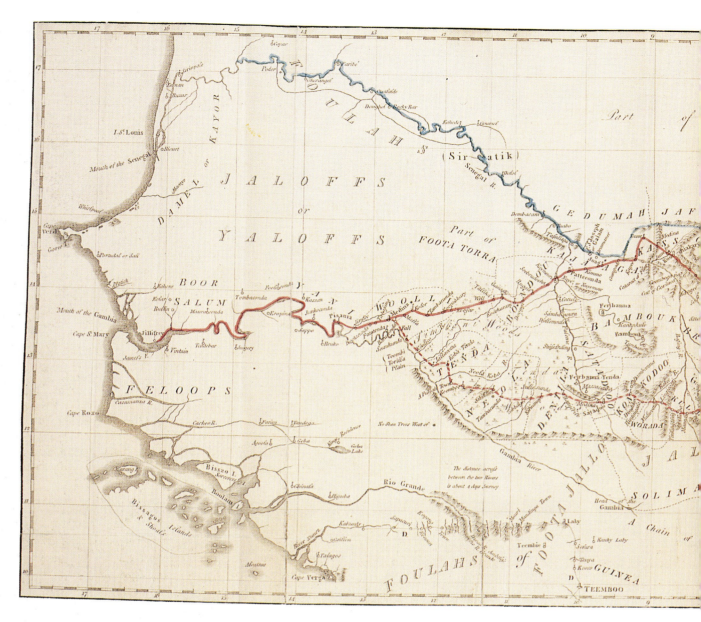

The Niger by Mungo Park, 1797. This map shows the course of Park's first great journey from the Gambia to Segu on the Niger.

explore the Senegal River into the Bambouk region, where they heard the first modern reports of the River Niger leading to the great Saharan trading centre of Timbuktu.

The region of Africa which attracted a special degree of European attention however was Ethiopia, indeed, like Cathay, it enjoyed an existence in the European mind that was quite separate from real knowledge of the place itself. Ethiopia is unique among African countries in tracing its history into antiquity and in preserving its original identity into the twentieth century. A Christian kingdom from the fourth century AD, it had become by the middle ages a Christian island on the edge of the ocean of Islam. When contact with Christian Europe was re-established in the fourteenth century, it seemed that the kingdom of Prester John – the fabled Christian ruler of the east – had been found in Africa rather than in Asia; when the Portuguese arrived in the Gulf of Aden and opened relations with Ethiopia in 1520, the event seemed almost as startling as the discovery of America. Franciscans and, later, Jesuits were eager to explore the country; Francisco Alvares published the first

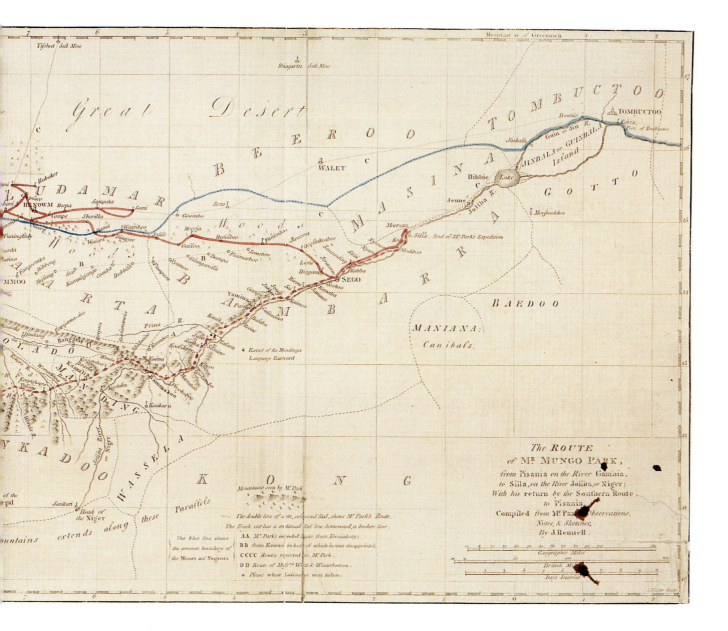

European account of Ethiopia, entitled significantly *The Prester John of the Indies*. In 1613 Pedro Paez travelled the highland region near Lake Tana and found the source of the Blue Nile – two springs said to be unfathomable. A map drawn from Portuguese sources and entitled 'The Kingdom of Prester John' was published by Ortelius from 1573 onwards, and was copied for the next two hundred years, its most striking feature being its enormous exaggeration of the size of the kingdom, filling a third of Africa. The more accurate maps made by the Jesuit Manoel de Almeida around 1640 were little known and of little influence. Nevertheless Ethiopia, or Abyssinia, was long identified as the most civilized region of Africa, so that in the eighteenth century both Voltaire and Samuel Johnson could use it as the setting for philosophical novels on man's search for happiness and wisdom.

European interest and exploration in Africa underwent a sudden acceleration in the late eighteenth century, and there were two quite clear reasons for this. First there was the contemporary sense that exploration was an intellectual challenge which a scientific age must meet, that the great blank on the map of Africa was 'a reproach upon the present age'. This spirit found expression in the founding in London in 1788 of the 'Association for Promoting the Discovery of the Interior Parts of

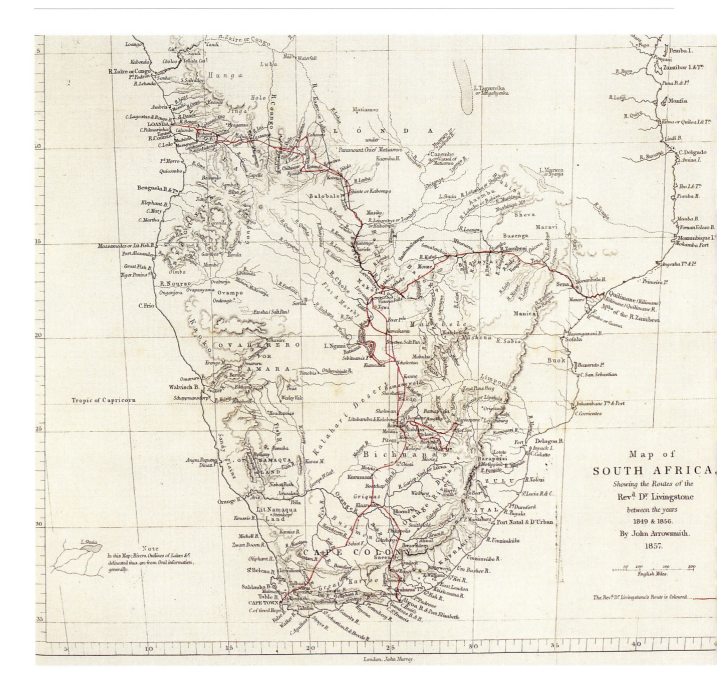

Livingstone's first journey, mapped by Arrowsmith, 1857. In three years Livingstone covered some 5,000 miles on foot and by canoe following the Zambezi west to Luanda and back, the first recorded crossing of the continent.

The British Library 1560/292.

Africa', which was to sponsor many new expeditions in the following fifty years. After 1830 its functions in this respect were taken over by the Royal Geographical Society, which became a great focus for African exploration. Equally important was the growing movement towards the abolition of the trade in slaves, an aim which was achieved in Britain in 1807, in the United States in 1808, and in the Netherlands and France in 1814. In the decades preceding abolition, a high degree of geographical factfinding was required about the mechanics of the trade, and afterwards the European powers sought other forms of commerce to succeed that in slaves, as well as seeking to maintain their relations with the African kingdoms. Moreover the enforcement of the slavery ban, carried out by the British navy for example, required the presence of numerous officers and missionaries in Africa. Sierra Leone was chosen by the British as the site for the repatriation of freed slaves. The iniquitous three hundred year old trade was succeeded by more direct forms of European intervention in Africa, political, economic or religions, in all of which improved geographical knowledge was an essential precondition.

The first explorer in the newer, scientific spirit was James Bruce who travelled from Cairo in 1769 to Ethiopia's Red Sea coast, and inland to the mountains, in a deliberate search for the source of the Nile. Unaware of their earlier discovery by the Portuguese, he reached the springs at Geesh in November 1770, which he grandly described as 'that spot which had baffled the genius, industry and enquiry of both ancients and moderns for the course of near three thousand years.' Bruce's adventure inspired further exploration in Ethiopia, but the London African Association was more interested in the west, in the reports of the River Niger, and the possibility that it would provide a route to the great African interior. The earliest attempts were unsuccessful and cost several lives, before Mungo Park trekked east from the Gambia and in July 1796 reached Segu, where he saw 'with infinite pleasure the great object of my mission – the long-sought-for, majestic Niger glittering in the morning sun, as broad as the Thames at Westminster, and flowing slowly to the eastward.' Park returned to England and became famous, but his work was only half completed, for he had not traced the course of the Niger beyond Segu, nor established its outfall, whether into a great lake or into the sea. In 1805 he returned with a much larger expedition, again to Segu where he embarked on a down-river journey. Neither he nor any of his party was ever seen alive again, but later explorers pieced together the story of his thousand-mile descent of the river as far as the rapids at Bussa, where he was killed in a skirmish with some natives; the problem of the Niger remained unsolved for a further twenty-five years. Significant exploration in West Africa was resumed in 1820s, when Hugh Clapperton journeyed south across the Sahara from Tripoli to the kingdoms of present-day Nigeria. Dixon Denham made a reconnaissance of Lake Chad in 1824 which showed that it was unconnected with the Niger, and in 1826 Alexander Laing became the first European of modern times to reach Timbuktu by land (Park must have passed through it in 1805) but he was killed during the return journey. In 1830 two brothers, Richard and John Lander travelled from the Benin coast north to Bussa and descended the last five hundred miles of the Niger to its mouth in the Gulf of Guinea, thus disposing of many long-standing geographical myths, that the Niger flowed into the Nile for example, or into the Congo, or into a great inland lake.

The British had by no means the monopoly on African exploration, indeed it was a determined young Frenchman, René Caillié, who realized the European dream of reaching Timbuktu in 1828. He travelled north-east from Sierra Leone, and, equally important succeeded in returning safely to France via Morocco. Timbuktu was one of those cities, like Lhasa, which had become almost the object of a mythical quest, but Caillié experienced the same disillusionment that awaited those who reached Lhasa: poverty, silence and squalor were his chief impressions of what ancient writers had represented as a golden city. A few decades later, a great German explorer, Heinrich Barth, was only slightly less critical of the city, which he visited in 1855 in the course of a trans-Saharan journey from Tripoli. Like the Arabian peninsula, the Sahara is not exactly an easy place to map, but after journeys such as those of Caillié and Barth, the main desert routes and features appeared on maps – the eastern route due south from Tripoli to Lake Chad, the western route from Morocco via Taoudenni to Timbuktu, and the Hoggar and Tibesti Mountains. As in Asia and the Americas, this mapping process marks simply the adoption by European geographers of knowledge that had been in native hands for centuries, so that the term 'exploration' is culturally limited here.

In the extreme south of Africa, the early decades of the nineteenth century saw a complicated process of migration and settlement played out among three groups of people: the original Bushmen and Bantu inhabitants, the Dutch colonists of the Cape, and the British who became masters of the region in 1806. The mutual pressures exerted among these groups led all of them to explore and settle the high veldt inland from the coast. The most celebrated movement was the Great Trek in 1836 of the Boers, seeking to escape British control by crossing the Orange and Vaal Rivers, although they found that British power still pursued them. British responsibility for the Cape Colony, with its complex racial and political tensions, drew a new breed of European missionaries devoted to 'the heathen in his blindness', and whose motive was to explore Africa in order to Christianize it. One of the earliest was John Campbell who between 1811 and 1813 explored the course of the Orange River and found the source of the Limpopo. The most tenacious and celebrated missionary was David Livingstone, who became one of the heroic figures of Victorian Britain. Livingstone equated civilization with clothes, Christianity, medicine and monogamy; he had a profound horror of the slave trade, which was still conducted in the secrecy of the African interior, largely through Arab intermediaries, and he believed that only by opening Africa's heartland to the light of international judgement and supervision would this evil be rooted out. 'I view', he wrote, 'the end of the geographical feat as the beginning of the missionary enterprise'. His first historic journey in 1853–56 was to cover almost 5,000 miles, on foot and by canoe, on the upper Zambezi, and west across Angola to Luanda, then to return across the entire continent to the Indian Ocean coast, the first recorded trans-African journey, during which he was the first European to see the Victoria Falls. In 1858 he returned and attempted to navigate the Zambezi by steamboat, but was blocked by the Quebrabasa rapids, and turned north to explore Lake Nyasa. His final expedition between 1866 and 1873 in the Lake Nyasa and Lake Tanganyika region turned into a prolonged quest for the source of the White Nile, which he was convinced lay much further south than previously guessed. This quest was ultimately fruitless but it placed on the map the complex territory around Lake Mweru, Lake Bangweulu and the Lualaba River; these Livingstone believed drained into Lake Albert and hence were the true headwaters of the Nile, whereas in fact they are the source of the Congo, or Zaire River. Livingstone's achievements, his fame and his missionary earnestness, helped to shape British attitudes to Africa for years to come: through the territory which he disclosed and through his cultural preconceptions, he inadvertently prepared the age of European imperialism that was about to sweep through Africa.

Livingstone's uncertainty about the Nile was the legacy of the expeditions of John Hanning Speke and Richard Burton in 1858, in the course of which they had discovered Lake Tanganyika, and Speke, during a lone detour, had discovered Lake Victoria. Driven by intuition rather than evidence, Speke proclaimed Lake Victoria to be the source of the Nile, but Burton strongly disagreed. Speke's return to the lake in 1860–63, and the further discovery of Lake Albert by Samuel White Baker, still failed to settle the problem because they did not trace the connecting rivers with sufficient exactness. It was Henry Morton Stanley who circumnavigated Lake Victoria in 1875 and, after examining the river that flowed from its northern edge, confirmed that Speke was correct in his belief. Stanley was the antithesis of Livingstone: brash, worldly and mercenary, his reputation was built on his encounter with Livingstone in 1871, which made him as famous as the lost missionary. But he went on to become a highly effective but ruthless explorer in his own right. He spent two years in 1877–78 making the first descent of the Congo River, from its source to the Atlantic Ocean. Failing to enlist British interest in the Congo, he worked to open up the region in the service of King Leopold II of Belgium, thus laying the foundations of the Congo Free State. Later, in 1889, Stanley discovered the Ruwenzori, the snow-covered glaciated mountains lying directly on the equator, and the Semliki River flowing between Lakes Edward and Albert. The Ruwenzori range was identified as the 'Mountains of the Moon', and its snows did indeed feed the headwaters of the Nile as classical geographers had imagined.

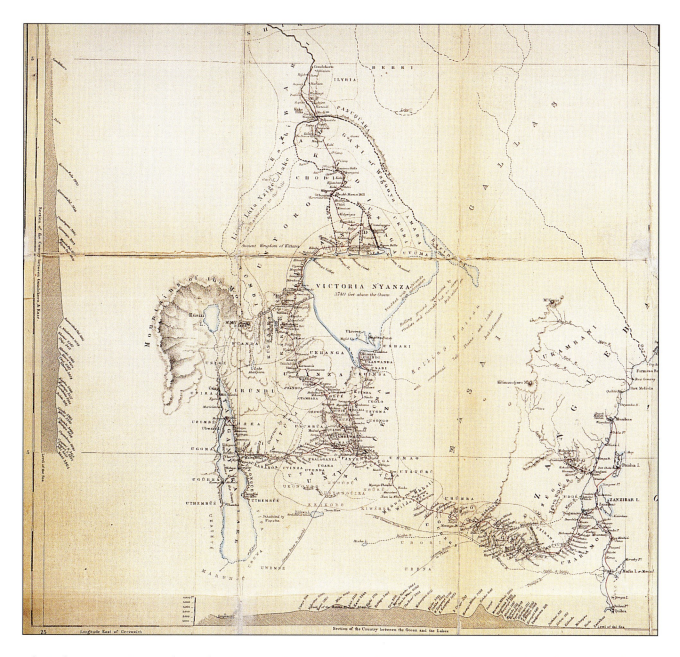

The Lake Victoria Region, by Speke, 1863. Speke believed that the Lake was the source of the Nile, as shown here; he was correct, but his claim was not finally proved until Stanley fully circumnavigated the lake in 1875.

The British Library 2358.e.15.

Stanley's career marked the close of a 'heroic', freelance, non-political period of exploration in Africa, a period which had seen the major river systems – the Niger, the Nile and the Congo – placed on the map. The political aftermath of this exploring activity was swift and far-reaching: in the space of the two decades 1880 to 1900, every region in Africa, except Ethiopia, Libya and Morocco was under the dominion of European governments, and of these the last two would hold out for only a dozen more years. France, Britain and Germany were the leaders in this scramble for African territory, with Belgium, Portugal and Italy also involved. Even now, one hundred years later, it is difficult

[*173*]

to explain exactly why this happened, exactly what the European powers thought they were gaining when they claimed Angola, or Togoland or Rhodesia, for reconnaissance in these countries had not yet revealed any great sources of wealth. The real explanation is that these territories had become pawns in the power-game that was being played out by the European powers, and the important thing was to occupy territory before it was claimed by your rivals. The game had begun in the 1850s and 60s in West Africa, where British and French traders came into conflict, and the only answer seemed to be for each nation to create formal colonies in order to protect their interests, as happened in Senegal, Lagos and the Gold Coast. In Africa as in the Americas and in the Pacific, the traditional political order had become powerless in the face of European pressures – pressures technical and economic. The more frantic phase in the scramble for colonies is considered to have begun with the French reaction to the British occupation of Egypt in 1882, and the rivalry between France and Belgium in the Congo region a couple of years later. It was the arrival of German treaty-makers in Togoland and the Cameroons in 1884 which really galvanized the British into securing their African colonies. These events lay behind the Berlin West Africa Conference of 1884–5, in which Bismarck exploited the colonial issue for the purposes of his European diplomacy. During World War One of course these pawns were seized and redistributed. But, ultimately none of this explains what the politicians in London, Berlin or Paris really thought they were gaining as they traced their borders and their spheres of influence on the map of Africa. If modern theorists are correct, at the heart of the imperial impulse lies a class instinct to find new lands and new peoples to govern and command. Colonial activities such as farming and mining were secondary to the central impulse to conquer and rule. Africa was systematically explored only in the nineteenth century, and it therefore received the full force of European technology and political ambitions. Whatever the ideals with which explorers like Bruce, Park or Livingstone set out, ideals of serving geographical science or obeying a religious imperative, it was impossible that their discoveries would not be used to further European economic aims and political rivalries.

AUSTRALIA

Australia was the last inhabitable continent to be found, explored and settled by Europeans. Its first outstanding characteristic was its isolation – isolation in two senses: global remoteness from other civilizations or trade routes, and the isolation of settlements that were established within the great land-mass itself. Its second characteristic was the aridity of most of its surface, an aridity matched only in central Asia and North Africa. It was these two characteristics which protected Australia for so long from outside interest, for after its shores were first sighted a century and a half passed before any attempt was made to settle the land. The significance of Captain Cook's brief visit to the eastern coast, near the modern Sydney, was that it revealed for the first time fertile, inhabitable regions of the continent, which had previously been been dismissed as near-desert. He claimed the land for Britain and named it New South Wales, as distinct from New Holland in the west – the name Australia was adopted by international consent in 1817. The British policy of using New South Wales as a penal colony was conceived a decade after Cook's return: convicts were to work on government farms, while freed prisoners of good conduct would be allowed their own plots of land. The first fleet of eleven ships carrying some 730 convicts and 250 government servants and marines commanded by Captain Arthur Phillips arrived at Botany Bay in 1788. They removed almost immediately to the better location of Port Jackson – the modern Sydney Harbour – and ironically one of Phillips's first actions was to establish an outstation on Norfolk Island, 1,000 miles across the Tasman Sea, as a prison for those who misbehaved in Australia.

Other penal colonies followed in New South Wales, in Tasmania and in 1827 at Albany in

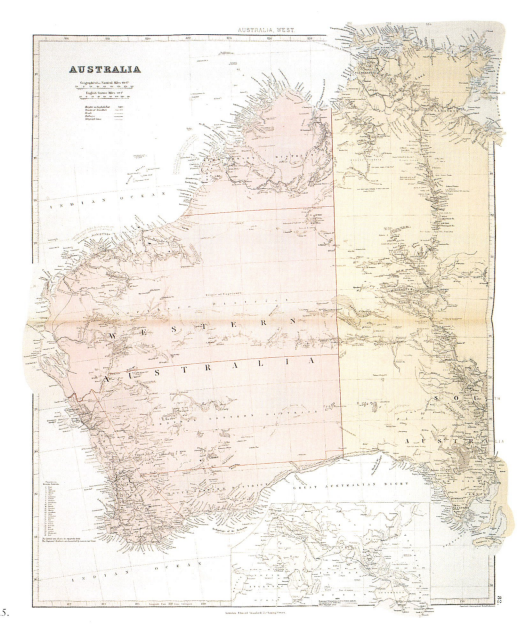

Central and Western Australia, by Stanford, 1887. The mapped portions of the desert interior are in fact the tracks of the explorers, Stuart from south to north, Giles and Forest from west to east; huge blanks still remain on the map.

The British Library Maps 46.f.5.

Western Australia. In 1825 the Governor's commission was extended to 129 degrees east, in order to include settlements on Bathurst and Melville Islands in the north, and by 1830 Britain claimed sovereignty over the whole of Australia, having realized its strategic value as base for British sea power in the entire Pacific-Indian Ocean region. In the 1830s settlement by non-convicts opened a new chapter in Australian history, so that population in 1851 was 450,000 and ten years later had reached 1.1 million. When Captain Phillips landed there may have been between a quarter and a half a million aboriginal people in Australia, whose culture had developed in isolation from the other peoples of Asia and the Pacific. They were semi-nomadic hunter-gatherers, whose culture rested on balance and continuity rather than the technology and change espoused by Europeans. Inevitably, their world was transformed as they were dispossessed of their land, and their only response was a kind of guerilla warfare which lasted until the later nineteenth century, although individual groups of aborigines would often display friendship and accommodate themselves to the newcomers. The worst relations between Europeans and aborigines were in Tasmania where persecution and disease effected a slow genocide between 1810 and 1860.

From the early years of the nineteenth century, as soon as the colonies were firmly established, the desire arose to explore beyond the narrow coastal plain of the south-east and investigate what lay beyond the mountains. With the spread of settlements however, there was to be no single frontier, as there was in North America, but rather a series of margins behind each coastal area, which were gradually penetrated in the course of approximately eighty years. The outstanding geographical problem swiftly defined itself as the interior: were there rivers, inland lakes, tropical forests or rich grazing lands, a possibility suggested by the westward-flowing rivers from the wooded mountains of the Great Dividing Range? And were there routes across the interior which would link all the settlements of the east and south with those of the west and north? In addition, as the population expanded from the 1830s onwards and sheep-rearing became the mainstay of the country, new grazing lands were always being sought. From around the year 1810, by which time the coastline of Australia had been explored and charted to a high degree of accuracy, most notably by Matthew Flinders, a series of overland journeys set out deliberately to answer these questions. The names of some of these explorers, such as Eyre and Sturt, are now preserved on the map of Australia, but many other features commemorate contemporary governors like Darling, MacDonnell and Ayers.

The process started in 1813 when Gregory Blaxland and William Wentworth made the short but highly important first crossing of the Blue Mountains, inland from Sydney. In 1817 John Oxley explored the region they had found – the Bathurst Plains and the Lachlan River – and in the 1820s he commenced the first systematic surveys of it. Oxley was accompanied by Allan Cunningham, a trained botanist, who in 1828 explored the Darling Downs inland from Brisbane, where he found 'extensive tracts of clear, pastoral country'. The most important of these early journeys were those of Charles Sturt who in 1830 followed the Murrumbidgee–Murray rivers to the sea east of the modern Adelaide, and of Thomas Mitchell who between 1830 and 1836 explored the tributaries that feed the Darling River, then struck south from the Murray River to Portland Bay. Sturt and Mitchell revealed large, potentially rich grazing lands which were rapidly settled. West of the Flinders Range was explored in several journeys by Edward Eyre in 1839–41, in the last of which he crossed the great arid Nullarbor Plain close by the southern coast, reaching King George Sound. This was one of the first of the many agonizing desert journeys endured by Australian explorers as they revealed that much of continent was indeed uninhabitable because of its heat and drought.

This experience was repeated in the first of the attempts to penetrate the heart of interior, that of Charles Sturt in 1844–45. From Adelaide Sturt and his party moved north into the Sturt and Simpson Deserts, where they suffered agonies of heat and thirst before making a desperate retreat. Exactly contemporary with Sturt was the Prussian, Ludwig Leichardt, whose ambition was to cross the continent from east to west. From Brisbane Leichardt trekked more than 2,000 miles via the Gulf of Carpentaria to the north coast of Arnhem Land. On a subsequent journey in 1848, Leichardt and all his companions disappeared without trace, creating one of the classic mysteries of Australian exploration. One of those who was to travel in search of Leichardt was Augustus Gregory, who in 1855–56 had trekked eastwards across the entire Northern Territory and Queensland.

Sturt's journeys had cast grave doubts on the potential of Australia's interior, but it was in the 1860s that an entire north-south crossing was finally achieved, and that any hopes of rivers or lakes were dispelled. The expedition of Robert Burke and William Wills in 1860–61 has entered Australian consciousness, in the way that Scott's South Pole expedition has entered the British, because both were magnificent failures, and because both were documented in great detail, allowing fatal misjudgements to be studied and argued over. Burke and Wills succeeded in their aim of crossing from Melbourne to the Gulf of Carpentaria in six months. On their return journey, their fate hinged on the departure from their mid-point depot at Cooper's Creek of their support party, only eight hours before the exhausted explorers arrived there. A third member of the party, Charles Gray, had already died, and only the fourth member, John King, survived by living with the Aborigines until help came four months later. There is a semantic argument about success and failure here, since they did indeed cross the continent, but failed to survive the aftermath, like Scott and his men in the Antarctic.

Where Burke and Wills 'failed', John McDouall Stuart succeeded, travelling from the Spencer Gulf in the south to the Van Diemen Gulf in the north, which he reached in July 1862, more than a year after Burke and Wills. But Stuart survived a harrowing return journey, indeed he is said to have arrived back in Adelaide on the very day that the funeral procession of Burke and Wills was moving through the streets. Within ten years the telegraph line from Adelaide to Darwin was laid, following Stuart's route, connecting Australia with Singapore and thus with Europe; today this is the route of the main transcontinental highway via Alice Springs. The vast expanse of bush and desert that is Western Australia was penetrated in the 1870s by the brothers John and Alexander Forest, by William Gosse who was the first European to set eyes on Ayers Rock in 1873, and by Ernest Giles, who later wrote some of the most dramatic of the many descriptions of the tortures of Australian desert travel.

By around 1880 the map of Australia was generally complete, although some desert areas would not be finally explored and surveyed until the mid-twentieth century. The intuition of the early discoverers was correct, that much of the continent is uninhabitable. Yet there are also huge grassland areas where stock could be reared, and the barren interior had proved valuable after all in its great mineral wealth. The penetration of Australia was a concentrated problem of reconnaissance, solved over a period of sixty years, and in this it was quite different from the exploration of any other continent. In another respect, the impact on the native peoples, the pattern was familiar, as the Europeans became the agents of a process of cultural extinction, which they calmly regarded as inevitable.

Ross's ships before Mount Erebus, 1841.

The British Library 2374.f.6.

POLAR EXPLORATION

Penetration into the Arctic and Antarctic in the nineteenth century marks very clearly the transition from the historic pattern of European exploration, whose motives were trade or conquest, to a purer form of exploration for its own sake, where geographical knowledge was the motive. In this phase, every tract of land or sea however inhospitable, must be explored, must be forced to yield up its secrets, simply because it was there; a blank upon the map was intolerable to the civilized mind. At the same time international rivalry played a strong part, especially in the race for the Poles. Great significance was attached to whether the prizes of exploration were claimed by an Englishman, or a Norwegian or an American, for this form of exploration was an opportunity to demonstrate superior skills, courage,

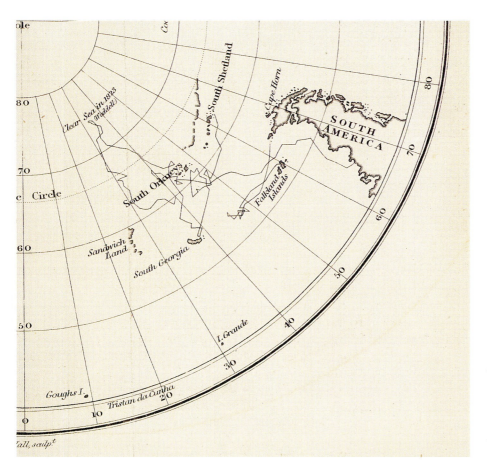

Part of the Weddell Sea in 1823, with Weddell's note that there was 'clear sea' at 75 degrees south, deep into the area normally impassable with ice.
The British Library 1045.g.18.

or endurance. Although Polar exploration was unconnected in the strict sense with imperialism, there was still a kind of imperialism of the mind, a sense that the most savage places of the world had somehow been tamed, and compelled to acknowledge the authority of the European nations. The technical skills of the European navies increased rapidly in the early nineteenth century, and after the removal of the Napoleonic threat, there were many tough, expert officers available who helped to build up a culture of exploration.

The historic quests for the North-West and North-East passages were abandoned in the face of insurmountable difficulties: the Arctic seas were literally unnavigable by the sailing ships of the sixteenth or seventeenth centuries. It was much later, in the eighteenth century, that Captain Cook sailed deep into Antarctic seas, and concluded that a southern polar continent might exist, but that it must be so barren that 'the world will derive no benefit from it'. Cook believed that the ice of the Antarctic had its origin on this continent, but that it would never be explored. Yet it was Cook's discovery of South Georgia and the South Sandwich Islands, and his reports of sighting many whales and seals in the South Pacific, which drew more ships to the region and led to some important discoveries. In 1785 the London whaling firm of Enderby first sent its ships to hunt in the Southern Ocean, and Enderby Land was named in 1831 by one its employees, John Biscoe. In 1819 an English brig sailing due south from Cape Horn sighted land at 62 degrees south, which the skipper, William Smith, reported to the British navy in Chile. Together Smith and Commander Edward Bransfield returned to the South Shetland Islands, and continued on to the nearby mainland at 64 degrees south, which they named Trinity Land. Their landing in 1820 on the north of the modern Graham Land was the first recorded landfall on the Antarctic continent.

The voyages of these private vessels were not necessarily all recorded and charted. A major Russian Antarctic expedition was mounted in 1819–21 commanded by Fabian von Bellinghausen, which covered 242 degrees of longitude south of the sixtieth parallel, almost circumnavigating the continent. Yet Bellinghausen was staggered when, in January 1821 off the South Shetland Islands, which he imagined he had just discovered, he encountered an American sailing ship, captained by the youthful Nathaniel Palmer, who informed him that an American fleet was at work among these uncharted islands. The Russian Admiral was distressed that his imperial fleet should have been forestalled in this way by a commercial skipper, but he paid generous tribute to his young rival, and both Bellinghausen's and Palmer's names are perpetuated on the map of Antarctica. Further Russian expeditions followed, such as Frederic Lutke's in the 1820s which resulted in an important commemorative atlas.

The greatest difficulties in the mapping of Antarctica were to distinguish the land itself from its surrounding ice-walls, and to determine whether ice-covered promontories were part of the mainland or were islands. Almost all the place-names of Antarctica tell their own story, commemorating explorers or their monarchs. In 1822 an officer of the Enderby company, James Weddell, working off the South Orkney Islands, sailed south-east into open sea for a further 500 miles, to an astonishing 74 degrees south, where still 'not a particle of ice of any description was to be seen'. Only contrary winds forced him to turn back, and Wedell was led to believe that this sea might continue to the Pole itself; yet no later skipper was ever to find the Weddell Sea so clear of ice again. The whaling potential, and the undoubted existence of a southern continent now inspired a number of official naval expeditions. In 1840 Dumont D'Urville, who had earlier made important voyages in the Pacific, attempted to locate the South Magnetic Pole. He was unsuccessful but named the Antarctic territory in which he was searching, Terre Adélie, after his wife. Just a few days later the French encountered an American ship, part of the fleet of Lieutenant Charles Wilkes, some of whose discoveries were later discounted, because what he took for continental features were ice-walls, but whose name still remains on the largest tract of Antarctica. Exactly contemporary with these French and American expeditions, two ships of the British navy under the command of Captain James Clark Ross set out with mainly scientific objectives, including the location of the South Magnetic Pole. Searching due south of Tasmania, Ross penetrated the pack ice and entered the sea which now bears his name, He sighted two huge volcanoes which he named after his ships *Erebus* and *Terror*, before finding his way blocked by the Ross Ice Shelf. They had sailed to 78 degrees south, before turning their attention to the Weddell Sea, but here they were checked at 71 degrees, and concluded that Weddell had been 'favoured by an unusually fine season'. After these three expeditions there was a lull in Antarctic exploration for almost half a century; private whalers and sealers continued to use these waters, but governments evidently had come to agree with Captain Cook in his assessment of the polar continent.

In the Arctic at this time, British interest in the North-West Passage was rekindled, partly for scientific reasons and partly for political ones. The Second Secretary to the Admiralty, Sir John Barrow, argued in 1818 that 'The North Pole may be approached by sea' and that 'a communication in all probability exists between the Atlantic and Pacific Oceans.' Shipbuilding, navigation, naval discipline were all considered to have improved enormously since the search for the Passage was abandoned almost two centuries earlier, therefore a series of Polar expeditions was launched in the next decade to test these theories. There was also a certain anxiety that American or, more important still, Russian fleets might discover and exploit the Passage first, and with Russia actually claiming sovereignty over Alaska, the prospect of her controlling the northern access to the Pacific was viewed seriously. To Barrow 'The discovery of a North-West Passage to India and China has always been considered an object peculiarly British.' While it was possible or even probable that the Passage did exist, navigators were aware that the difficulty lay in locating the channels which were open when the pack-ice melted, for the pattern altered from year to year, and no permanent passage could be guaranteed. Since the mid-seventeenth century, when the Hudson Bay and Hudson Strait were found to be dead-ends, it had been clear that if such a Passage existed, it must he sought via a north-westerly exit from Baffin Bay. In 1818 Captain John Ross (uncle of James Clark Ross of the Antarctic) made for exactly this point and entered the all-important Lancaster Sound. After sailing westwards for fifty miles however, Ross saw, or thought he saw, that he was in a bay blocked by a 'chain of mountains' stretching from north to south, which he promptly named the Croker Mountains, after the Secretary of the Admiralty, and sailed back to England. Flattered as he was no doubt, John Wilson Croker's satisfaction lasted only until 1820, when Captain William Parry's expedition proved the mountains to be a mirage or hallucination. The bizarre story of 'Croker's Mountains' made the unfortunate Ross a laughing-stock among geographers and naval officers for years to come.

Parry's was a far more successful venture, for he penetrated to 112 degrees west of Greenwich, much further than any previous voyage (incidentally collecting a £5,000 reward offered by Parliament for reaching this point within the Arctic Circle), and due to Parry's outstanding leadership, the men passed an excellent winter anchored at Melville Island. Parry returned to the Arctic on two further expeditions, in 1821–22, and in 1824–25. During the earlier voyage he discovered a new channel leading out of the Hudson Strait–Foxe Basin which would connect with Lancaster Sound. He named it Fury and Hecla Strait after his two ships, but although it gives theoretical access to the North-West Passage, it is extremely narrow and almost invariably choked with ice. Parry studied with interest the Eskimo way of life – the way they dressed, travelled and hunted, but he failed to draw the conclusion that Europeans in the Arctic might copy their survival techniques. Parry later made the first deliberate attempt to reach the North Pole, across the pack ice north of Spitzbergen. He and his party reached 82.5 degrees north, but found that their progress was counteracted by the southward drift of the ice. In 1828–33 John Ross seized the chance to expiate his 'Croker Mountains' blunder; accompanied by his nephew James Clark Ross, he explored the Boothia Peninsula, located the North Magnetic Pole, and after their ship had been frozen in the ice, survived an overwintering and a nightmare journey by sea and land to Lancaster Sound where they were rescued by a whaler.

The British Admiralty was still far from satisfied with its incomplete charts of the Arctic, and still fearful of Russian intentions, a further attempt to reach the Bering Strait from the east was launched, the ill-fated expedition led by Sir John Franklin in 1845. Franklin had earlier explored by boat and on foot 500 miles of the North Alaskan coast from the McKenzie River to Point Barrow, which he reached via the river itself, and the mouth of the McKenzie was a mere 500 miles from the point in Melville Sound reached by Parry, so there were theoretical grounds for optimism. But Franklin must also have known that a few hundred miles of Arctic ice can become an eternity, the difference between life and death. Franklin used Ross's ships from the Antarctic, *Erebus* and *Terror* and sailed in May 1845; they were seen by a whaler in July west of Greenland, before the ships and their crew vanished forever. What happened to them was pieced together ten or more years later by search parties. In the summer of 1846 Franklin's ships had passed Lancaster Sound, Peel Sound and Franklin Strait, and were poised to commence the final westward section of their journey to the south of Victoria Island, when they became beset by ice in the Victoria Strait, which receives the full force of the Polar ice flow driven down from the Beaufort Sea. Here they remained for twenty dreadful months, during which Franklin himself and twenty-four other men died, before the crews abandoned their ships and attempted to march south, hoping to find a Hudson's Bay Company post. All 105 men died en route, unable to make contact with the Eskimos in that area whose survival skills could undoubtedly have saved them. The nationalistic psychology of Polar exploration was plainly revealed in the aftermath of these events, when the dead of the *Erebus* and *Terror* were said by Franklin's widow to have 'laid down their lives in the service of their country as truly as if they had perished by the rifle, the cannon-ball or the bayonet . . . they forged the last link of the North-West passage with

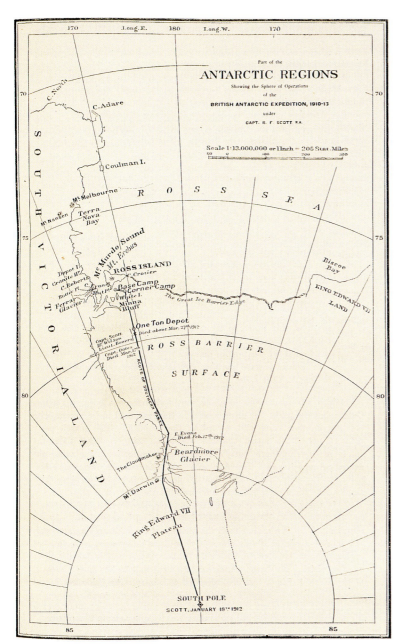

British Antarctic Expeditions, 1910–13. Among those parties that failed to reach the South Pole, Shackleton's came closest in 1909, less than 100 miles short.

The British Library Geographical Journal vol. XLI, 1913.

their lives.'

The Franklin affair was the greatest disaster in the history of Polar exploration, yet in drawing dozens of search-parties to the region in the 1850s, it was responsible for completing the map of Arctic. One of the searchers, Robert McClure, entered the Beaufort Sea via the Bering Strait and after abandoning his ship, joined a sledging party north of Banks Island, and joined with a ship from the east. Thus McClure became the first man to traverse the North-West Passage, but in reverse and partly on foot. He was also the first man known to have circumnavigated the entire American continent, north and south. His route via McClure Strait, Melville Sound and Lancaster Sound is in fact the obvious one from the modern map, but its ice rarely disappears altogether, even in summer, and the route south of Victoria Island is more practical. This would be the route finally taken by the Norwegian Roald Amundsen in 1903–6 when he at last navigated the North-West Passage in a small motor vessel. Amundsen's route differed only in one vital respect from that of Franklin: he passed east of King William Island, avoiding the Victoria Strait which had been Franklin's grave. In 1875–76 George Nares and Albert Markham explored the Ellesmere Island and North-West Greenland region, establishing the insularity of Greenland. Markham reached further than 83 degrees north on sledging excursions from his ship, and pointed the way in which the North Pole might be reached.

The North-East Passage had always been guessed to be even longer and more arduous than the North-West, and only the advent of steam-powered ships made it possible. In July 1878–79 the Swede Adolf Erik Nordenskiöld sailed from Tromsö in a reinforced whaler, the *Vega*, and made for the Kara Sea with the object of finally traversing the Arctic Ocean eastwards. Two months later he anchored at Cape Chelyuskin, the most northerly point of Asia. Sailing on, by the onset of winter they were within sight of the Bering Strait

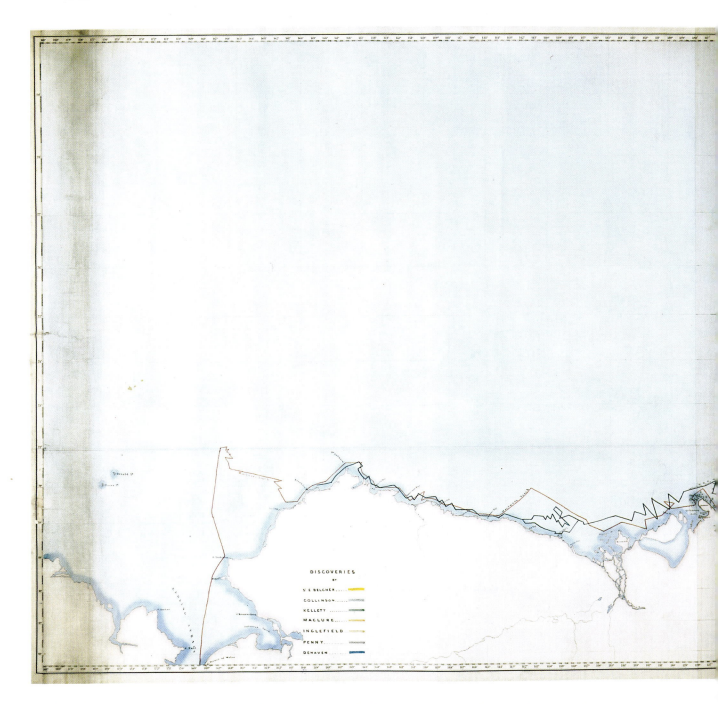

The Beaufort Sea, 1854. Among the expeditions which searched for Sir John Franklin was that of Robert McClure who sailed east from the Bering Strait, and whose tracks are marked here. He was forced to abandon ship but was picked up off Banks Island and became the first man through the North-West Passage, although in reverse.

Hydrographic Office, Taunton

when they were beset by ice, which they could have avoided had they been a day or two earlier, and were forced to remain for almost ten months. They made contact with the Siberian Chukchi people, the most remote inhabitants of Russia, who herded reindeer and traded in skins and furs from Alaska. In July 1879 Nordenskiöld was free of the ice, and passed the Bering Strait into the Pacific. The *Vega* continued south and west, making the first circumnavigation of the Old World, more than three hundred years after the Elizabethan seamen had set out confidently for the North-East Passage to Cathay. An equally historic north-eastern voyage was made by the Norwegian Fridtjof Nansen in 1893–96. Nansen had conceived the theory, based on observation of the drift of Polar ice, that the

Arctic was not a true continent but a vast ice-cap. To test this he planned to allow his ship, the *Fram*, to become frozen in north of the Lena estuary, convinced that it would drift west and be freed into the Greenland Sea. This plan was perfectly fulfilled, and while some of the crew remained with the *Fram*, Nansen made a remarkable overland journey, to 86 degrees north, passing within 240 miles of the North Pole, and pressing on to Spitzbergen. The understanding of the Arctic Ocean that came with these two journeys made it certain that the once-unnavigable North-East Passage would one day be used by shipping.

The final, if irrational, goals of Polar exploration – the reaching of the Poles themselves – were achieved within five years of each other. Robert Peary, an American naval officer had twice crossed the Greenland ice-cap before turning to the challenge of North Pole. He led three expeditions between 1898 and 1909, learning the skills of Arctic navigation and sledge-travel, before his tenacity was rewarded in April 1909, when he reached the Pole, accompanied by Matthew Henson and four Inuit. The speed with which Peary travelled from his final base at Cape Columbia, in the extreme north of Ellesmere Island, to the Pole and back, led some to doubt Peary's achievement, doubts which have never been entirely dispelled.

In the final decade of the nineteenth century, scientific and geographical societies took a revived interest in the Antarctic, wishing to establish at last the extent and nature of the continent. In 1897 the crew of a Belgian ship had survived the first overwintering in the Antarctic, a feat repeated in the Ross Sea two years later by a British team which was financed by a newspaper. The British landed dog teams and explored inland, reaching 78 degrees south; the possibility of travel on the Antarctic continent was obviously a reality. By 1905 German, Swedish, French and British expeditions had all arrived in Antarctica, with the unspoken ambition of preparing to gain the South Pole first. In 1908 Ernest Shackelton with three companions passed 88 degrees south, and were a mere 97 miles from the Pole, when they turned back and barely survived the 800-mile return journey. Had this expedition enjoyed another few days' grace, the next few years of Antarctic rivalry would have been different. The race for the Pole in 1912 between the Norwegian Roald Amundsen and Captain Scott has been narrated many times. Both men had extensive Polar experience, but Amundsen's journey seems to have been better planned and equipped, and was significantly shorter in its chosen route. Amundsen, with his clear-sighted tenacity and already world-famous for his North-West Passage, is worthy of his place in history; but Scott's heroic failure has somehow entered the history of exploration even more securely. He and his companions were exhausted and ill, but they were a mere eleven miles from their base camp and probable safety, when they were imprisoned in their tent by blizzards, and forced to wait for certain death. Scott's last diaries and notes are unforgettable, as he attempts to rationalize what is happening – 'We are showing that Englishmen can still die with a bold spirit' – yet all the ambiguity of this form of heroic, irrational combat with the natural environment is disclosed in his pathetic, reiterated concern for their familes, that surely 'a great rich country like ours will see that those who are dependent upon us are provided for.' And finally his unemotional, officer-trained mask drops away as he confronts the futility of his ambitions: 'All the day-dreams must go . . . Great God, this is an awful place.'

EXPLORATION IN THE MODERN WORLD

Mount McKinley at dawn: the mountain world that draws the modern explorer into its solitude.

'To my joy and relief there was nothing but a little crest, a short snow slope only a few yards long, easier now, easier . . . I was on the highest point of the mountain, the summit of Nanga Parbat, 26,620 feet above sea-level. Nothing went up further anywhere. There was a small snow-plateau, a couple of mounds, and everything fell away on all sides from it. There I was on that spot, the target of my dreams. I was the first human being since creation's dawn to set foot there . . . I felt as if I were floating high above everything, out of all relationship with the earth, severed from the world and all humanity. To the north, a hundred miles away, great ranges melted into the distance; to the east a similar sea of peaks, innumerable, ice-clad, unapproached. . .'

These were Hermann Buhl's thoughts in July 1953 on becoming the first climber to reach the summit of Nanga Parbat, the giant Himalayan pinnacle which had already claimed more lives than any mountain outside Europe. Buhl was a tough young Tirolean peasant who had conquered all the great Alpine rock-faces, and who now made history on his first visit to the Himalayas with his almost incredible lone ascent of this savage mountain. His achievement and his reflections on it bring into sharp focus some fundamental questions about exploration in the twentieth century, not least whether it really exists any longer. Five hundred years ago no one on earth knew, by experience or by report, what more than a quarter of the world was like. Now the unknown, untrodden areas of the world are tiny and must be deliberately sought out. Objectively there is no more exploration to be done, for the map is complete, and no one can venture into the unknown in the way that Magellan or Cortes or Orellana did. By an intriguing paradox, the modern explorer knows exactly where he is going before he sets out. Arguably, the word exploration now belongs to history, and should be replaced by adventure travel.

But what remains – and this is what stands out clearly in Buhl's memoir – is the subjective experience of discovery. We can still leave the safety of the civilized world and confront alien land-scapes and alien cultures. We can enter an existential unknown in which the avowed aim is to find some 'other', but at a deeper level it is to find the self. The path to such self-discovery typically takes the form of physical struggle against a hostile environment, an experience of the elemental forces of solitude, cold, darkness or fear, forces from which we are largely insulated in our daily lives. Something in modern civilization plainly feeds this need to escape from safety into risk, from servit-ude into freedom, from the familiar into the unknown. 'In this modern age,' wrote the French climber Gaston Rébuffat, 'very little remains that is real: night has been banished, so have the cold, the wind and the stars ... What a strange encounter then is that between man and the high places of his planet, up there, surrounded by the silence of forgetfulness.' Mountain heights are the classic location for such experiences, with the unspoken suggestion that the man who conquers them takes the place of the gods who were once believed to inhabit their peaks. Whether the elusive self is finally discov-ered, or whether the climber simply finds a renewed sense of balance with the natural and human world, the experience is clearly addictive, drawing people back again and again to the mountains, even at the risk of death; four years after his triumph on Nanga Parbat, Hermann Buhl was killed while climbing on Chogolija in the Karakoram.

It would be easy to say that the desire to penetrate and explore the world's wild places is a fundamental human impulse, but in fact mountaineering was unknown before the later eighteenth century, and the almost mystical response to solitude and wilderness evident in Buhl's text would also have been unthinkable before that date. The culture of exploration seems to have undergone a profound change in the era of Romanticism, so that the aesthetic response to nature came to be emphasized very strongly, while the psychological experiences of isolation, danger and suffering were acknowledged to be central in all travel narratives. Is this subjective experience of discovery depend-ent on being the *first* to reach a certain peak or goal? Logically the answer should be no, but the psychological intensity of such experiences depends partly on their uniqueness: the traveller or climber is engaged in a deliberate search for the void that lies outside civilization, and being the first to penetrate a mountain or wilderness where no human being has ever set foot becomes an essential part of the story. In contemporary travel writing, commercial pressures drive the explorer into an increasingly desperate search for novelty and first achievements, reversing what should be the natural order of experience and literature: one now travels and suffers in order to write about it. The very history of mountaineering consists of a chronicle of first attempts, notable failures, and triumphant first ascents. It was in the eighteenth century that European scientists and naturalists began to explore the higher regions of the Alps, collecting plants and minerals, or observing glaciers and weather patterns. But as far as we know the idea of climbing a mountain peak for its own sake was virtually unknown before Bénédict de Saussure became determined to reach the summit of Mont Blanc in the 1760s. Saussure spent many years studying the Alpine environment, and it was he who introduced the word geology into scientific literature, but it was many years before he was able to ascend beyond

Maat Mons, Venus, mapped by radar. Maat is an eight-kilometre high volcanic mass near the equator of Venus; the terrain is covered with lava flow.

S.P.L.

the mountain's lower slopes and make progress in the unfamiliar world of snow and ice. Although a dedicated scientist, he was also the first to write about mountaineering in modern terms, indeed the desire to climb Mont Blanc became an obsession with him. 'I could not even look upon the mountain,' he wrote 'without being seized with an aching desire to ascend its heights'. In 1787 he achieved his ambition, but he was not the first to do so, for in the preceding year Michel Paccard and Jacques Balmat of Chamonix, the one a doctor the other a hunter, had succeeded in reaching the summit. These ascents, with the published accounts which followed them and the interest they aroused, are generally taken as the starting-point of the history of European mountaineering.

The development of this new psychology of discovery did not of course mean the end of objective geographical exploration, indeed it was during the later eighteenth and early nineteenth centuries that the aims and methods of precise surveying and mapmaking were developed in Europe and applied in her colonial territories. Geographical exploration was gradually redefined in this period, for it was no longer sufficient to know in a general way that a territory contained rivers, plains or mountains. The scientist, the soldier or the colonial governor required precise distances, elevations, terrain features and names so that they could exercise their power over the landscape, whether that power was intellectual or military. Judged by this standard, even by the year 1850 vast areas of the earth remained virgin territory. The fact that a world map of that date appears virtually complete is somewhat misleading, for it was the coastlines which had been so comprehensively charted, leaving

Route Map from Kathmandu to Lhasa, 1868. One of the surveys made by the spies trained by the Survey of India.
The British Library Maps 159.38.

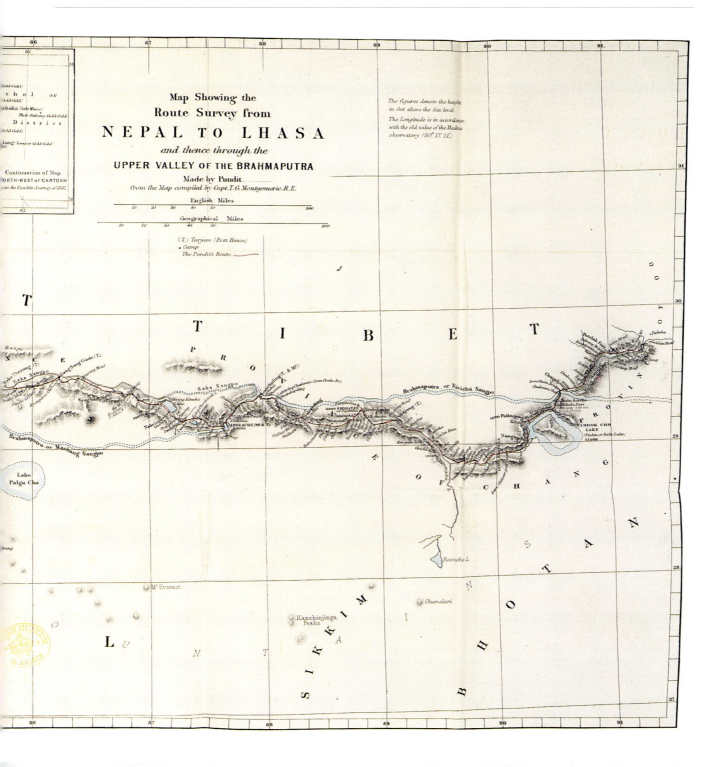

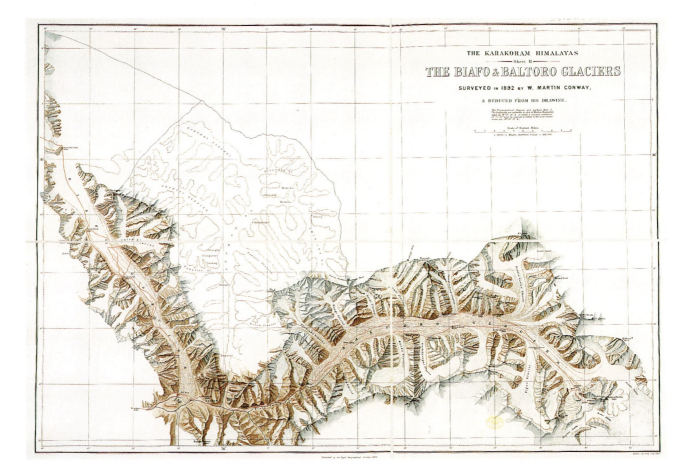

Baltoro Glacier with K2, mapped by Martin Conway in 1892.

The British Library Maps 46848(3).

Right: Triangulation network of the Survey of India, 1876; imperial and scientific motives came together to map the sub-continent.

The British Library Maps Ref.K.5.(9).

an enormous amount of interior exploration to be done. For example New Guinea, which had featured on sea-charts since before 1600, was totally unvisited by Europeans before the 1850s. The British in India and Australia, the French in West Africa, the Dutch in the East Indies and the Russians in Siberia were all in a position to undertake long-term, systematic surveys which emulated the methods and completeness of the European national map surveys. Where such surveying was not possible, individual travellers with surveying abilities produced route traverses, with sightings of prominent features such as mountains and rivers, the whole being tied to reasonably good latitude and longitude bases. Such route maps would be reconciled as accurately as possible with existing base maps, and the result was the characteristic mid-nineteenth century map of large parts of Africa, Asia or South America, in which detailed strips of territory alternate with blank spaces where no terrain features are shown.

The aim of removing these blanks on the map became a deliberate and perhaps the dominant motive for European expeditions throughout the world. The context of this work might be land settlement or colonial administration, as in North America or Australia, where it was followed by the

building of railways or telegraph lines. It might be missionary, as it was in Africa, where the opening of the interior was seen as the essential prelude to the bringing of civilization. It might be scientific, as in northern India where the geographical problems of the Himalayas were formidable – it was as late as 1913 for example that the source of the Brahmaputra was traced to the Tsangpo in Tibet. Whether the motive was scientific or imperial, it is hard to see the process of exploration and mapping, as it gathered pace in the later nineteenth century, as anything but the 'Europeanization' of the world map, the landscape analysed and captured in grids and contours, the tribes named and subjugated, the railheads established. This was surely the culmination of the process that had begun when the first European navigators began to extend their world maps beyond the North Atlantic.

Parallel with the exploration of the physical world, European scholars in the nineteenth century used their new freedom of world travel to re-interpret human culture and history through the emerging sciences of anthropology and archaeology. The earliest explorers had paid little attention to the native peoples they encountered, classifying them merely as naked savages. The recognition of the diversity of human cultures followed from the rational spirit of eighteenth century travel, while the loosening of religious dogma facilitated the study of man as a species, whether in England, in Africa or in Tahiti. Darwinism provided a convenient conceptual framework for the study of human diversity: 'It is undeniable', wrote one pioneer anthropologist 'that portions of the human family have existed in a state of savagery, other portions in a state of barbarism, and still other portions in a state of civilization . . . these three distinct conditions are connected with each other in a natural as well as necessary sequence of progress'. Traveller's accounts of 'primitive' customs and beliefs were used to develop this linear view of cultural development, and the associated concept of cultural diffusion. This type of anthropology was rejected by twentieth century scholars, who based their more pluralistic view on original field-work, Boas and Benedict among the Indian tribes of North America, Mead and Malinowski in Oceania. The newer understanding of non-European culture that resulted was summed up by Malinowski, who insisted on the principle that 'In every type of civilization, every custom, material object, idea and belief fulfils some vital function, has some task to accomplish, represents an indispensable part within a working whole'. The search for these exotic ideas and beliefs, the encounter with alien lifestyles, the desire to shed the skin of European culture, have become leading themes in modern exploration literature. Almost as challenging to the traveller as the overseas peoples themselves, were the material remains of their predecessors. In the Indus Valley, in the Yucatan Peninsula, in the jungles of Cambodia, have been found archaeological remains which have forced a re-evaluation of the history of entire regions and epochs; that perennial lure of explorers, the lost city, often proved to be a reality after all.

Prior to the twentieth century, the explorer's environment was restricted to the surface of the earth. Technical advances have now added two new elements that offer a limitless field for research – the sea and the sky. The American navy officer Matthew Maury is acknowledged to be the pioneer of oceanography, producing in 1854 the first map of the North Atlantic seafloor. It was in the 1870s that the British oceanographic research vessel HMS *Challenger* carried out systematic soundings over thousands of square miles of ocean and revealed the complex pattern of the ocean bed – the continental shelves, the mid-Atlantic ridge and the plunging coastal trenches. The mapping of the ocean floor became possible only with the discovery of sonar in the early twentieth century, which is based on the fact that sound can be detected through thousands of kilometres of water, while visible light penetrates at most a few hundred metres. This technique underlay the first generation of seafloor maps produced by oceanographers in the 1950s. This form of mapping has been an important tool in understanding the nature of the earth's crust and in working out the all-important theory of plate tectonics. Sonar has been superseded by remote sensing as a mapmaking method, which has revealed that the sea's surface is warped by seafloor features: huge ridges cause the sea to bulge over them, and trenches cause the sea's surface to sink. This has made possible a new type of gravity map of the seabed composed from satellite data, accurate to a very high degree, and far more comprehensive than sonar surveys taken from on board ship. This form of exploration is of course highly cerebral, analysing huge amounts of scientific data, but at the same time the desire to explore the sea-bed in person led a few pioneers to enter a Jules Verne world of undersea trenches and mysterious life-forms. In 1960 Jacques Piccard descended the Mariana Trench in his bathysphere to a depth of 35,000 feet, into a world of perpetual darkness where the hostility of the environment is such that the human presence can accomplish little, except to claim the achievement of having been there.

The distinction of being the 'final frontier' is usually accorded to the world of space. Over five thousand years of intellectual history, astronomy had been unique among the sciences in that its object of study was forever out of reach: it was purely an observational science and never an

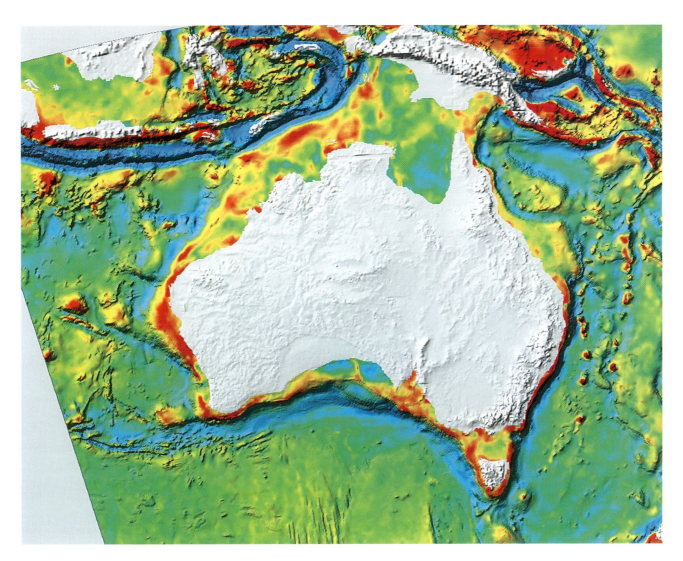

The Ocean floor around Australia, composed from Seasat imagery. The deep blue feature at the upper left is the Java Trench, where the Indo-Australian tectonic plate meets the Eurasian; at the top right is the New Guinea Trench.

S.P.L.

experimental one. This changed significantly with the first manned spaceflight in 1961, although whether the change will be decisive remains to be seen. It seems impossible for example that the fundamental problems of cosmology can ever be solved by personal exploration in space, since the scales of time and distance involved dwarf not merely human life but the whole of human history. In some ways it is difficult to see space travel as the heir to the long centuries of geographical exploration, because the massive technological weight of the project diminishes the human element: if any one of a thousand complex electronic systems malfunctions, the expedition cannot succeed, and the human role is to monitor and conform with these systems. Rather like polar adventure a century ago, space travel has represented a pure form of scientific exploration, but complicated by political rivalries. With the end of the Russian-American confrontation, the future of space travel looks very uncertain, for its continuation is dependent on the political will to invest unimaginable sums in the pursuit of scientific achievement for its own sake.

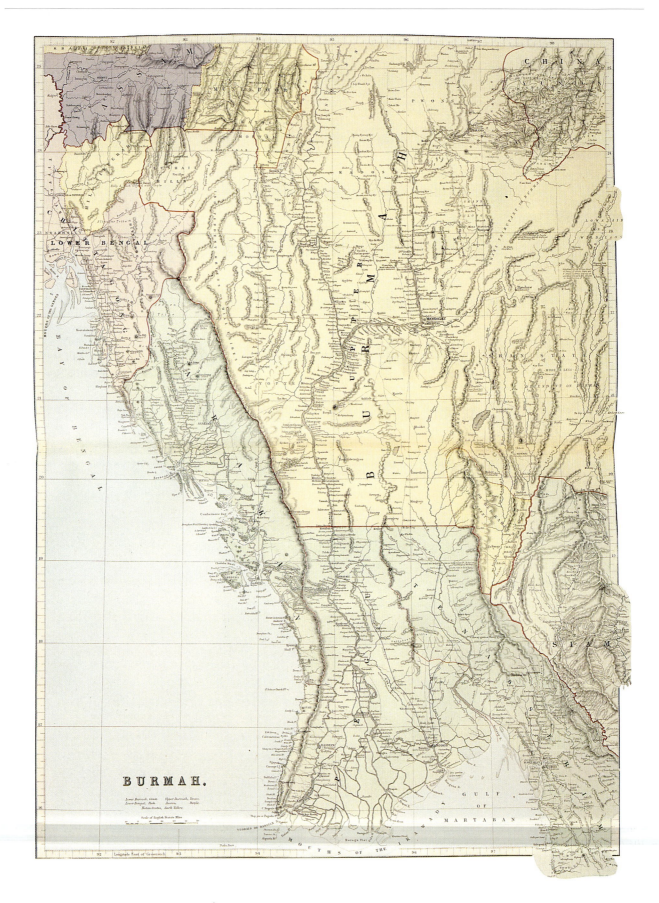

BURMAH.

Lower Burmah, Green.   Upper Burmah, Brown.
Lower Bengal, Pink.   Assam, Purple.
Native States, dark Yellow.

The history of exploration, like the history of science or of art, acts as a window into the fundamental problem of man's relationship with his world. In what we may call the classical period of European exploration – from the Renaissance to the late nineteenth century – that relationship was essentially a quest for dominance, the dominance of nature and of other nations. The immediate motive was overwhelmingly mercenary, the pursuit of gold, spices or slaves; but mercenary motives alone cannot explain the career of a Columbus or a Cortes; only a culture of crusade and conquest can explain them. European dominance was first achieved through military means, although indigenous social systems also found it virtually impossible to survive the pressures of European commerce. Later both science and religion were employed to secure a more pervasive cultural domination. When the anthropologist Frederick Errington visited the Melanesian island of Karavaria in 1968, the inhabitants told him that their history had begun in 1875 when the Christian missionary George Brown first landed on their island. Before that date, they believed that a condition of savagery had prevailed that was dark, timeless and unbroken. Through prayer and superior magic, Brown had exorcized the evil in the island, and inaugurated their modern history. Could there be a more telling example of European cultural dominance than this, a dominance Cortes or Pizarro would have envied?

By the time this event occured, far-reaching changes in the European outlook meant that travellers, exploring the territories opened for them by their more ruthless predecessors, were seeking a very different relationship to their world. There was a retreat from domination into genuine discovery, both of the outer world and of personal identity. This they pursued in the solitude of the mountains, deserts or polar regions, in an experience described by Nansen as 'This dark, deep, silent void like the mysterious, unfathomable well into which you look for that something which you think must be there, only to meet the reflection of your own eyes.' It is difficult to avoid applying the word mystic to such passages, for all practical or intellectual aims are plainly dissolved in the solitude-experience itself. This motif of the inner journey has become characteristic of modern travel literature. Inherent in it is a desire to escape from the social and intellectual anxieties of the modern world into a realm of purer choices. Its psychological roots have been analysed simply and forcefully by one distinguished writer, Freya Stark, immediately after World War One: 'It seems to me that the only thing for a pacifist to do is to find a substitute for war: mountains and seafaring are the only ones I know. These substitutes must be something sufficiently dangerous not to be a game. . . There must be something heroic in life, and no amount of enthusiasm over material things will give this heroic life to more than few people. In fact there must be danger, and the problem is to find a sufficiently dangerous alternative to war'.

Alongside this intense and intellectualized encounter with the natural world the rise of global tourism has created a feverish vogue for travel, in which the remoteness of the destination is highly prized. The relentless pressure of fashion drives millions of people to criss-cross the earth in a restless search for the new and exotic. In an age when global tourism can convey anyone in a matter of hours to the Himalayas, the Kalahari or even the Antarctic, what, objectively, can be the future of exploration? That future lies in teaching us not about the world, but about ourselves and our relationship to it, for if there is a final frontier, a final unknown shore, it is surely the human psyche itself. How different is the modern traveller's insatiable desire for new lands and new experiences from the supreme detachment of the oriental sage to whom 'The next place might be so near at hand that one could hear the cocks crowing in it and the dogs barking, but one could grow old and die without ever wishing to go there.' This spirit is fundamentally opposed to the European drive for knowledge and

Burmah, by Stanford, 1887. The mapped portion of the terrain follows established routes; at this date large areas of the world still remained effectively unmapped.

The British Library Maps 46.f.5.

for the power that knowledge brought with it. All the various phases of European exploration – military, commercial, scientific, romantic – have their memorial in the history of the gradual completion of the world map. But the narratives of the men who acted in this long drama, their motives and their achievements, belong not solely to the history of geography, but form a revealing index to the dynamic but flawed psychology of European civilization.

'And the end of all our exploring
Will be to arrive where we started
And know the place for the first time.'

BIBLIOGRAPHICAL NOTE

The literature of exploration is very large, and becomes enormous if one includes the related fields of economic, colonial, maritime and cartographic history. Many important original exploration narratives have been made available by the Hakluyt Society in their 300-plus volumes published since 1847, and these form the basis for any history of the subject. A number of general works are so comprehensive that they never seem to be superseded, among them are J. N. L. Baker: *A History of Geographical Discovery and Exploration*, 1937 and subsequent editions; R. A. Skelton: *Explorers' Maps*, 1958; and B. Penrose: *Travel and Discovery in the Renaissance 1420–1620*, 1952. There have been a number of impressive illustrated 'Atlases of Exploration', among them *The Times Atlas of World Exploration*, 1991, edited by F. Fernandez-Armesto, and the excellent *World Atlas of Exploration*, 1975, edited by E. Newby, which quotes generously from original sources. The ancient period is studied in J. O. Thomson: *A History of Ancient Geography*, 1948.

Among the many regional studies S. E. Morison: *The European Discovery of America* is supremely readable, appearing in two parts – *The Northern Voyages*, 1971, and *The Southern Voyages*, 1974; W. P. Cumming et. al.: *The Exploration of North America*, 1974 deals with the interior of the continent. G. Schilder: *Australia Unveiled*, 1976, is authoritative for this region. The political and maritime context of exploration was brought out in some classic works such as J. H. Parry: *The Age of Reconnaissance*, 1966; and C. R. Boxer: *The Portuguese Seaborne Empire 1415–1825*, 1969, and *The Dutch Seaborne Empire 1600–1800*, 1965. For the cartographic history R. W. Shirley: *The Mapping of the World*, 1984 and subsequent editions, is always indispensable.

The literary and philosophical aspects of travel are now growth areas, and recent titles of interest include N. Rennie: *Far-Fetched Facts: the Literature of Travel and the Idea of the South Seas*, 1996; and S. M. Islam: *The Ethics of Travel from Marco Polo to Kafka*, 1966; both books exploring the psychology of travel. Theories of imperialism are discussed in J. A. Hobson: *Imperialism*, new ed. 1975. Finally, for anyone interested in understanding the 'Age of Discovery', Camões's *Lusiads*, the Portuguese national epic, is essential reading.

INDEX

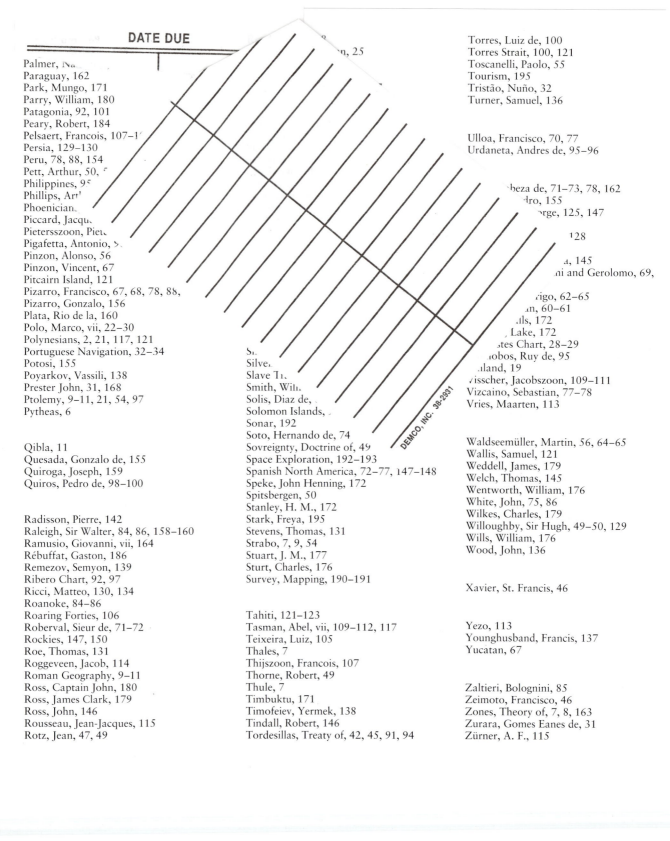